JUST SEA & SKY

England to New Zealand the hard way

A VINTAGE CRUISE THROUGH THE SOUTH SEAS

BEN PESTER

Introduction by Dick Durham

ADLARD COLES NAUTICAL
LONDON

Published by Adlard Coles Nautical
an imprint of A & C Black Publishers Ltd
36 Soho Square, London W1D 3QY
www.adlardcoles.com

First edition published 2010
Reprinted 2011

ISBN 978-1-4081-2855-8

A CIP catalogue record for this book is available from the British
Library.

This book is produced using paper that is made from wood
grown in managed, sustainable forests. It is natural, renewable
and recyclable. The logging and manufacturing processes
conform to the environmental regulations of the country of
origin.

Design by Susan McIntyre
Typeset in 10 on 12pt Minion
Printed and bound in Croatia by Zrinski

Note: while all reasonable care has been taken in the publication
of this book, the publisher takes no responsibility for the use of
the methods or products described in the book.

By the same author

Through the Land of Fire
Published 2004
A cruise through Tierra del Fuego, Patagonia
and around Cape Horn.

Contents

DEDICATION

To Peter, my crew, companion and friend whose unstinting contribution ensured the success of our adventure together. His competency as a seaman, unfailing good humour and enduring equanimity made the cruise so enjoyable. I was immensely fortunate to have had him with me.

And to the many people we met throughout the cruise who went out of their way to offer help, friendship and hospitality. Quite a few have featured in the text but there were too many to mention individually. To all of them my heartfelt thanks and appreciation.

I have the hope that some of those whom we met will read this book or it will be of interest to their descendents.

I have special appreciation for the encouragement of my wife Susan and my daughters Anna and Jane to write this account to preserve the memories from being lost.

Ben Pester
Falmouth
December 2009

About the Author

Born in New Zealand in 1924, Ben Pester came to England in 1943 to serve with the Royal Navy. He was granted leave to sail his 10 ton yawl *Tern II*, of Claud Worth fame, out to New Zealand in 1953. As an engineering officer in the New Zealand Navy, his last appointment was as commander (E) of the cruiser *Royalist*.

In recognition of the cruise of *Tern II* he was awarded the Royal Naval Sailing Association's Hammond Cup.

He left the navy and joined Alcan Aluminium Limited of Canada, holding managerial positions in New Zealand and Australia before becoming chief executive of companies in Nigeria, Indonesia and Malaysia.

Retiring to Falmouth in Cornwall in 1990, he set up a small sail training school with his McGruer 36 foot classic sloop *Marelle*. In her he sailed down to Patagonia to see in the millennium and to round Cape Horn – described in his book *Through the Land of Fire*.

Until his sudden death in May 2010, at the age of 85, Ben continued to sail the coastal waters of Cornwall all year round in his beloved *Marelle*.

Author's Note

Every man thinks meanly of himself for not having been to sea.

DR JOHNSON

In writing this account of an adventure, an ocean voyage in a classic yacht, I have enjoyed myself. It has been fun. Hopefully it will also be fun for the reader.

Much mention has been made in the text of traditional seamanship, an art not practised so much today, with frequent reference to sailors of earlier times. They have bequeathed, I believe, a legacy of ongoing value. They were consummate seamen and we all have much to learn from them.

I have included quite a few extracts from *Tern*'s log as, apart from being a record of events, they help, I think, to convey some of the reactions of her crew to situations encountered throughout the voyage.

The sources for material used in the text have, where relevant, been acknowledged but two particularly important works were Charles Darwin's *The Voyage of the Beagle* and Captain Cook's *Three Voyages Round the World*, edited by Lieutenant Charles Low.

My special thanks to Dick Dickinson for the use of his dramatic shot of a trade wind squall, the quality of the photograph being far beyond the capabilities of the black and white 35mm Leica I used in *Tern*.

A special mark of appreciation is due to Amanda Major who, despite her experience with my first book, once again put my heavily 'cut and paste' manuscript onto disc and still kept smiling.

Michael Bradley also once again and with good cheer made a valued contribution with his computer graphics and photographic work.

Finally my deep appreciation to Dick Durham for his generosity in undertaking the somewhat daunting task of writing the Introduction. News Editor of *Yachting Monthly*, a magazine of today, he is nevertheless a long standing traditionalist. He had the unique, on my part envied, experience of being the last mate of the celebrated Thames barge *Cambria* in the final days of the sailing trading barge era.

Ben Pester

Preface

It is as hard to describe the fascination of the sea as to explain the beauty of a woman.

CLAUD WORTH

As recently as fifty years ago deep water cruising yachts were a rarity. Today their number is legion, made possible by the giant strides of scientific development. Wind and sea, the elemental underpinnings of sailing, have of course not changed, but otherwise almost everything connected with the pastime has been transformed.

This account of a passage made in a traditional sailing yacht in those earlier years aims to bring to life the way it was when blue water small boats had the oceans largely to themselves, with the arrival at each stop on passage being an event for locals and crew alike.

The story is as much about those locals as well as on sailing in a small boat the way it used to be in more relaxed times, untrammelled by the clutter of the push button world of today. It records a way of life that will never be seen again.

Tern II, taking two young men half way round the world, was a classic example of a Victorian gentleman's yacht, graciously well proportioned with a feel of the gentility and good manners associated with that era. By great good fortune she is still in existence.

In her fifty fifth year she was not much changed from her early days. She had sometime back been given an engine, an innovation frowned upon by the purists of the day, which seemingly had been something of an unwelcome guest on board. So was ours. We had a successor, a little 8 HP petrol/paraffin affair, hand cranked and hardly used but we had to live with it, being mandatory for the transit of the Panama Canal. We had no electrics, let alone electronics. All lighting, in the cabin and on deck for navigation, was by oil lamp. The only batteries were those in our torches and in a portable radio receiver, the principal purpose of the latter being to obtain time signals.

During the passage out from England to New Zealand nothing of note on board went wrong, because there was nothing much to go wrong. Navigation was by sextant and chronometer watch, satellites did not exist and had yet to be invented. Distance run and deduced speed were by towed Walker patent log, with depths taken by hand lead and line. No self steering devices were carried. Except when she sailed herself every mile was hand steered.

We had no radio transmitter. To identify ourselves, if need be, we hoisted our signal flags. Weather forecasting was by the barometer, the look of the sky and run of the sea but in the end we just took what came along. Advance warning by radio would have been of no real value, only serving either to lift our spirits or alternatively thoroughly depress us. Foul weather gear was a long oilskin coat and bare feet.

Since those days the development of ocean sailing has been staggering, made possible by the explosion in technology, but one has to wonder if perhaps some of the plot has been lost? Sailing, after all, is essentially a basic art. The modern boat is stuffed full of the latest, must have, electronic equipment but how much of it is really necessary or even desirable? The seductive power of this wizardry to induce total dependence on it is to court disaster. What better authority to refer to than Sir Robin Knox-Johnson who, in a recent ocean race, complained '…the… phone kept cutting out – more bloody useless expensive electronics. It was all easier 38 years ago when none of these gadgets had been invented, so one did not miss them'.

If freed from the grip of ever better and better technology, with its all pervasive and intrusive domination, one can then experience the simple pleasure of sailing the way it was once enjoyed. That is what this account is all about.

> *Some day the history of the sea will be divided into two great periods.*
> *The Age of Simplicity and the Age of Complication.*
>
> FELIX RIESENBERG, AUTHOR AND MASTER MARINER

Introduction

by Dick Durham

I would like to have sailed with Ben Pester, but I was only two years old in 1953 when he was looking for a crew to join him aboard *Tern II*, his 39ft gaff yawl, for a 14,000 mile cruise from Plymouth to Auckland, New Zealand.

However having read *Just Sea and Sky*, his compelling story of that voyage, I now feel I *have* sailed with him. Ben has the gift of bringing the reader along for the passage and his prose leaves as clear a wake in your mind as *Tern II*'s long keel does across the ocean.

Ben, a New Zealander, himself, came to the UK in 1943 to serve with the Royal Navy. His droll and free-thinking antipodean views about the origins of World War II: 'There was in the aftermath of the war a view that Churchill had resolved a conflict which he had played a major role in starting in the first place,' came as something of a shock to an Englishman brought up on the chauvinistic propaganda that Winston Churchill was the saviour of the sceptred isle. The green and pleasant Jerusalem promised to returning warriors was in fact a monochrome and bankrupt land inhabited by disillusioned people from among whose ranks came a bulging post-bag of respondents to Ben's advert for a crew.

The one he chose was Peter Fox, a Portsmouth-based yachtsman, and it is with him the reader shares their first landfall in the Canaries from the deck of *Tern II*, the thoroughbred Victorian gentleman's yacht, which once belonged to the legendary yachtsman and author Claud Worth: 'It was a beautiful night, soft and warm but impenetrably black. We needed the (leading) lights. Peter went up forward to get a clear view under the foot of the jib. "Got them! One, two, three, four…seven, eight, nine, ten. I give up there are hundreds of the b***** things!" the explanation soon became clear: close by were dozens of fishing boats all using red flares.'

The author treats the reader to historical asides which put the cruise into cultural, political and sociological context. Whether it's the moribund sight of a Grand Banks schooner arriving in Lisbon with its holds full of fish; the sourness of the slaving legacy behind the sweetness of West Indian

Calypsos, or the misguided do-gooding of European missionaries in the Pacific, Ben always provides a greater picture thereby bringing gravitas to a privileged voyage.

Along the watery highway Ben introduces great figures from the past who have helped fill the psyches, of those of us who've never been there with exotic images of these enchanting isles. Literary giants like Herman Melville, pirates like William Dampier, the unique Charles Darwin as well as other cruising sailors from William Albert Robinson to Eric Hiscock all join Ben's cruise at appropriate stages.

Then there is the adventure itself, from the swim *Tern II*'s crew made in mid-Atlantic watching the gaffer's 'shapely form as she rolled showing her red, anti-fouled under body, then to roll back towards us revealing the gentle sweep of her deck,' to the unexpected lunar eclipse they witnessed en route to the Galápagos. 'We watched the slow progression in sharp relief of the earth's shadow across the amazingly brilliant surface of the full moon. As it did so the shining white surface gave way to a warm copper glow.' We share the sheer wonder of *Tern II*'s crew at their surroundings: 'We were the minutest of specks sitting on top of an enormous volume of water at the bottom of which was an unknown world, completely devoid of light and occupied by creatures beyond anything we could imagine. Beneath us were depths of 35,000 feet or more … the thought of sinking down through this vast abyss to total black oblivion was frightening to contemplate.'

But the reader is just as close to the action when disaster beckons. I was on the edge of my bunk when Ben described falling overboard with *Tern II*'s helm pegged while the boat was doing six knots and Peter was asleep below. I will not spoil the story but let the reader discover what saved the author. His subsequent view on the wearing of lifejackets is enlightening and as relevant today when the RNLI is behoving us to wear one at all times. Aboard *Tern II* were no lifejackets, no harnesses, no liferaft. Ben believes it made them follow the age-old rule of 'one hand for the ship and one for yourself.'

'The danger is one can become careless if there is a feeling of false security fostered by the wearing of safety gear. Safety was not then the God it has now become.'

But as with all real sailors, as well as the polemic there is the confession. Such as the near miss they suffered because Ben was 'too lazy' to fill the oil navigation lamps, clean their glasses and trim the wicks: 'Why should we? We were in our own private playground,' he remarks sarcastically and after the tanker passes them very closely to starboard, adds 'black and menacing she rapidly merged with the night. It was as though she had never existed. She appeared to have altered course but of this I could not be too sure...'

Or the night they both turned in leaving the boat hove-to in a flat, calm sea in the Tuamotus. Ben was confident he had measured the boat's drift and leeway. But lying in his bunk: 'I was aware something had changed. The boat's motion was more lively and from outside there came a strange, continuous roaring sound.' On deck they found a reef just yards under their lee with the ocean sending up breakers on it.

The reader will agree with the author that noise is possibly the most frightening feature of a gale and 'a gaff rigged boat's mass of standing and running rigging produces a sound like a musical instrument.' Here let me throw in an excerpt from one of my own favourite passages: the thoughts of a Tall Ship skipper who Alan Villiers interviewed for his memorable book *The War With Cape Horn*.

'In the tumult of spray and hail and tremendous ear-assaulting noise, I noticed the higher sound of the wind's scream at the rigging screws, the deeper roar of that mighty orchestra in the powerful shrouds and backstays.'

Ben's voyage helped bring about the Ocean Cruising Club when its founder, Humphrey Barton of *Vertue XXXV* fame, called for a club record which would detail ocean cruises.

I started by saying I would like to have sailed with Ben and especially on a boat as beautiful as *Tern II*. To my surprise I discovered in this book that he has a hankering for a craft I once sailed upon: *Cambria* the last of the Thames spritsail barges. Certainly my old skipper Bob Roberts sailed without any mod cons at all, as I reported in the biography I wrote about him: *The Last Sailorman*. Like *Tern II*, *Cambria* had no electrics 'let alone electronics'; like *Tern II*, *Cambria*'s weather forecasting was by the barometer and the look of the sky and run of the sea. Like *Tern II*, *Cambria*'s foul weather 'wardrobe' were old fisherman's style oilskin coats and bare feet in summer, or clogs in winter. *Tern II* had an engine of sorts, although for all the use it was she might as well have been like *Cambria* and not had one at all.

The good news for people who share Ben's passion for these very different but great sailing machines, is that both *Tern II* and *Cambria* are being rebuilt. The bad news for me is that it comes too late for that sail.

Chapter One

Genesis

*We who adventure upon the
sea, however humbly, cannot
feel but we are more fortunate
than ordinary people.*

CLAUD WORTH, *YACHT CRUISING*

'I don't care,' Peter said, 'whether we go to Alaska or New Zealand. I just want a good sail.'

I liked it. Straightforward. No hint of a secret agenda. Here, I thought, was someone to whom I could relate and get along with over an extended ocean passage, and more importantly there was a suggestion that he might even get along with me. The setting for this conversation was in an officers' club in London's Cromwell Road and it was Easter 1953. This 'constructive dialogue' was one of several held with a variety of people over that weekend, the objective being to find someone prepared to throw their lot in with me on a small boat passage from England to New Zealand via the South Seas. I was not certain, though, how successful this quest for a crew would work out. It might be a tall order to find individuals prepared to give up their present settled existence and sail off with a complete stranger to the other side of the globe to a totally new life. It could be assumed that if there were any such souls, they would be thinking in terms of a one-way passage. In those days, the protracted time as well as the cost involved in overseas travel by ship severely restricted people's ability to travel. Here, however, in the form of Peter, I had someone who was relaxed about all this: he just wanted 'a good sail'. Great!

The wonder is always new that any sane man can be a sailor.

R WALDO EMERSON

I had hoped that a 'crew wanted' advertisement in the appropriate media might perhaps unearth what potential there was – expected, at best, to be small. If any correspondence ensued it would be followed up by a face-to-face meeting with the brave hearts who responded. As it was to turn out, the problem was not in getting a response but in dealing with the numbers who did respond. One difficulty was my own position in the scheme of things. As an engineer officer with specific flight deck responsibilities in the new aircraft carrier HMS *Eagle*, my time was not my own. The *Eagle's* role was to facilitate the changeover in the navy's air arm from propeller propulsion to jet power. As this involved a considerable amount of sea time, face-to-face interviews with potential crew were difficult to arrange.

The quest for a crew was another step on the road to achieving a long-held ambition to experience the joys or otherwise of long-distance cruising under sail, and more especially in my own boat. Since a young age I had read most of the books of small-boat voyages, commencing with the pioneering Captain Joshua Slocum, whose entertaining account of a remarkable, and at the time unique, circumnavigation (published by Adlard Coles Nautical in 2003), had set the pattern for an elite group of adventurers: Voss, Robinson, Gerbault and the like. Independently minded and self-reliant, they achieved their 'groundbreaking' goals unaided and unsupported. They were a world apart from their modern equivalents who are armed with unbelievably clever navigation and communication aids, coupled, moreover, with constant contact with outside assistance the moment something goes wrong. Reading those historic accounts, the essential difference between then and now jumps. The early sailors were at one with the sea and the elements around them. Their world was what they could see, hear and feel on a flat disc surrounding them of three miles radius. They were completely alone in that world. Not any more. Technology has put paid to that oneness with the elemental world. It was to be my good fortune and happy fate to participate in and enjoy small-boat cruising the way it was, before the explosion in scientific development was to sweep away that simple empathy with the sea.

I had joined *Eagle* in Belfast when she was still in the hands of her builders, Harland and Wolff, during the 'troubles'. The ensuing commission in her had been a rewarding and eventful experience, but that was now coming to an end, with my presence being required back in New Zealand to join another ship. What better way to make that journey than in my own boat? That would satisfy that long-dormant desire for an ocean passage under sail. The rather tortuous path to fulfilment now got under way.

Before anything could happen I needed approval from my overlord, the navy. The normal mode of travel in those days was by passenger liner, long-haul flying being still in its infancy. As an ocean liner passage from Southampton via the Cape of Good Hope to Auckland was, in any event, going to take many weeks, I harboured the thought that the naval authorities in New Zealand might be sympathetic to my alternative transport proposal. They were. The Admiralty was also co-operative, in that I was loaned the two essential tools for ocean voyaging; an Admiralty-pattern micrometer sextant and a chronometer watch. The choice of timepieces lay between a deck watch and the more accurate chronometer watch. The former was frequently used in ships to take the time of the astronomical observation out on deck and relate that to the more precise time kept by the main chronometer down below. The deck watch would have done the job if fairly frequent radio time signals could have been procured, but as I could not be too sure about this I asked for and received the more accurate and correspondingly more expensive chronometer watch. Their Lordships were most obliging. Would the MOD be so today?

Approval had not been a foregone conclusion by any means, as 'human resource management' to foster personal development through adventure activity was not then the fashionable concept that it is today. A condition of approval, however, was that for the duration of the trip I would not enjoy receiving any pay. Also I was not to dawdle on the way, indulging myself on a supposedly carefree jaunt whilst my fellow officers were sweating it out on the job. However, there was an upside, in that I would be given a lump sum of cash, the equivalent of what my fare would have cost in a passenger ship. This was most welcome, as the expected outlay on the venture could raise the distinct possibility of an invitation for a chat, probably unsatisfactory to both parties, with the bank manager. The no-pay ruling was presumably based on the principle that whilst out of the mainstream of naval service, gratifying a personal whim, I was contributing nothing to the defence of the realm. However, the same could be said for the period I was out of the front line whilst enjoying shipboard romances and equally not in circulation in an ocean liner, unable to respond to a call to arms. Accordingly it might have been arguable that I could reasonably have expected to have been paid for the anticipated time such a passage would have taken. However, not wanting to push my luck, I did not advance this proposition.

Armed with the necessary approbation, I could now proceed with the twin basic tasks of finding a crew and a boat.

The start point for the crew search would seem logically to be the yachting press. Sure enough, as soon as the advertisement 'Crew wanted by young naval officer for small-boat passage to New Zealand' appeared on the shelves, it brought a response: not the trickle I expected but a veritable flood. The letters just kept rolling in. All ages, working people, retired, both sexes and a surprising range of backgrounds. What I was looking for, of course, were those whose principal motivation lay in sailing, and although those individuals were naturally well represented, the correspondence began to reveal there were wider issues at stake. It became apparent that there were many 'out there' within the public at large who wanted badly to emigrate to the New World, particularly the Commonwealth, and this was a way to do it within reach of their pockets. In the context of post-war Britain, the urge to get away, if it could be afforded, was so understandable. The state had not yet stepped in with subsidised travel and assisted overseas settlement – 'the '£10 Poms'.

The quest for a crew was to put me in touch with a wide section of everyday existence. Widespread dissatisfaction with the aftermath of the war, pessimism about the future, ongoing food and commodity shortages and an overall lack of faith in the country's governance were very evident. Disillusionment with what their political leaders had brought about was dominant in the mood of many. Two world wars had been fought. Why? The origins of the 1914–18 Great War had never been clear, but what was clear was that it should not have been fought.

It was easy to apply the same scepticism to its successor, World War II. At its end, Great Britain had seemingly been victorious, but in terms of people's daily lives the perception was different. The country was bankrupt, vast numbers had lost their lives and the ranks of the young were decimated.

The population as a whole had made tremendous sacrifices, all in the cause of achieving security. So where was the security?

The international tensions that had been building up between the two world wars were now re-emerging yet again, albeit with different principal actors, but deepening in a form far more sinister and threatening. So much for the security that the British people had been assured twice during the century would be their reward for going to war. They had been told that defeating Hitler was necessary to save them from death and destruction. The policy makers brushed aside the fact that Hitler had made it clear enough that he did not want a fight with Great Britain, stating repeatedly in speeches and writings that his objective was to defeat Communism and expand Germany eastward by taking land from Russia. The Russians, the real enemy, were in his sights, not the British. On this premise there was a body of opinion that claimed Britain would have been better advised not to have declared war on Germany in 1939, but instead to have stood aside and left Germany and Russia to fight each other to a standstill and complete exhaustion. Britain, Europe and much of the world would then have been spared the horrors of total war.

The post-war threat now looming on the horizon was infinitely worse than the pre-World War II threat: total nuclear annihilation. So what had the blood, sweat and tears been all about? No wonder disillusionment with the 'Establishment' had become the popular attitude. Churchill, far from being appreciated as the nation's wartime saviour, was thrown out in the 1945 end-of-war general election. It was he who had been a dominant proclaimer of doom in the 1930s, leading the non-appeasement lobby with an aggressive, hostile policy towards Nazi Germany – an attitude not universally adopted by the British population. Included in the dissenting ranks, it would seem, was Aneurin Bevan, the father of the NHS.

'Winston Churchill does not talk the language of the 20th century but that of the 18th. He is still fighting Blenheim all over again. His only answer to a difficult situation is to send a gunboat'.

There was, in the immediate aftermath of the war, a view that Churchill had resolved a conflict which he had played a major role in starting in the first place – all, it could be argued, in his pursuit of personal ambition for power and influence at a time when his political fortunes were at a low ebb. The returned servicemen and women, coupled with those who had taken the strain at home, had had enough. They had been asked by the politicians to endure the dangers and hardships:

Till we have built Jerusalem
In England's green and pleasant land.

But what they had been promised had not happened. It was not surprising that I had received such a positive response to my advertisement.

However, I was not setting myself up to resolve these social problems by supplying an emigration facility. I was primarily seeking to make contact with those who had an overriding interest in ocean voyaging. If this offered an opening to a new life, that would be all to the good. A bonus.

To sort out the motivation behind the applications, a shortlist was compiled which entailed a not inconsiderable volume of correspondence; so much so that 'postie', the ship's postman, was overheard to make an expressive comment when delivering the wardroom mail about my personal responsibility for the unwanted addition to his workload. But then he always seemed to convey the impression that having to handle mail was an unfair imposition on him.

The respondents had included in their number several females. I pondered long and hard on this. In the 50s, attitudes to mixed crews in the confines of a small boat, particularly on an extended voyage, were very different to what they are today. Although the war had removed many of the taboos, there was still a degree of conservatism in society's feelings about such questions. There being a certain ambivalence on my part, I decided to play safe and have an all-male crew.

Nubile young women would not necessarily be out of place, but if I needed any further reassurance about my decision, a prescient philosopher added a timely warning:

> *It was a blonde. A blonde to make a bishop kick a hole in a stained glass window.*
>
> RAYMOND CHANDLER

With the list of possible candidates having been compiled, the next step was to interview them. I was quite well known in that London officers' club, and having secured the secretary's interest, a phased programme of meetings was set up with the candidates over the Easter weekend, *Eagle* being in harbour for this event. To put some consistency into the interviews and provide a basis for subsequent analysis of the responses, the methodology was to draw up a list of set questions to be asked of all interviewees. One such question, bearing in mind Dr Johnson's observation that 'being in a ship is being in a jail, with the chance of drowning', was 'Why do you want to set off on a long ocean cruise with all the discomfort, risk and restriction of being stuck in a small boat, miles from any land and no means of escape?' I must admit this was a question to which I personally had no ready answer. The last question on the list, and probably the most important, comprised: 'After our chat, how do you feel about having to live with me, with no respite, for a month or more way out at sea?' Unsurprisingly everyone was most tactful when answering this one.

Peter Fox came out clearly the front runner. I felt happy about him and I sensed he harboured the same sentiment in return. He was employed as a quantity surveyor with Portsmouth City Council, was single and hence had no family commitments.

One of the stock questions put to all concerned their state of health. In Peter's case he was all clear, apart from the occasional bout of asthma. We had both heard it said that a complete change of environment was beneficial. What could be more of a change than exchanging urban life for one on the ocean wave? We decided that his unfortunate complaint would not be a problem. In fact, although not occurring all that often, it was to cause difficulties.

Following the weekend's interview I had the task of breaking the news to the unsuccessful ones. I did not enjoy this. There had been so much hope. I had not been relaxed during the interviewing sessions, which had left me with the uncomfortable feeling I was some sort of jumped-up Lord Muck, holding ordinary people's future in my hands. I sought consolation in the thought that for many of them the likelihood was that escaping from home would not in reality have fulfilled their hopes.

The crew question resolved, it was a matter of settling on the boat. By now, this was in fact well under way.

'Don't mind if I do, sir. Mine's a mild and bitter. A pint. Me mates 'ere will have the same, thanking yer kindly.' Alf and his friends were helping me cope with a raw winter's evening huddled in the near warmth of a public house in Woodbridge on England's east coast. It was mid December and it was cold. Very cold. That part of the country has a special brand of bleakness. The all-too-frequent wind comes off the North Sea, cutting into one's bones, as Masefield would say, 'like a whetted knife'. The flat countryside offers no protection to the strong onshore winds from the North Sea that mercilessly sweep over the mud flats, up the rivers and across the low contoured land.

Tern II had recently become mine and was lying in a mud berth in Robertsons Boatyard, up the Deben River and near to Woodbridge town centre. I had a week's leave in the run-up to Christmas and had a plan to spend it in the boat, getting to know her. To this end, I had acquired a paraffin heater and some bedding, and after laying in basic food stocks, I moved in. Night comes early in midwinter, particularly in those parts, and by late afternoon the yard was immersed in darkness and deserted. I suddenly felt very alone. The only sound was a low whining, the wind playing amongst the masts and threading through the rigging of the boats laid up in the yard. The steady inhuman note emphasised that aloneness. Despite the heater giving its utmost, the boat was cold and so was I. I retired to the pub. This was to become the pattern for the rest of the week.

Alf and company were pleased to see me. Strangers were always welcome, particularly when they had the chance to assist with the flow of beer. I also provided them with the lucrative opportunity to impart their pearls of public bar wisdom on a captive receiver.

Alf and his mates were good company, and the outlay on all that beer was well worth it, saving me from the cold, lonely nights in that dismal, dark boatyard. They were practised tellers of entertaining salty yarns of doubtful veracity, or perhaps one should say brackish yarns, as Woodbridge and its pub are some way up the Deben.

The search for the boat had turned out to be quite easy. Snatching weekends away from the ship, I had looked at several, principally through another advertisement I had placed in *Yachting Monthly*. Post-war England was a buyers' market. Up came a boat further along the coast. She was called *Petula*, and I liked her but decided against. As it happened I was to meet with her again. That was to be in Lisbon and again in the Canaries.

Tern II then came up on offer and it was love at first sight. She had an air about her and I liked that air. She looked strong, with beautiful, classic lines. Moreover, closer inspection indicated she was in good condition and her gear sound. She had obviously been well looked after and cared for throughout her life. To do 'the right thing', I called in the local boat surveyor. He was young and relaxed, joining me for a beer and a chat. After a stroll through the boat and opening a few cupboards he pronounced her 'fit for the purpose'. She had, he said, 'a good smell about her'. After presenting his bill and being paid, he departed, leaving me wondering if I was in the wrong profession.

Tern II was the second of the well-known series of boats of ever increasing size owned by the legendary Claud Worth, author and doyen of cruising sailors in the first part of the 20th century. *Tern III* was to be lost at sea, but *Tern IV* and *Tern II*, at the time of writing, are mercifully still with us. My *Tern*, a gaff yawl, 39 foot on deck and built in 1899, was straight of stem, with a long graceful counter and long straight keel, deep enough to allow a flush deck with skylights. Although born in the 'plank-on-edge era', narrow and deep in section, she had more beam than others of her kind; consequently there was more space down below without, moreover, the same proclivity as others of the type to go 'on her ear' when sailing on the wind. Now well into middle age, she was little changed from Claud's days. The galley was forward in the bows, which also contained a fold-up pipe cot which would have allowed for a paid hand to get on with the cooking without intruding on life in the saloon.

Crew and the owner's ensemble, of course, did not mix. The saloon was a delight: two settees with brocaded squabs. The backrests formed the base of pull-down bunks, which remained discreetly out of sight when not in use, putting on display the beautifully grained, polished, wooden joinery of Spanish timber. The boat's interior, although faded and darkened with age, was still elegant, with a warm intimacy, particularly at night under the brass oil lamps. Between the saloon and the forepeak was the heads compartment, closed off by doors on its forward and after ends, fitted out with a hanging wardrobe with mirrored panelled doors, and drawers in a sideboard. A tip-up washbasin emptied into the toilet bowl. This was a space which enabled the owner, owner's wife and guests to change their attire in privacy, considered essential in those days. The compartment was referred to by Claud Worth in his writings about the boat as 'a commodious dressingroom with a separate skylight'.

The bringing of *Tern* round to Plymouth from Woodbridge was an educational experience, involving a study of human performance, whilst engaged at the same time with the practice of coastal navigation and getting to know how the old lady liked to be treated.

For this exercise I could not complain about being undermanned. As Peter could not sail with me, he sent along a close friend, another dinghy sailor, Harry. He was to prove a real asset. In addition, there were two serving naval officers who were to prove decidedly non-assets, at least during the early part of the ensuing passage. They tended to reinforce the old maxim about the three most useless objects in a small boat being a naval officer, a wheelbarrow and an umbrella. I am not sure where this leaves me, though.

The Deben has its fair share of shallow patches and we found them in the most positive way. We stuck on them.

We emerged, however, into the North Sea relatively unscathed, apart from a little emotional wear and tear, and turned south to negotiate the Dover Strait, with its sandbanks and the perils of shipping congestion. It was getting dark, damp and raw with, of course, that penetrating east wind. In other words, a typical east coast night was drawing on. I can defend that statement on the basis of previous experience sailing those waters. I had been there before as a voluntarily unpaid mate of a trading Thames barge, *Clara*. One of the last of her kind, a true 'spritty' as the bargemen would say, earning her living carrying cargo, frequently wheat, in and out of London Docks, engineless and with the bare minimum of crew. Built in 1896, of 60 tons and carrying more than twice that in cargo, she had remained largely unchanged over the years. In her and under her skipper/ owner, the incomparable Captain Banyard, I learned about real sailorising. I also learned something about the shifting sands in those parts.

In a night similar to the one we were about to experience in *Tern*, we put our deeply laden barge firmly on to the seaward end of a sandspit and there we stuck; the prospects, at least as they seemed to me, were not promising. Aground on a lee shore, a hefty wind blowing us further on, dismal, drizzly rain, and the night as dark as 'the inside of a cow'. No engine and no radio to seek help, as we would do in present times. Our fate lay in the hands of my captain, who turned not a hair. 'Nothing more to do now, lad, until the tide makes again and we sail off. Time we had a mug of tea down below.' Sail off she did. *The Magic of the Swatchways* may have immortalised that sailing area but there was little evidence of any 'magic' during our dismal night. In the times I sailed with him, not once did he ever raise his voice, no matter how adverse the circumstances. Like the rest of his breed, he was 'imperturbable and solid'.

The London River, and particularly the dock systems then, were unbelievably different to the nothingness of what they are today. In the '50s Britain was still a major maritime nation, and London Docks the centre of the shipping world. The congestion of craft was bewildering in variety – passenger liners, cargo ships, tugs, lighters, barges, and coastal vessels of all sizes and shapes in the Thames waterways. Through this lot in the river and the docks themselves, filled with ships, bow to stern, the humble barge under sail alone had to find her way, relying solely on the skill of master and crew. It seemed there was a permanent war between the different denizens of the river. Lightermen, in particular, seemed to go out of their way to make life difficult for the bargemen.

I had my first encounter with the docks way of life when I joined *Clara* on a damp, unpromising evening as she was finishing loading a cargo of wheat. On my way down to where she had been loading, I had noticed one or two little groups of men engaged in earnest discussion, the reason for which was explained to me later. They were concerned about a particular instance of docks thievery and corruption, not with a view of finding a way to correct an undesirable situation, but rather what damage limitation exercise should be mounted. Bulk cargoes, such as wheat, were loaded into barges and lighters via a chute fed from an elevated hopper, each installation being under the control of a loading master. There was no independent monitoring of what he actually loaded and what he said he had loaded. Systematic abuse, in sophisticated ways, of the loading regime had been standard practice for a long time but beneficiaries of it had suddenly become worried. One loading master had recently 'got religion' and now felt it was his God-driven mission to spill the beans, hence the groups of concerned men.

We put the hatch covers on and sailed at midnight. With the tide under us we breasted the broken waters of the river with the wind fully in our teeth. It was uncomfortable going, the night raw and miserable in the persistent drizzle. When going about, the mate's task was to tend the foresail, and to do so he had to get forward. With the head sea we were taking solid water on board, filling the decks and sluicing over the hatch. Waiting for the barge to lift and throw off the load of water, it was a question of judgement when to make a dash for the mast, running along the top of the hatch cover. Meanwhile, the master was putting the wheel over to bring the bows through the wind. As the barge came head-to-wind the foresail would come aback, held by a bowline, blowing the bows over onto the other tack. The mate then released the bowline, the foresail crashing over to fill on the new tack. Its sheet was a bight of chain running on a massive wooden beam across the foredeck. It was a big, heavy sail and one had to be careful to keep well out of its way when it came hurtling across, otherwise there could be an unwelcome outcome.

In the early hours, the tide turned against us and it was a case of anchoring to hold our ground. This was again an operation not without its risks. The mate was also central to this somewhat cumbersome procedure. The main bower anchor, a big fisherman type, was permanently over the side, close up to the bow, held there by the anchor chain. This had three turns round the horizontal wooden drum of the windlass which could only turn in one direction: to heave in. To let the anchor go, the turns were lifted off with one's fingers, whereupon the cable rushed out. The mate's part in the working of a barge was exacting and at times downright dangerous.

Compare the scene with today. The waters of the docks are dead, apart from brave attempts at yacht berths. The soul has gone, replaced with graceless high-rise buildings, an ill-conceived dome, a glitzy exhibition building and not much else.

At the beginning of the 1950s, when I became involved with Thames barges, there were 50 or more, mainly wooden, still trading under sail alone, with the first built in 1889 and the last, in steel, in 1925. It was sad that these graceful craft were vanishing, taking with them the sea lore and the skills needed to sail them. It is of some consolation that quite a few have survived in the form of auxiliary yachts, but it has to be accepted that the essential spirit of the time-venerated Thames spritsail barge, the spritty, has gone.

I was so privileged, albeit in a small peripheral way, to have experienced, in the form of barging life, commercial sail before it vanished for ever. When I had a couple of weeks' leave coming up I would contact Captain Banyard, who always seemed happy for me to join him. At the time, true sailing barges were giving way to motorised versions, hybrids which retained the main gear but had the mizzen mast removed, a wheelhouse erected in its place and a diesel engine installed. I was to sail once in one and life was certainly much easier on the mate, but the barge had lost its heart. This transition saw a change in the character of the young man contemplating a career in barges. Progressively, those offering themselves for this vocation were disinclined to take up the life of third hand or mate in a sailing barge with all that that entailed in hard living and hard work. Motor barges were vastly easier, the work less demanding and less skilled, as well as better paid. This was the situation facing my captain, who remained true to the profession in which he had been brought up. *Clara* was continuing to make a profit and he saw no reason to change. He was not afraid of hard work. He was, however, experiencing the increasing problem of getting a mate and, if he got one, keeping him. The problem became so acute that over one winter he sailed *Clara* single-handed. How one man managed to get a heavily loaded barge in and out of London Docks under sail alone and then handle her on the coast in all weathers was quite beyond me. This, however, did lead to an intriguing situation in which, in due course, I was to become involved.

With some leave once again coming up, I was in touch with the captain, who advised he would be loading in Rochester for London and I would be most welcome.

'And where's ee goin' ter sleep?' enquired the stevedore of his mates at large as I walked off. I had just been directed to where *Clara* was lying, wondering at the rather curious question but giving it no further thought. She was unchanged since I had last been on board, or so I thought. There was no one around as I went down into the little cabin to await the master's return. The interior was as before, but there was something different which became apparent as I looked more closely around me. Bright curtains were up, on the table was a gaily patterned table cloth and most strange of all, there were vases of freshly picked flowers. What had happened to the man I thought I had known? The basic, no-frills, very utilitarian cuddy had been transformed into a HOME! I was pondering on this mystery when I heard voices topside. One was the captain's and the other decidedly female. The owners of these voices then appeared down below. The female voice belonged to a strong-looking young woman, most pleasant and personable. This was Marion. It was evident that she was very much a member of the barge's complement. Enlightenment began to dawn. The significance of the stevedore's query was now becoming clear.

Over tea, with cups and saucers in place of the more familiar mugs that had become stained through long use, and with little cakes laid out, the captain explained it all. I must say I was now relaxed, knowing that he had not undergone some metamorphosis of personality. The need for a full-time mate becoming pressing, it being too much to ask anyone to keep on sailing a barge single-handed indefinitely, he had placed a simple advertisement in the London papers, but one which said it all: 'Mate required for working Thames sailing barge'. Several replies were received, most being transparently inappropriate, but one did catch his eye. It was so different to what he had expected. The applicant was a London typist who had become disenchanted with the tedium and parochialism of City office life, banging away all day on a typewriter. She badly needed a change in lifestyle. What greater change could there be than a barge, actually being on the river rather than just catching the odd glimpse of it? An interview was set up at which she and the captain experienced an immediate empathy. The subsequent arrangement had worked out well. In addition to introducing the benefits of a warm 'woman's' touch to the barge's routine, she had proved most competent on deck, providing that extra pair of hands that was so needed. There were many occasions when her presence made all the difference, such as taking the wheel when some particularly heavy task had to be undertaken.

That night we went ashore to the wharfside pub for a drink. There was the slightly bizarre scene of *Clara*'s crew sitting in a row on a bench, the captain and the third hand, myself, drinking pints of bitter, and between us the mate drinking Pimm's No1 and reading *Vogue* magazine. 'The mate of the *Clara*' was the talk of the London River, a situation unheard of in recent memory. That night I put my head down in the tiny accommodation, hitherto unused, right up forward. I was not, unfortunately, to have the occasion to put the stevedore's mind at rest.

It is interesting to compare yachtsmen's attitudes now with those prevailing in earlier eras. It may be satisfying to the older generation of yachtsmen to maintain that sailors of today 'ain't what they used to be', but if 'seamanship' is defined as an integral part of the safe conduct of a vessel, then 'starter button seamanship' can be considered good seamanship.

Frank Carr's monumental work, *Sailing Barges*, had featured so prominently in my early reading programme to learn about sailing, and had been the successor to a quite marvellous book entitled *Cruising and Ocean Racing*, published on behalf of the Lonsdale Library and which included contributions from the likes of EG Martin and John Irving, the predecessors of Eric Hiscock. The latter book was in the library of my school and I studied every word from cover to cover. Viewed through modern eyes it was unbelievably traditional, all about 'housing topmasts' and 'reefing bowsprits'. Those two books hooked me and provided me with a sound basic grounding, if that is the right word, to launch me into sailing.

In *Tern*, as we rushed south in the brisk onshore wind, the memories of earlier occasions in a barge in those selfsame waters were vividly before me. Now I was reliving the conditions in my own boat. The deteriorating weather was starting to take its toll on my crew. The professional duo of David and John, almost as one man, took to their bunks and there they stayed throughout the night. It was not until breakfast time next morning, after we had passed down through the Dover Strait and were well into the Channel off Eastbourne, that two wan faces appeared. The sea by then had gone down, the sun was peeping through and the misery of the night forgotten. They had given up completely at a time when their help would have been useful, but such is the crippling effect of that universal killer, seasickness. Not so, Harry. He and I had shared that damp, dreary and vigorous night, across the Thames Estuary and through the strait with their sands and ships. I had felt a great sympathy for our two sufferers and had tried to give them comfort in the midst of their woes, but in reality that had been the wrong approach. If they had been forced onto their feet and made to play an active role in the handling of the boat and participated in her pilotage, it would have been so much better for them. This was a lesson I had yet to learn.

Later in the forenoon we made a pit stop, welcome to all hands, in the Solent, anchoring off Cowes. By prior arrangement, the previous owner – a retired army officer, Lieutenant Colonel Brodie – came on board to meet up with me first-hand to pass on tips and advice based on his experience with *Tern*. With wife and child he had spent a happy time living on board in the Mediterranean, the cruise earning him the Royal Cruising Club's cup. He had a great affection for the old boat, and his words of encouragement on the forthcoming adventure were very well received. It had been a worthwhile stop, with smiling faces all round on board once again, the acute discomfort of the night completely forgotten.

With the crew now fully recovered, we arrived in good order in Plymouth Sound to go on to pick up a pre-booked mooring off Mashford's Boatyard at Cremyll and started on the programme to prepare for the passage ahead. That delivery trip had confirmed I had a good boat, and furthermore, judging by the performance of his close friend, the indications were I was going to have a good crew in Peter. The portents for the passage ahead were promising.

Chapter Two

The Joining Up

*The sea finds out everything
you did wrong.*

FRANCIS STOKES

'PLYMOUTH TO NEW ZEALAND IN 39FT YAWL. YOUNG LIEUTENANT SAILS IN MONTH'. So the *Western Evening Herald* proclaimed to the world. We had no option now but to go through with the venture. However, armed with the confidence that goes with youth, I was feeling reasonably relaxed about the undertaking. In its planning and the attention needed for its successful execution, I had benefited greatly from serving in one of Her Majesty's vessels. In this regard I was fortunate in having a co-operative executive officer, he who is second in command to the ship's captain. *Eagle*'s executive officer, known by his rank as the commander, was the late Peter Hill-Norton, destined to achieve the highest pinnacle of his profession. The commander was interested in what I was doing and that made not a little difference. One of my concerns was how to tackle the crucial, if not *the* crucial question of provisioning and all that that entailed. What had to be arrived at was a best guess at how much of what would two hungry men consume in the way of non-perishable foodstuffs over nine or ten months. The intention was to store fully before we left Plymouth, and it had to be assumed that space would be found on board *Tern* to stow it all away, as it was recognized that boats of that era and type were not expecting to make long passages between stopovers. A matter for particular consideration in my situation was where and when to purchase our stocks, and moreover where to accommodate them in advance of being able to get them on board *Tern*. Associated with storing a large quantity of tinned produce was the requirement to preserve it against the ravages of a sea air environment over a considerable period of time. Perceived wisdom was to remove the labels, paint on the tins the code reference for the contents and then apply a couple of coats of varnish. It could be argued there was a case for not removing the labels. When inevitably these came off, the contents of the cans would then have constituted a mystery. The unexpected results would have presented a challenge to the cook, adding interest to what might otherwise have been a less exciting meal, its preparation entailing an excursion into the unknown. The can treatment operation required space to lay it all out. If I had been living ashore this would have been more straightforward, but I was faced with the limitations of shipboard life. However, all was to be well.

We were due to call in to Gibraltar for fuel and stores replenishment. This could be the time to lay in my own stores. The commander demonstrated his co-operation with, 'You can have the cabin that young soldier never used and keep your grub in it for as long as you like'. When the marine contingent had come on board at the time of our commissioning in Belfast, there was included in their number a subaltern of exceptional dimensions: thin and excessively tall; so much so that the standard bunk fitted in cabins was far too short. As it was impracticable to lengthen the bunk in his allocated cabin, or the bunks in the other available cabins, the shipbuilders constructed especially for him a cabin with a bespoke bunk. This was to my advantage. I now had a space large enough to store all my tins and, moreover, with room to spread them out for the preservation treatment to be affected. *Eagle* was a large ship and a stable platform, so all those loose tins would not be all over the place in a seaway.

By now I knew what had to be purchased, having spent some considerable time studying what various ocean voyagers had written about their provisioning experiences – good and bad – including detailed suggestions on what to carry on a long ocean passage. I assumed Peter was not pernickety about his food. I was right in this assumption, but what I did not know was that I was to benefit from having a good cook on board – something that I was not. Peter had been living a bachelor's life for some time and during this period had acquired a culinary skill of some note, having developed an interest in that art. To have someone in a small-boat's crew who knows about cooking is, I have learned over the years, an asset beyond price.

I had further support from the commander (S), head of the department responsible for what we would know today as 'services' and that overworked word, 'logistics', the 'S' after his rank standing for 'supply'. He, along with the supply organisation as a whole, was known universally as the 'pusser', the successor to the original 'purser', the old name for individuals appointed to dispense pay, provisions and clothing in naval vessels. In doing so, these grace and favour appointees, known also as 'paymasters', were all too frequently more in receipt of opprobrium than approbation, many becoming very rich men at the expense of the unfortunate common sailor. Until reforms, stemming back to Samuel Pepys, gradually came into place, much of the unrest in earlier naval times could be attributed to the flexible way the purser dispensed in practice the Admiralty-laid-down scale of daily rations. Happily, the modern breed of pusser is looked upon with more favour and affection. The improved grading in the villainy scale is evidenced by the word 'pusser' coming into use as a synonym for the adverb 'proper'.

Stores and general provisioning being very much within his authority, our pusser was happy for me to ride on the back of the ship's storing programme, lumping in my requirements, albeit miniscule in comparison with the ship's orders, on the shoreside supplier, and moreover enabling me to enjoy the bulk purchase price spin-off. The trader would also deliver my goods at the same time as those for the ship. All I had to do was pay for mine. Everything was dropping into place. There would appear to be advantages in being a member of the naval system.

They were interesting days and rewarding ones. My sailing plans were coming to fruition and I was enjoying serving in *Eagle*. She was very much under scrutiny throughout the fleet and her performance closely watched. An occasion for this was the Home Fleet regatta held at Invergordon, the centrepiece of this being highly competitive intership whaler racing. Ships carried the Montague whaler as their sea boats, these being slung out in their davits and ready for immediate use at sea as safety boats for such emergencies as man overboard. Twenty-seven foot long, clinker built of wood and with no engine, they were pulled by five oars. This was a carry-over from an era when manpower was considered more reliable in an emergency, when the chips were really down, than this newfangled motor power. Additionally equipped for sailing with a standing lug yawl rig, they were used both as working boats and for recreation. They came into their own at regatta times and, being of standard design, provided keen competitive racing. Each ship entered pulling crews to represent individual departments, including wardroom officers' crews. Rivalry was intense, and winning was of great importance to the ship's complement, from the commanding officer down.

Because of her status, in no ship within the fleet was it of more importance to win than in *Eagle*. This was doubly so for Hill-Norton. To win the regatta was not only a litmus test of the organisation and training given the crews, but a highly visible indication of the ship's spirit and morale. A large measure of this was generally considered to be attributable to the executive officer. Success in the regatta could only serve to assist him up the promotion ladder. Ours took a keen interest in the training of the various crews, with a particular focus on the wardroom crew, of which I was a member, pulling at number three. Having him as our cox, we were to feel the full effects of this interest, with training sessions at every opportunity, the ship's routine being made to suit. Taking it one stage further, out of his own pocket he had arranged to be made for each of us Nelson-era sailors' outfits, and for himself an officer's rig of the times, complete with cocked hat. We had no option but to win.

The great day came and late in the forenoon our moment of truth was upon us. Over the ship's broadcast system came the pipe:

'Away wardroom racing whalers crew. Man your boat!'

Down the gangway we filed to be met with a no-nonsense look on the face of our cox. We pulled out to the starting line and went on to win. The ship, moreover, won the regatta overall. Hill-Norton was on his way up the promotion ladder and we had helped to put his foot on the next rung up. He was to end up Admiral of the Fleet Lord Hill-Norton, and I, for one, was happy for him.

It was party time in the wardroom and quite a party it was too. The commander being the president of the mess meant there was little difficulty in keeping the bar open. Late in the evening someone was heard to remark, 'Anyone seen the commander recently?' No one had, so a manhunt was mounted. In due course, there, behind an anteroom settee, was a recumbent figure, flat on its back with a happy smile on its face. As the winning crew we were given the honour of carrying its owner up to its cabin and putting it to bed. It was a kinder variation on the traditional practice of the successful crew throwing their cox over the side. It had been a good day for the commander, as it had been for the rest of us. Next day it was business as usual.

In my own personal world, my act was beginning to come together. Boat and crew were now in place and the bulk of the provisioning complete. It was now time to put in some details on the passage plan, which currently consisted of not much more than showing a departure point of Devonport, England, and arrival in Devonport, New Zealand. There was some filling in to be done. Primarily, what would call the tune was, of course, the wind. To be taken into account was the risk factor of the likelihood of tropical storms, but the overriding consideration was to choose a route and time to make the optimum use of the wind patterns in the two oceans we would be traversing: the North Atlantic and the South Pacific. In view of the time I had available to me, the clear choice of routes was via the Panama Canal. First off, to ensure enjoyment of the so-called Portuguese Trades, fresh northerly or north-easterly winds blowing down the Iberian coast, a yacht should aim to leave English shores by the end of August. Much later than this the frequency of gales starts to rise, as does the greater likelihood of south-westerly winds. This timing fitted in well with the temporary cessation of my naval activities. A non-stop run to Madeira, and then a period in the Canaries before making the Atlantic crossing in the north-east trade wind belt, would ensure we arrived in the West Indies after the hurricane season had pretty well run its course. On entering the Pacific at the beginning of the following year, the Doldrums belt should be narrow, allowing us to get through them fairly quickly, and thence into the south-east trade winds on the eastern side of the ocean. By the time we arrived in April in the region north of New Zealand and east of Australia, the cyclone season should have expired and the South Pacific winter conditions should not have yet developed. Accordingly I advised the New Zealand Naval Board that I would leave Plymouth at the end of August and arrive in Auckland at the end of the following April. With the uncertainties of sailing, and in particular long-distance voyaging, this confident prediction might have been seen as being unrealistically precise, with more faith than certainty. But we certainly aimed to meet this timetable, even though adjustments were to be needed en route, to the passage plan.

There were two doctors on board, one of which, Surgeon Lieutenant David Perrins, was of gynaecological fame, and was a personal friend and member of the family in that well-known British institution, Lea and Perrins, with their unrivalled Worcestershire sauce, 'The Original and Genuine.' He assumed the role of medical adviser to *Tern*'s crew and set about assembling a medical chest so comprehensive that every ailment and physical misfortune that could possibly overtake us would be catered for with no difficulty. With the contents went detailed instructions on how and when to use them. These guidelines were incorporated in a copy he edited of the *Ship Captain's Medical Guide*, the 1946 18th edition. It was a small, plain, closely printed, modest publication and totally unlike the glossy, colourful version of today. The first edition had been produced in 1868 at the behest of the Ministry of Transport to help masters of vessels not carrying a doctor. That was us. Apart from invaluable advice on all manner of ills, it contained a wealth of helpful observations such as: 'How to detect horse flesh... The carcase of a horse can hardly be mistaken for that of an ox'. And again, what every young sailor needed to know: there was a full description of making 'cunji water for an invalid'. Inside the front cover David had included various observations of his own: 'You will find the book suggests a purge for nearly every condition; this is a relic of the old empirical days and is not considered very important these days.' He ends on an encouraging note, at least for the faithful: 'The Almighty is the best physician and nearly all conditions will eventually cure themselves in the end.' As it happened, except on just one or two occasions, we did not have to open the lid of this medical treasure trove or seek divine assistance but we were well set up. We needed to be, as with no radio communication to call for help as one would today, we were very much on our own, medically speaking, both at sea and in many of the places where we called.

I was also helped in other ways. To avoid dragging a fixed-bladed propeller, with the consequential loss of miles made good, I fitted a self-folding type. Not particularly efficient and pretty hopeless when going astern, but it certainly improved sailing performance. The design of the boss of the new propeller required the remachining of the existing propeller shaft. Where else but *Eagle*'s extensive machine shop? In the course of going on board to check on progress I was to overhear the machinist, a senior engine room artificer, complaining to a mate nearby about having 'to turn on *Tern II*'s f****** propeller shaft'. I was very happy to hear this. It has long been a navy adage that 'when Jack stops complaining is the time to start worrying'.

This was followed by yet another call on the ship's capabilities. One of *Tern*'s wrought iron floors, the heavy metal straps that secured the boat's frames to the wooden keel, had wasted badly over 50 years. Through the floor went a bronze keel bolt, with the result that galvanic action had caused the iron to corrode. I procured some bar stock and made a template from which the ship's blacksmith forged a new floor. It fitted perfectly.

In the context of attitudes prevailing today, I suppose there would be accusations of misuse of government resources and I would have faced a court martial: at best thrown out on my ear, being marched out of the dockyard gate, medals and buttons ceremoniously ripped off, to the slow roll of a drum. In those days there seemed to be a more relaxed attitude to such matters. The navy was then always referred to as 'The Service' and this was a meaningful expression. Personnel of all ranks had a great sense of belonging to something bigger than oneself, transcending personal interest. The Service came first but in turn was expected to look after its own. To balance this unstinted dedication to the concept of service, perhaps a little something coming back on occasion could be condoned. Fanciful rationalisation perhaps, but then again perhaps not.

To get halfway across the world, covering two oceans, a knowledge of nautical astronomy was self-evident, and this is what I did not have, being an engineer officer by specialisation. Officer cadets, joining the navy in what was known as the Special Entry Scheme, underwent the same initial training, but this did not embrace the intricacies of celestial navigation. This so-called black art I now had to address. At that time there was no way of finding one's way over the world's open seas out of sight of land other than by deriving the ship's position from sextant observations of the heavenly bodies. There was, of course, no shortage of textbooks on the subject, including the easy-to-read *Admiralty Manual of Navigation: Volume 2*. These all explained the theory adequately enough, but I felt the way to drive it into my head was to practise worked examples over and over again to become as proficient as possible in converting theory into practice. To achieve this I needed to be disciplined, and the way to do this, it seemed to me, was to take a correspondence course, which would involve receiving a string of questions which had to be answered and numerically worked, thence to be sent back for marking. I selected a programme run by Captain OM Watts from their upmarket chandlery in London's Albemarle Street. It was excellent value for money and gave me a grounding in a subject that I found fascinating, imparting a deep interest in astronomical navigation which has remained with me ever since. The wealth of exercises involved the working up of the full gambit of sights of the sun, planets, stars and the moon, leading me to become word perfect, as it were.

Watts himself was something of a legend. A young master mariner, bright and enterprising, he had left the sea in 1927 and, in the early 30s, in conjunction with Thomas Reed and Co, compiled, edited and published *Reeds Nautical Almanac*. The choice of publisher was a good one. The family-owned business, later sold to Adlard Coles Nautical, was generally accepted as being the world's longest-established nautical publishing house, dating back to its founding in 1782 by the original Thomas Reed. For many years this was the principal almanac for home waters. Containing a wealth of accurate data, it was used by the great majority of yachtsmen as well as commercial craft. It reigned supreme. In addition to coming out with the ubiquitous almanac, Watts produced one of the best books around on the sextant, entitled *The Sextant Simplified*. This was a worthy companion to the Watts correspondence course and is still in print today. Additionally, I was to get practical help from *Eagle*'s navigating officer, who loaned me a sextant to get a feel for using this vital organ. Ignoring the inevitable snide comments from onlookers, seemingly with nothing better to do, I gained invaluable practice in the actual taking of sights. In using the flight deck as an observation platform at sea I was well aware, however, that this would be appreciably easier than using a sextant on the deck of a yacht jumping up and down in a seaway, but I got the idea. I subsequently worked the sights up on graph paper in the privacy of my cabin away from prying eyes. Astronomical navigation I was to find a deeply satisfying experience. There is beauty and elegance in the process of determining one's position out at sea by commune with celestial bodies. They are part of a system which, being of 'God's creation', has a soul which cannot exist in the man-made world of satellites.

With departure time near and the work programme completed on *Tern*, I moved her round from Mashford's yard to the basin in Plymouth's Barbican, where Peter joined me to live on board. All stores had been moved from *Eagle* and stowed on board our new home. Miraculously they all went in, filling every conceivable space, with nothing left over. The poor old girl's waterline vanished, not to be seen again for some time, becoming home in the meantime to marine life.

Shortly after the move into the basin, and when we happened to be below, there was the slightest, gentlest of bumps alongside, with a voice hailing us, 'Are you on board, sir?' Emerging on deck I found the admiral's barge from *Eagle* alongside. The barge was, if anything, bigger than *Tern*, all gleaming dark blue and white enamel with impossibly bright brassware. The owner of the voice, its impeccably turned out petty officer coxswain, delivered a message from the admiral requesting our company to take tea with him in his quarters on *Eagle*. Our programme that day was somewhat busy, with goods being delivered and a long list outstanding of jobs to be completed. I sent a message back to the great man explaining, as respectfully as I could, that we were rather busy and it was not convenient to accept his invitation. The barge departed to the sound of the roar of powerful engines and the crew, with guardsmen-like precision, going through their ceremonial boathook drill.

It was then it hit me what I had done! A request from an admiral is synonymous with an order, but here was a mere lieutenant saying to an admiral 'thanks very much for the thought but I have not got the time to see you'. The arrogance of youth! In a very short time the barge was back, and for an anxious moment I thought it would be the bearer of a short, sharp message from him. But no. The same sparkling clean coxswain handed over a large package and a letter. The admiral fully understood the urgency of last-minute pre-departure preparations and wished us well with our forthcoming adventure. The package was presented with his compliments but with the stern admonition that it was not to be opened, unless in dire emergency, until we arrived safely in New Zealand. It turned out to be a case of champagne. As it transpired, the barge was to make yet another trip round to *Tern*, this time with the admiral in it. On the immediate eve of our departure he came out to visit us, coming on board to have a look at the boat and to convey personally his best wishes. I was somewhat flattered at this and further much relieved as it confirmed we had been fully forgiven for having stood him up over his invitation to tea.

As the Home Fleet's Heavy Squadron flagship, *Eagle* carried an admiral. Vice-Admiral J Hughes-Hallett was a formidable character. Tough and uncompromising, he had a tendency to give those immediately under him a hard time. He was, however, a very hands-on senior officer, and although not directly in charge of what went on domestically on the ship – that was the captain's backyard – he nevertheless wished to keep in close contact with the ship's affairs. To this end it would seem he did not want to have everything filtered through the captain. The tactic adopted was for the admiral to invite small groups of the younger officers in turn to join him for dinner. Instructions were given to his steward that glasses were never to run dry. As the evening progressed, tongues became loosened and gossip flowed. The admiral was in touch with the ship's deep pulse.

Although a strict disciplinarian, Hughes-Hallett was an appealing personality, exemplified by an occasion when we were alongside in Portsmouth. Called to London for a meeting at the Admiralty, he decided, rather than take the train, he would use his own car, this being carried on board. It was lifted out onto the jetty, but neither his driver nor he could get it started. Likewise, the full resources of the ship's extensive engineering department were unable to persuade the engine to behave, the commander (engineering) losing some face in the process, having been summoned to take charge personally of the situation. Undaunted, the admiral ordered his motorcycle to be hoisted out. Despite the unfriendly weather – wind and driving rain – he would ride to town. Reappearing in full bikey gear – leathers, boots, goggles and leather helmet, the lot – he was piped over the side for the second time by the full quarterdeck staff under the officer of the day, with the captain and commander in attendance. Mounting his big, powerful machine, he kicked it into life and roared off to London. One could imagine that if his motorcycle had in its turn not performed, he would have purloined 'postie's' bicycle and set off across the Portsmouth cobbles to London town.

After leaving the ship and before facing up to the relative inconvenience of life living in *Tern*, I needed a few weeks of living ashore. Once again the service looked after me. On the edge of the dockyard in the Devonport suburb of Keyham was located the Royal Naval Engineering College, HMS *Thunderer*, in which, sometime earlier, I had undergone training. The captain of the college very kindly provided me with accommodation in the staff house, where the instructing officers lived. It was an enjoyable time, as had been my earlier experience in the establishment as an OUI (Officer Under Instruction). It was sad to learn that some years later, as part of the restructuring of the armed services with the advent of the Ministry of

Defence, the long-standing college was closed down. The rationale was that efficiency gains would result from the amalgamation of technical training within the three services into one scheme. It could only be hoped that the destruction of an integral component of what comprised the Royal Navy was to be to the combined operational good and not just a cost-saving measure. I have my doubts, though. The soulless, faceless MOD, riding over the wishes of many senior officers, would no doubt claim it had all worked out nicely.

Whilst indulging in the comfortable, relaxed environment of the staff house I took the opportunity to renew acquaintance with an old friend from past times. The college maintained a boathouse on the banks of the Tamar close to the dockyard, in which was kept a variety of recreational sailing craft and dinghies of one sort or another. In my time at the college I had kept a private dinghy in this boathouse and as a result had got to know well the chief petty officer pensioner in charge. He was still there and it was good to meet up with him again. He was a product of the pre-war navy and typical of the type of senior rating who had made up its core. He had known no other working life apart from the service. It was his world and he was devoted to it. He welcomed me with great warmth. He had heard about my forthcoming trip and said he had something for me. From a cupboard in his little office he handed to me a plain, unvarnished box bearing on it a plaque with the German eagle and swastika. It was a sextant. A Plath, a top-of-the-range make, issued to U-boat commanders in the recent war. It was in perfect condition. The chief did not comment on how he had acquired it and nor did I ask. I was very moved.

At the end of hostilities, the German Navy's fleet of submarines surrendered and were escorted to the west coast of Scotland and taken into care by the Royal Navy. A member of the receiving team was Mike Richey, who subsequently became director of the Royal Institute of Navigation. He was also widely known later as the last owner of the famous, ill-fated, wooden, junk-rigged *Jester* and an early fellow member of the Ocean Cruising Club. An article written by him in more recent times for *Yachting Monthly* magazine throws some light on what was no doubt the background to my sextant.

'…One of my duties was to be present during the interrogation of the captains. Another was to take charge of the navigational instruments. Some of these were of great ingenuity… but it was the sextants that caught my eye: black, beautifully machined, very light and with an enormous horizon glass. The instruments (in the interests of protecting British nautical-instrument manufacturing) were all destined for destruction, but I was able, more or less with official connivance, to "liberate" – to use the cynical expression then fashionable – a single sextant, the centring error zero and the swastika emblazoned on the index arm. It was the finest instrument I have ever used and I used it for close on 45 years. The last time I saw it was amid the sodden debris of *Jester*'s final knock-down.'

What the tortuous path had been that had ended up with my taking possession of one of these sextants I know not, but it came into a good home where it resides to this day. I have used it for years and it was a joy to do so. Like Mike, I had the same experience of finding it light, easily read and virtually error-free. Certainly over the years it never gained any index error. It did all it could to make the life of this particular navigator as pain-free as possible.

Our departure time was nigh, and on the scheduled date of 30 August 1953 we sailed, there being no game of bowls on Plymouth Hoe that had to be finished. The event of our leaving was recorded in a letter home which I wrote later from the Canaries.

'We cleared the Barbican after a hectic week of final preparation, storing, watering and showing the boat to what seemed a ceaseless stream of visitors and friends of both of us. There was a very large contingent out of *Eagle*, from the admiral to my chief ERA (Engine Room Artificer), who had worked so closely with me on the flight deck. I was delighted that he had come out to see us. He supplied us with enough vegetables for three weeks, refusing any question of payment. We eventually got away after lunch, accompanied by a press boat taking photographs and bearing a host of friends and relatives.'

The boat stayed with us as we crossed Plymouth Sound, only turning back as we approached the point which in navigational terms we would take as our 'departure', the eastern end of the breakwater. It was a wise decision on their part. We were to discover yet again as we emerged into open waters that the sea harbours no sentiment of kindliness to those who invade its domain.

Chapter Three

The Iberian Experience

The sea has formed the English character and the essential England is to be found in those who follow it. The sea endures no makeshifts. If a thing is not exactly right it will be vastly wrong.

JOHN BUCHAN

'There should be nine buoys with flashing red lights coming up pretty soon, Peter. As soon as we get past the ninth we can turn into the harbour round the end of the breakwater.'

It was close to midnight and we were in the approaches to Puerto de la Luz, the port for Las Palmas on Gran Canaria. We had arrived in the Canaries and were decidedly pleased to be there. It was a beautiful night, soft and warm but impenetrably black. We needed those lights. Peter went up forward to see them better, taking up station forward of the staysail to get a clear view under the foot of the jib.

'Got them! I've picked up those red lights. One, two … seven, eight, nine, ten, eleven, twelve. I give up! There are hundreds of the bloody things!' The explanation soon became clear. Close by were dozens of small fishing boats bobbing up and down under oars and all using red flares, which would seem to be part of the fishing process.

Apart from this navigational difficulty, conditions were perfect for a night entry under sail into a strange harbour. The freshly blowing trade wind that had brought us through the eastern group of islands had died with the setting sun, giving way to a gentle whisper off the land, but with enough body in it to give us adequate steerage way. We were being allowed enough time to take stock of our surroundings and keep check on our position without undue pressure.

Threading our way through the silent fishing boats we brought up out of the night the shape of the breakwater, dark against the lights of the town spread out behind it. We would soon be enjoying the luxury of the whole night in our bunks…or so we thought. We were tired. Under easy sail of jib, mainsail and topsail, we slid across the quiet, silky, shimmering surface of the inner waters of the harbour to the spot we had pre-selected for anchoring. Down went the CQR bower anchor in four fathoms and we were at rest. It was midnight. We had successfully completed the first leg of the journey and a sense of well-being flowed over us, but the peace that had entered our souls was short-lived.

Out of the night appeared a large motor launch which attached itself to us, its crew assaulting our ears with a barrage of loud, unintelligible Spanish. Prominent amongst this group of uninvited guests was a large figure in a strikingly impressive uniform – all blue and white with a mass of gold trimmings. It was no less a person than the harbourmaster himself. He was quite drunk, but pleasantly so. On board he came and dived straight down below, making it clear he was in need of further refreshment. Peter and I had, prior to the arrival of this gentleman, been talking about cocoa to soothe us into our bunks, leading into long, restful sleep. Now whisky was the order of the day. We felt intuitively that a nice hot cup of cocoa would not be adequate for the occasion. The problem associated with having, at short notice, to break out the whisky bottle was that we had to pull down the back of one of the settees, which revealed for all to see that there was not a shortage of this commodity. Our guest was an interested observer.

Our new-found friend had some English, with which he dominated the conversation, interspersed with assaults on the whisky bottle. Peter and I had some difficulty afterwards in recalling what he had been on about in the course of the general conversation, but we remembered well the pantomime performance over passports and ship's papers. The latter involved perusal of the crew list, which we did not have. Unfortunately, I had not prepared one in advance, not thinking this of too much importance, there being only the two of us. The compiling of this document, which we now had to undertake to his satisfaction, gave the harbourmaster the excuse to delay his departure. I made a note not to repeat this mistake in the future and to have a ready-prepared formal-looking document, albeit bearing just two names. We were despairing of him ever going, but eventually, when he did make a move to leave, it was evident he wanted us to go with him. For some unexplained reason we could not remain anchored where we were and must move further into the docks area, just where we did not want to be – amongst all the shipping congestion, where our vulnerability would have been of concern, which was what I had tried to avoid. It may have been that in going straight to our self-selected spot we had bypassed his authority. He was now about to rectify this. We were told to get our anchor and then, secured alongside his craft, we were taken to a new berth of his choosing. Still full of good cheer, the decider of our fate vanished into the night. Where he had been before boarding us was not clear, but judging by his condition we were not the only vessel he had been on board that night. We were not to see him again. Whether it was because he had enjoyed our company so much, or our brand of Scotch, or both, we were not to know, but certainly we never received any demand for harbour dues. Waiting until we were confident that our affable and progressively less coherent guest had gone for good, we picked up our anchor for the second time and moved back to our original spot close to the western shore, over by a group of local trading schooners. As we sank into the embrace of our bunks, dawn was beginning to make its presence felt.

Catching up on our desperately needed sleep was to be a short-lived experience. At 0800 we had two further visitors. Customs and the Mafia. It had to be assumed that the arrival in short order of these two parties was coincidental, there hopefully being no common link in their interests. Unlike the earlier session with the colourful representative of the harbour authority, the customs event was unremarkable, proceedings being conducted with no comic-opera effects or need for any lubrication. The visit of the other party was to prove a somewhat different story.

Las Palmas was at the time famous and infamous on widely different fronts. Looking at its better side it had long been noted for the beauty of its women and the quality of its abundant, readily available fruit. Offsetting these features, both highly desirable to crews of visiting vessels, yachts included, was the reputation the place enjoyed for the pollution of its harbour water and rampant waterfront thievery. This mixed bag of characteristics coloured our stay in Gran Canaria, the negative certainly outweighing the positive.

Of immediate interest from the moment of our arrival was the risk of the boat being plundered. Stories abounded of the misfortunes that had befallen yachts there before us. Boats left unattended at anchor, their crews ashore, had been boarded and broken into and everything moveable cleaned out. At night, with the occupants turned in and deep in slumber, anchor chains had been severed by bolt cutters, or rope rodes cut. On drifting ashore the boat was at the mercy of shoreside gangs with the manpower to overcome the yacht's crew, the plunder then being easily removed and taken off. Little help could be expected from the police, who were both poachers and gamekeepers. About all this we were apprehensive but need not have been. Help was nigh. The second boat to call on us on our first morning contained, as we were soon to gather, members of the local Cosa Nostra, the Mafiosi. One of them enquired politely in passable English if they could come on board. The question was only too obviously purely rhetorical. Ensconcing themselves in the cabin, their leader, a godfather figure, explained in courteous and most polite terms what it was all about. In view of the dishonesty that sadly prevailed on the waterfront, they were there to look after our welfare. We could put our trust in them. In return for a fee, which we had to admit as being quite modest, we would have their full protection. This would entail one of his men moving on board full-time, taking up residence 24 hours a day, living at our expense, and we could be assured of not being molested. He emphasised that acceptance or not of the arrangement was entirely up to us, but it was quite evident that if we declined, our future would be very uncertain indeed. We agreed. The negotiations, something of a euphemism for a rather one-sided discussion, had been conducted in a gentlemanly manner. We parted company on the most amicable of terms. The individual selected to watch over us would remain on board for the remainder of that day until nightfall, returning the following morning to commence his full-time duties.

After their departure we planned a day of idleness and sleep, having survived, we thought with some satisfaction, the perils of both the deep and the shore. But first a visit ashore, the boat now in the hands of our guardian, to change money and call on the British Consul to collect, hopefully, our mail. This was there with him, but additionally we had to get hold of the mail that we had directed to be sent to Madeira, where, due to the change in the passage plan, we had not made the originally scheduled stop. We were told that this mail could be put on board the next plane from Madeira to the Canaries. There was a weekly flying-boat service, the next scheduled flight of which was expected on the coming Sunday. We left the necessary arrangements in the hands of the consular service but had some reservations about the outcome. They seemed to have a somewhat third world approach to such matters.

Back on board and in the absence that night of our watchman, we recommenced keeping watches so that we had someone awake on deck during the dark hours, the particularly dangerous period. Feelings about this chore are contained in an entry in my journal:

What a tremendous bind this is, and at 0330 here am I writing up my journal by the light of the moon and the Bialaddin (pressure lamp). I feel aggrieved, perhaps irrationally, and a sympathy for poor old Peter sleeping soundly down below, as he is soon to be awakened rudely and be up here. Hopefully he will gain some solace from the beauty of the night. Any lingering doubts we may have harboured about succumbing too easily to the iron-fist-in-the-velvet-glove "persuasion" by the Mafiosi to accept their offer of complete day-and-night surveillance are now totally allayed. Guard duties at night are not on. Watchkeeping at sea, with associated broken sleep, is one thing but not in harbour.

I was feeling sorry for myself. As it was to turn out, the investment in 'our man' proved to be a good one, with him going beyond just the call of duty.

Our arrival in the Canaries was more or less on schedule, and marking the completion of the first stage meant we had achieved the first significant milestone. It was a fitting moment to look back on the passage, evaluate the performance of the boat and her crew and review what lessons had been learned. All of this would help in our preparations for the next big leg – the Atlantic crossing. What was gratifyingly evident was that we had complete confidence in the boat, but more importantly we had that same confidence in each other. There was a mutual respect, and it had been established we could work well together under trying circumstances.

The first test of boat and crew had been off Ushant following an uneventful crossing of the Channel from Plymouth. We were too close in to that lump of land, Ushant (Ile d'Ouessant), sitting offshore from Brittany and getting in our way. We had not taken into account the effect it has on the run of the sea and the disturbance to the tidal stream flowing past it. We were to pay the price for this error in judgement and were also about to experience our first gear failure. The boat's log tells all:

Tuesday 01 September 1500 Close-hauled on the port tack under all plain sail, punching into a most unpleasant sea with little progress. Sea short, confused, with wave fronts running at different angles. Bows burying themselves, totally submerging the bowsprit. Water all over the deck.

1600 Link parted in bobstay chain. Bowsprit bending upwards alarmingly under pull of No 2 jib. Just saved spar from breaking. Rigged purchase to hold down bowsprit. Wore ship and headed for Brest for permanent repairs.

2100 Hove-to under staysail hauled a-weather and five feet of mainsail rolled in. Strong wind from the south and heavy rain. Without large-scale chart prefer to make Brest approach in morning.

02 September 0600 Eased sheets and ran into coast. Little wind. Boom swinging in allowed mainsheet to catch under starboard lifebuoy fitting pitching the buoy into the sea and lost. Someone will find it with *Tern*'s name on it and be left wondering. Too difficult in the sea running to try to recover it. Rigged boom guy. Must always do this in future on all points of sailing except when close on the wind. That boom is lethal.

1400 Goulet de Brest ahead. Set spinnaker. Dipped ensign to five French Navy vessels in line ahead passing down our port side. No response.

2100 Dropped spinnaker. Breeze failed. Started engine with difficulty having carelessly stopped it on paraffin when we left the Barbican.

2200 Anchored in Brest Harbour. Missed not having large-scale chart. Made do with the Admiralty *Channel Pilot.*

The fact we were in such close proximity to Ushant was not entirely due to human error. By that I mean mine. It was also due to the danger posed by passing ships. Because of the very real risk to us in *Tern* of either being run down by a ship coming up astern or run over by one from ahead, we tried to keep out of the way by hugging Ushant. The dangers associated with the close-quarters situation in which we found ourselves with ships all around us were not a modern phenomenon. As far back as 1878 that doyen of early cruising folk, R McMullen, wrote: 'If large steamers only ran down small vessels, it might appear to gentlemen of advanced opinions as if only small vessels were in fault; but, in fact, large steamers exhibit a commendable spirit of impartiality and fair play by running down each other.'

At the time we were rounding this southern gatepost to the English Channel, the International Regulations for Preventing Collisions at Sea, the ColRegs, were the only form of control. Vessels bound south on leaving the Channel, or heading north to enter it, would bend their tracks as close as possible round Ushant Island to save distance. The traffic flow was considerable, and in those days a significant proportion were British flagged ships heading to or coming from major ports such as Southampton or London Docks. A state of chaos also tended to exist in other congested areas where shipping converged in 'narrow seas'. Because of the steadily rising casualty rate, highlighted by some spectacular disasters, the brilliantly clever idea of keeping ships in clearly defined one-way lanes was dreamed up. The world's first TSS (Traffic Separation Scheme) was set up in the Dover Strait in 1967. Others, including Ushant, quickly followed, but too late for us. All ships were in due course required by international law to stay in their correct lane throughout its length.

The next morning, after our safe arrival in Brest inner harbour, we moved alongside the quay in No 2 basin in the Port de Commerce, where we sorted ourselves out, fitting a new bobstay chain which we had bought in the town. The lack of bureaucracy during our stay was remarkable. No charges for being there were made, and we came and went with no one questioning us.

Today we would have been in the marina, with admittedly all conveniences, but regulated. I preferred the way it had been for us: free of interference, unmindful of any lack of amenities. It had been a relaxing experience, as reflected in a letter home to my folks. 'We appeared in the local papers, ate a lot of good French food, drank a lot of good French wine and spent too much money but had enjoyed ourselves.' Today, there being a large number of foreign yachts using the Brest facilities, the arrival of two young men in the course of an ocean cruise would attract no attention, but not so then. Accompanying the articles in the Brest newspapers were photographs of *Tern* and the happily smiling faces of *les deux matelots britanniques.*

The time arrived for us to sail, but in the meantime we had made a major change to our route plan. We would cut out going to Madeira and make the Canaries in one leg, our schedule having taken a dent in its timing. We needed to catch up. The demands of the navy, and more importantly the dictates of the weather ahead of us, were calling the tune.

The parting of the bobstay chain had been a frightening experience. *Tern,* typical of contemporary design, had a very fine entrance and consequential lack of buoyancy in the bows. Heading into the disturbed waters off Ushant she was making wet work of it, the bows plunging into the sea, totally immersing the bowsprit. Disaster struck. The bows lifted and the spar came out of the water with the bobstay chain hanging down from its outer end, the sprit bending upwards in a great curve under the pull of the jib. I was steering at the time and just had time to put the helm up to take her off the wind. It was amazing that the spar had not broken off at the gammon iron as it emerged from the water, and I was still expecting this to happen at any moment. The way it was bending filled us with dread. Having got the jib off and saved the situation, we had to rig a temporary bobstay, using a luff tackle, a difficult job involving lying stretched out along the bowsprit and being almost completely underwater as it plunged into the sea, the threat ever present of being washed off.

Another lesson we had learned from the passage was the need for discipline in engine-operating procedures. The engine ran on paraffin, but as it would not start on this it was necessary to use petrol in the first instance and then change over to paraffin. Before stopping the engine, a change back to petrol had to be made to ensure the carburettor and fuel system was full of petrol. If it was stopped on paraffin, the whole of the system had to be drained out and refilled with petrol. Messy and irritating.

I was not alone in being disenchanted with our engine. The original owner but one of *Tern II,* Claud Worth, wrote of his frustration in the course of a cruise to Brittany:

'While drifting up with the tide we nearly fouled a buoy, so brought up and tried to start the motor. We got it to work slowly for two or three minutes, then something smashed, and it was found that a vital part of the machine had given way. So we turned off the water cocks, closed the doors of its cupboard, and agreed not to mention the dreadful thing again. RIP. We felt much happier after it was all over.'

If it had not been for the Panama Canal regulations I would also have been happy to have dispensed with the pleasure of the company of our 'dreadful thing', particularly when having to cope with its idiosyncrasies over petrol and paraffin.

05 September 1210 Sailed from Brest under engine. No wind.
1600 Slight breeze from NNW. Set all plain sail and Yankee jib.
1930 Gybed ship. Wind ENE freshening. Took in Yankee. Streamed the log and took our departure from the Goulet for the Canaries. Set course to round Finisterre.

We were following in Worth's track in those waters when in 1912 he did a west coast of France cruise in *Tern II*. His crew included Mrs Worth (the 'mate'). Throughout his writings Mrs Worth is always referred to as Mrs Worth. She did not seem to have had any other name, presumably having been born Mrs Worth.

Their cruise would appear to have been most successful and had certainly started off well enough. 'We picked up a mooring in front of the Royal Cornwall Yacht Club and soon the steward came off with letters.' The Royal Cornwall Yacht Club remains today an accommodating club, but Claud would be disappointed to know that sadly it is improbable a steward now would bring out his mail.

Within the relatively short history of amateur yachting there stands out a handful of individuals, dedicated to this interest, who had a marked influence on small-boat cruising. Three such sailors, outstanding in their achievements, were RT McMullen, Claud Worth and Eric C Hiscock. The example they set in accomplishing many fine offshore cruises and then writing very readable accounts of them did much to foster the development of a pastime so widely popular today. I, like countless others, benefited enormously from their teachings.

The first of these, and possibly the greatest, was the Victorian Richard McMullen, he being a true pioneer. An admirer was Arthur Ransome: 'Besides setting a higher standard in amateur seamanship than had been set before, McMullen freed small cruisers from the fetters and dangers of too close dependence on the shore.' 'I have always preferred the sea,' said McMullen, 'to the risk of entering or the misery of lying in a bad harbour'.

He lived all his life in the Thames Estuary, from which he embarked on many cruises, either single-handed or with friends and paid hands. Born in 1830 and practising as a stockbroker, he seized every opportunity to go sailing up to 1891 when, in the words of his friend, Dixon Kemp, '…he died upon the sea, sitting in the cockpit of the little *Perseus*, his face towards the sky, whilst he was sailing up the silver path of the moon, which seemed to unite heaven and the sea. After his spirit had gone forth the little craft sailed herself to the French coast…' He was found, sitting at the helm, by some French fisherman and taken into a nearby port – cause of death: 'failure of the heart's action'. He had gone the way he would have wanted to go: die on what had been his life, the sea.

A tough man, McMullen. He revelled in hard work, which he considered the right way, being part and parcel of sailing. In *Tern*, soon after leaving Plymouth we also were to carry away our topsail sheet. In our case we lowered the mainsail and, with the gaff on deck, rove a new topsail sheet. I felt doubly guilty about this. The first reason was that after reading McMullen I should have gone out along the gaff and kept the mainsail still drawing. The second was that it was my fault that we had lost the topsail sheet in the first place, since in the Barbican, Peter noticed the sheet was looking tired and had suggested it be replaced. In the interests of saving pennies I had not acted on this recommendation. The sea was to find me out.

A major contribution to furthering small-boat sailing was McMullen's *Down Channel*. An evergreen first published in 1869, with successive editions culminating in a second impression in 1951. The book is 'a good read', but more than that, it is an inspiration to all who sail small craft in the pursuit of the magic of cruising.

Overlapping him was Claud Worth, a giant in the sailing circles of his time, who contributed greatly, for many years after that, to the fostering of amateur and small-boat family cruising. Worth, a successful Harley Street eye surgeon, devoted himself to sailing, becoming a legendary figure, which had been fostered by his extensive cruises in his famous stable of successive *Tern*s. He passed on the benefits of hard-earned experience via his two influential books, classics in their own way: *Yacht Cruising*, coming out in 1910, and *Yacht Navigation and Voyaging*, published in 1927. All four *Tern*s were written up in great detail in these books. I consider myself privileged to have owned *Tern II* and in later life to have had the great pleasure of sailing in *Tern IV*.

Worth's health began to deteriorate, and on medical advice he gave up more serious sailing following his retirement from work in 1927, but not before sailing his much loved *Tern IV*, with his son Tom, who himself was to become a well-known world sailor, to the Azores and back. Despite suffering a broken boom, they made the return passage to the Lizard, south of Falmouth, in the respectable time of seven and a half days in tough conditions. Living in his big house amongst the trees overlooking the Helford River, immediately south of Falmouth Estuary, where he maintained a mooring, he daysailed until his death in 1936. He left an enduring legacy of cruising expertise and a depth of understanding of small-craft seamanship. He and Tom are buried in the graveyard of an old church, which fittingly also looks over the beautiful Helford River.

Following on from Worth was Eric Hiscock. Born in 1908 he acquired his first boat in his mid 20s, thereafter devoting his life to sailing and writing about it until his death aged 78. His many books on sailing offshore were widely read, providing a wealth of knowledge on all aspects of the navigation and handling of small cruising yachts, at sea and in harbour. In the sailing world he was a major player, a universally respected authority on the subject.

One boat in which Hiscock learned his trade was *Tern II*, and in her he made many passages before the Second World War. He wrote of his experiences in her in his *Wandering Under Sail*. Of these, one in particular had a special resonance with me in connection with our own Ushant ordeal. He records the difficult occasion when, heading out of the Solent in a fresh WSW, an unexpectedly large wave smashed over the starboard bow, with solid water coming onto the foredeck. 'In the succeeding trough she dived deep, burying her bowsprit and filling a large area of the jib with water. As she shook herself clear, there was a sudden thunder of flapping canvas, and it was just possible to see the dark shape of the jib, still tethered by sheet and halyard, flogging furiously from side to side. I was scared at the thought of muzzling that sail single-handed... But it had to be done.' Having got the jib off after a great struggle, the startling discovery was made that 'the bowsprit had broken off and was hanging below the waterline still held by the (jib) outhaul and bobstay... The spar itself had snapped at the gammon iron, where it was protected against chafe by a piece of copper sheeting, and it is interesting to note that the break had occurred exactly on the line of tacks that kept it in position; the wood, however, was perfectly sound'. It may have been that when we nearly lost our bowsprit in similar conditions the lower part of the jib had filled with water as the bows plunged down into the sea, adding to the load on the spar.

Like Hiscock I was also apprehensive about dealing with our bowsprit situation, eventhough ours had not actually broken off. Our bobstay arrangement, holding down 10 feet of bowsprit projecting from the bows, consisted of stout bronze rods and a length of chain which reached up to the crance iron at the outer end of the bowsprit. It was a joining link between the chain and a rod that had given way. What we were faced with after this had failed was a length of chain dangling from the bowsprit end and the bronze rods hanging down in the sea under the forefoot.

The first task was to lift the rods up clear of the water. This involved the use of a boathook, leaning over the bows with my head and shoulders being buried in the sea as the bows rose and fell. Having got the rods out of the water, the lower block of a luff tackle was hooked on to them. It was then a case of facing up to crawling out onto the wet, slippery bowsprit and lying along it with nothing, apart from the spar itself, to hang onto whilst hooking the upper block of the purchase into the crance iron. Having managed this, I edged back to the security of the foredeck whilst Peter heaved up on the tackle. Our bowsprit was now safe and we were exhausted.

I must confess there were occasions, such as changing headsails in deteriorating weather situations when on passage in *Tern*, that I swore I would not sail again with a bowsprit. Being perched out in space, way ahead of the boat, made for wet, hard work and was quite risky at times when changing sails. Many boats of *Tern*'s vintage carried bowsprits, these being a standard feature of Victorian design, and this was certainly the case in McMullen's day. His gaff cutter, *Orion*, only 3 feet longer than *Tern*, carried a virtual telegraph pole of a bowsprit, 16.5 feet outboard, over half as long again as ours. His, it would seem, required a lot of attention. It was McMullen's practice to reef the bowsprit, that is to reduce the length overhanging, when shortening sail in a blow to keep the sail plan balanced.

Handling *Tern II* was quite hard work but bore no comparison to what it would have been like in a McMullen-era boat. Reefing bowsprits and housing topmasts in heavy weather were standard practice, the 'know-how' for these laborious operations being fully described in manuals of yacht seamanship. 'The value of housing a topmast in heavy weather is self-evident. The weight aloft is reduced, the centre of gravity is lowered and the stability of the yacht enhanced. In the past, moreover, it was considered – and rightly considered – unseamanlike to sail about with two or more reefs down and the topmast still aloft; apart from this, it does not please the aesthetic eye of a seaman.' For the operation *to house a topmast*, detailed instructions are given, including for starters: 'When striking the topmast, the signal halyards, topmast stay, topmast shrouds and backstays must be eased up'. And so it goes on. The heart quails.

Clearing the Brest Estuary, the Bay of Biscay now stretched before us, and in view of its reputation we wondered just what weather lay ahead. With no access to weather forecasts we became committed barometer tappers. Its state was a regular entry in the daily log.

06 September Barometer 30.1 steady, fair. Beautiful day but stiff breeze from ENE.

07 September Barometer 30.1 steady, fair. Conditions much improved with both of us feeling happier with life. Hot and sunny – a lovely day. Took first forenoon sight for longitude and got good noon latitude. The first effort. OP (Observed Position) and EP (Estimated Position) worked in well together. Very satisfying. Having considerable difficulty avoiding fishing boats.

During the night we continued to have a big problem avoiding large numbers of fishing boats.

08 September Barometer 30.15 steady, fair. Fog, poor visibility. Wind very light NE dying. Gear and sails slatting unpleasantly.

1645 No wind. Unexpectedly found ourselves close to a dozen or more Spanish fishermen in small open boats which suddenly appeared out of the fog.

The appearance of these fishing boats so close was a cause for apprehension. We could well appear to be an easy picking, vulnerable to boarding, being outnumbered and unarmed. I had taken the decision not to carry a firearm on board, which seemed to be the consensus amongst cruising people. To use one could well trigger off, to use an expression, a situation in which we might be the losers, fatally. Faced with several persons not bent on furthering our welfare, we could be outgunned. If there was just one intruder, and in the course of protecting our rights we were to wound or even kill a local, we could well end up on the wrong side of the law, particularly where the judicial process was uncertain, as was to be the case in several of the places we visited.

The decision not to have a firearm would appear to have been vindicated in more recent times when there was the tragic case of my fellow Kiwi, Sir Peter Blake, the renowned world-circling ocean-racing yachtsman, who was shot dead after a gun had been produced in the defence of his boat in South American waters.

The tactics we adopted to discourage any malign intentions that the fishermen surrounding us may have had were to attempt to create the impression there was a veritable football team on board *Tern*. We adopted a comic-opera scenario, popping up through the forehatch and then appearing in the cockpit wearing a variety of different headgear. This may have achieved the desired effect, but again we might have been overreacting, as shortly after this encounter we found ourselves once more surrounded by fishermen in small rowing boats, dories. It was obvious there was nothing sinister about them and soon they were alongside trading fish for cigarettes.

The currency used throughout our trip was whisky as first option and then cigarettes, these two commodities being universally accepted for barter or payment for services rendered. In fact, it would appear there was another currency, which I only came across later. Sometime after we reached Auckland a fellow naval officer came in, single-handed, in a Folkboat, having also sailed from Plymouth. Widely known as Basher, because that was the sort of chap he was, he had a rather relaxed approach to life. Having made it to New Zealand, a very creditable effort in such a small boat, he thought it reasonable to make the most of the opportunity to enjoy something of the country and arranged to take himself off on a sightseeing tour. Unwisely, he communicated this to the Admiralty who had other ideas. He received a cable peremptorily ordering him to return forthwith to the UK by the first available ship. Unfortunately for him there was a passenger-carrying cargo liner sailing within days and inconveniently she had a berth available. Basher's last words were: 'Sort out the boat, take anything you want and sell her. Get the best price you can but don't worry too much about it.' He then left.

In the course of the sort-out, I came across quite a few sizeable chocolate boxes full to the lid with condoms. The number of these was somewhat in excess of what could be used by even the most virile of young men in the course of a couple of lifetimes. He hastened to assure me later that they had fulfilled a multi-purpose function, one of which was being used in the more mundane role of trading. I did notice, however, that he had converted the cabin interior in such a way that one of the bunks could be folded down to form a double bed. Retaining some of the contents in case they might come in handy, I emptied the boxes out onto the water around the boat. The world was not then subject to bullying by the environmentalists as it is now. The result bordered on the spectacular. The contents spread out to form a wide area. A large field of daisies slowly drifted down harbour on the tide and out to sea.

There is, however, a little more to the story. I arranged for the boat to be put on a mooring in the naval base, whereupon she was promptly attacked by a passing naval launch and dismasted. The New Zealand Navy did the right thing and had the mast replaced. I sold the boat quite easily and ended up with a mixed bag of ex-naval stores, comprising a .303 calibre service rifle, a Verey light flare pistol, an Admiralty-pattern barometer, which I am still using today, and some daisies.

08 September 2000 Thick fog but lifted momentarily to give a glimpse of a headland and what appeared to be a lighthouse.

2100 Saw Cabo Villano for about 30 minutes which confirmed our position before the fog clamped right down again.

2300 Visibility nil. We have ships all around, their fog horns sounding alarmingly close. This is going to be an anxious night.

09 September 1000 Fog cleared and turning into a lovely sunny day. Not a ship in sight! Where have they all gone? Only an hour or so ago they sounded everywhere!

2100 Went onto starboard gybe, course south and wind dead aft. During the course of this manoeuvre the mainsheet caught up and we had an involuntary gybe. Boom came heavily against the starboard runner. The shock load on the topmast stay caused the joining link on to the new bobstay chain to part again. For the second time we have a length of chain hanging disconsolately from the bowsprit end. Fortunately this time sea conditions are not as bad as off Ushant but nevertheless too rough to carry out immediate repairs. Took jib off and ran on. We have to do something about this weak link (literally) in the bobstay arrangement.

Wind increasing and following sea building up. Hove-to under staysail and mizzen with the helm lashed down, risking the plunging, weakened bowsprit. Conditions below most unpleasant with the boat's quick motion and dampness.

10 September 0830 Got under way under staysail and mizzen. Wind and sea moderating. Set reefed mainsail.

2300 Picked up Islas Berlengas light. Can no longer get BBC Home Service which may mean end of time signals for the time being until we can get the American broadcast on WWV. Course 180° and closing the Portuguese coast with Lisbon ahead.

At noon the following day we had Cabo da Roca close on the port bow. We also had a close-up view of bronzed bodies playing on the beaches in the sun. They were enjoying themselves. We were not. We compared their lot with ours and made the only decision we could make. Putting the helm down we headed for Lisbon.

Passing along the Costa do Sol, close into the beaches of Estoril and Cascais, we entered the approaches to Rio Tejo, the Tagus river. The shore was crowded, packed, we supposed, with sun worshippers and families on an outing by the sea, enjoying the beautiful day. We would have happily exchanged our situation for theirs, but as someone once said, 'It is all a matter of one's perspective.' No doubt quite a few of those on the beach, beset by fractious children and sand in their sandwiches, gazing on a yacht sailing serenely by on a quietly undulating, sun-speckled sea, would have thought how marvellous to have been us. For our part, we thought how marvellous to be viewing that self-same sea whilst lying comfortably on our backs under the sun on a gently sloping beach, wafted by the warm breeze. We badly needed a break from being on the sea. We had endured a somewhat trying passage. Although the Portuguese Trades had come in on cue, from just east of north, to give us a fair wind from Cabo Finisterre down the Portuguese coast, life on board had not been all that enjoyable. A feeling of dampness down below, uncomfortable boat motion and difficulties with the gear had taken the edge off our fun. Hence the peeling off into Lisbon, another unscheduled stop, but we needed that break.

We entered the river and anchored off the yacht basin. Ashore it was all very jolly with flags flying, it evidently being a gala day. For us, life was about to become difficult. A boatman came out indicating we should go alongside where customs were located. This we did, but it was not one of our most polished performances. With very limited astern power from our small engine driving the inefficient self-folding propeller, we were still developing our coming-alongside technique. The core of this was to get a stern line ashore before we did anything else. We could then control the boat's forward movement. On this occasion we did not get it right. As the log records with brutal frankness: 'Made a complete hash of coming alongside, ramming the stern warp of a ship alongside the quay ahead of us.' This brought us up short but put a fearful strain on the topmast stay and, for the third time, sheared the joining link in the long-suffering bobstay.

On arrival alongside we were arrested. Bundled into a vehicle ominously marked *policia*, filled with hard-eyed, armed men, we were driven to their headquarters in the old town where we were subjected to a surprisingly intense degree of interrogation. Why, was not made clear. The 'Inquisition' comprised an impressive assembly of maritime police, local police, international police, customs and a small group of unidentified individuals who played no part in proceedings but just sat around and said nothing. Peter and I were somewhat bemused by all the attention we were getting. Either we were considered important enough or looked sufficiently suspicious to warrant full investigation or, it appearing to be a public holiday, all these people had nothing better to do and we were a welcome relief from boredom. In due course, our papers standing up to a thorough poring over, and we apparently in the end not being seen as a threat to the national security, we were free to find our way back to the boat. We felt they could have at least given us a lift back to our berth, and although proceedings had been courteously conducted, there was a sense of threat in the air. We were glad to get back to the familiarity of dear old *Tern*.

Our welcoming reception having been completed, we were obliged to move off the quay and attempt the entry into the yacht basin. This operation looked as though it might have its share of problems, and it did. Blowing out of the basin was the very fresh northerly direction wind which had been building up during our recent incarceration. Flowing across the entrance was the full weight of the ebb tide. We were just off spring tides, the tidal stream flowing at such times at up to 3 knots. The combination of wind and tide was too much. As my journal records: 'The engine failed as we were halfway through the entrance, and missing the mole with its attendant rocks by inches we dropped anchor.

At 2300, wind having eased and the tide gone slack, we were about to move into a more comfortable position when we touched bottom. Got under way in the quickest time yet. With the engine now behaving itself we proceeded into the yacht basin to secure alongside an American yacht with a German paid crew who were most helpful with warps and fenders. They had recently, we were told, just painted her topsides, which no doubt helped their helpfulness. At last we turned in for a quiet night of rest.'

Like Portugal as a whole after the war, uncertain of itself, Lisbon was something of a Pandora's Box. Baedeker thinks highly of it: 'Thanks to its wonderful setting, Lisbon is rightly numbered amongst the world's most beautiful cities.' Maybe so, but at the time of our visit we could sense a darker side. There was a general air of suspicion, as witnessed by our arrival occasioning such intense police scrutiny. A feared secret police existed, the PIDE, and the silent men sitting in on our interrogation may have been these people. Portugal was under a Fascist regime, an authoritarian state looked at sideways by other European countries. Perhaps a resentful national reaction to this explained our reception. The police presence was everywhere and this included the yacht basin. Stationed at the head of the landing steps, giving access to the yacht berths, was an armed policeman who closely went through our passports page by page, supposedly to confirm we were whom we said we were, each time we left and entered. It was a tedious performance.

The basin was filled with large, very expensive luxury yachts, locally owned and which never moved during our stay. They were clear evidence of the enormous gap between the rich and poor that was so apparent all around us. Presumably the policeman was there to look after the interests of the wealthy, influential boatowners, no doubt being suitably rewarded for his efforts, as well as exercising police state surveillance of the likes of us. However, we were to receive individual gestures of friendship. The yacht club's commodore sent along Senhor Fragroso to make us welcome on behalf of the club. 'A very pleasant personality', I noted in my journal, and he was to prove most helpful in very many ways. The local Royal Naval Sailing Association representative, John Mitchell, made himself known and also helped to make us welcome, inviting us to dinner. He was doing his 'duty' as HLO (Honorary Local Officer), a worldwide network mainly of retired Royal Navy personnel who provide, on a voluntary basis, assistance to itinerant naval yachtspeople.

In general, though, we did not enjoy our stopover in Lisbon. However, it served its purpose. We were to get some essential repairs carried out and rectify weaknesses that this first leg had thrown up. The sea reveals all that is not right. A case in point was the mainsail, which had taken something of a beating as a result of frequent turning in of rolls in the reefing system. Because the foot had not been correctly laced to the boom, some of the lacing eyes had torn out. With the help of our little circle of friends, we got hold of a sailmaker who did a good repair job at a very reasonable price. We benefited from the economy not being strong, which kept charges down. We also sorted out the bobstay problem. The cause of the repetitive failures was the joining link which connected the length of bobstay chain to the bronze rods. The principle was a good idea in theory but bad in practice. The link, made in two halves along its length, when riveted over should have been as strong as a normal link. It wasn't, failing three times under shock load, although it could be argued that it is good in principle to have a known weak link in a boat's rig. We elected to discontinue replacing the split joining links each time they failed and replace with a standard galvanised shackle arrangement. Not as neat but stronger. We were not to have any further trouble, and in fact did not suffer henceforth throughout the trip any rigging mishaps of consequence. Lisbon was of value, not only in getting the boat sorted out but in giving us the opportunity to sort ourselves out. Peter gave *Tern* a thorough clean-out and we rearranged the stores for more convenient access, but importantly we were able to 'collect ourselves', taking time off to rest and catch up on sleep. Going into Lisbon had been a good move.

Shortly before our departure date came up, the British-owned *Petula* arrived in the basin. It was of interest to me to meet up with her again, the last time being when I had been inspecting her with a possible view to purchase.

She also was on her way down to the Canaries to be used as a jumping-off place for conducting ocean research into marine life, particularly plankton. To collect specimens they would be towing a large net, for which a slow-moving boat under sail would be ideal, quite apart from being cost-effective. We saw a lot of *Petula*'s team and were able to pass on what we had learned in doing business in Lisbon. As luck would have it, they had escaped the attention of the 'Inquisition'. She was the last British-flagged yacht we were to encounter until we reached Auckland, although we were to have the pleasure of her company again in Las Palmas. Being on a serious undertaking, she was not likely to fall prey to the fate that had befallen a collection of seemingly abandoned foreign yachts in the basin. Dreams that had shattered. These boats had left British and European ports to cruise the world, but crew incompatibility had taken its toll. Passages that had started out with high expectations had foundered so early into those passages. The boats had put into Lisbon, crews dispersed, with in most cases the owners going home, leaving the boats with an uncertain future. If anyone wanted a good, cheap boat, fully equipped and ready to sail away, Lisbon was the place to find one. An exception was our next door neighbour, the American-owned *Little Vigilant*, which we had met when we first arrived. We were impressed by the loving care bestowed upon her, and the dedication of her crew. She was a success story amongst so many failures.

The time for us to get on our way again was upon us. We were keen to get to sea once more.

16 September 1300 Got under way. Headed down river under all plain sail into light breeze from WSW. Beautiful day for our departure. Barometer 29.9 steady. Temperature 80° F. Weather looks all set fair.

Heading towards us, coming up river, was a truly magnificent sight, the significance of which we did not at first appreciate. We were privileged to be in the company of a Grand Banks schooner returning with her cargo of salted cod. We were so lucky to have seen her, as in a few short years she and her sisters would all have gone, swept from the seas by motor trawlers.

She passed close down our port side and we could see her in great detail. A four-masted schooner with towering topmasts and big sail plan. The topmasts supported large four-sided fisherman staysails set between the masts above the gaff-headed lower sails. These staysails were a feature of the schooners, providing immense reaching power whilst also being relatively easily handled from the deck. She had the lines of a yacht, with gently curving stem, and bowsprit steeved at the right angle to flow into the graceful sheer of the hull. Here was a big sailing vessel in all her glory, but also very much a working one. She would have been the best part of 200 feet overall. Her topsides were weather-stained and marked where her dories, loaded with fish, would have rubbed against them. Stacked on her deck were tiers of these 14 foot dories, neatly nesting in each other. There must have been 50 or 60 of them, the source of the wealth in the mother ship's fish holds.

The dories, open rowing boats with a small lugsail, were worked by one man 'shooting' long handlines baited at three or foot intervals to catch the bottom-lying cod. The practice was for the ship to launch her dories early in the morning, virtually regardless of the weather, recovering them as the dorymen filled their boats with their catch. It was a hard, dangerous life: fog and strong winds were frequent hazards.

Each year the major part of the fishing fleet would assemble in Lisbon – a big event being made of the occasion – to sail end of March, beginning of April, for the Grand Banks, the shoal area off the south-eastern corner of Newfoundland where the cod abounded, thence up through the Davis Straits to Greenland. When full of cod they would return home, usually in September. This is what we were looking at, the return of one of the Portuguese 'White Fleet', which had been fishing the cod banks over four centuries. She passed by, heading for the schooner anchorage off Belem and on her way into history. It was not to be known as we gazed upon her that not only were she and all of her kind doomed, but so was their very way of life, and shortly so were the fish themselves on which it all depended.

At the time there were over 30 schooners, divided fairly equally between three and four masters, sailing out of Lisbon. Of them, only four were built of steel; the remainder were wood, with several being of modern design constructed even after the steel vessels had been introduced. Included in the total fishing fleet were a few, comparatively small, powered trawlers. It was these that were progressively to kill off the sailing schooners and then in turn lead to the advent of 'factory fishing', which would change totally, with cataclysmic results, the way cod were caught.

In the 1950s industrialized fishing, in the shape of the factory freezer trawler, first arrived on the Banks, later to expand rapidly throughout the north-west Atlantic fishing grounds, which took in the major area for cod, Newfoundland's Grand Banks. The ships had become huge, dragging enormous nets along the seabed, scooping up the cod and every living organism in the process, destroying the ecosystem needed to sustain the fish. By the 1970s there were 700 or more large factory trawlers, more than half being Russian, dedicated to decimating the stocks of cod.

In the early 1990s the cod industry collapsed. There were no more cod. Today there is little sign they will ever come back in any numbers. In the space of 30 years man's greed and stupidity had destroyed 500 years of cod fishing, and the economy that had been built upon it since John Cabot in his little *Matthew*, out of Bristol with a crew of 18, had stumbled on to the untold wealth of the Banks in 1497.

16 September 2100 Perfect evening (hope it lasts) with gentle breeze from WSW. Boat close-hauled on starboard tack, lamps burning brightly, a good dinner inside us, calm sea and sailing gently down the path of a bright moon. This is one of those few occasions when one really enjoys sailing. The lights of Lisbon are astern and we are off for the Canaries.

'Where do you think we are?' 'Good question! With luck we are looking at the top of Lanzarote.' Five days out from Lisbon, uncertain of our position, it had been a great thrill to raise this piece of land on our port bow. Our last sight of land had been Cape St Vincent, the morning after sailing out of Lisbon, and I had taken our departure from the cape, our last link with Europe. Africa would be next on our port beam. During the passage the weather had not been a navigator's friend, overcast much of the time, with those heavenly bodies that lend themselves to astronomical observation being at a premium. I had tried for a Polaris shot to give us our latitude but with disappointing results. The Pole Star, being a second-magnitude star, is not particularly bright, and to quote the *Admiralty Manual of Navigation*, '…it does not appear to the naked eye until the horizon has become indistinct in the gathering dusk'. This is certainly what I experienced, my efforts not being helped by intermittent cloud. Experienced navigators work back from the DR latitude, presetting the approximate altitude on the sextant. The azimuth being precisely known, the star can then be picked up in the sextant's star telescope whilst the horizon is still clear cut.

A day or so later I tried for a forenoon shot of the sun for longitude and a meridian altitude for latitude, but my efforts were once again noteworthy for their lack of success. I was to notice later how frequently clouds come up at midday, obscuring the sun at the vital moment, but my particular problem was lack of experience. The passage to the Canaries had ended up being a dead reckoning exercise, hence the uncertainty about what piece of land it was we were gazing on. However, as the morning progressed and visibility became clearer, it was evident we were sailing down the west coast of Fuerteventura, the second largest island in the Canaries Archipelago and quite distinct. The land now on our port beam fitted the description shown in the Admiralty's *Africa Pilot*. What useful books these are! Although they are intended for 'vessels of 12m or more in length', *Tern*, at 11.9, more or less made this criterion. The books provide a wealth of completely reliable information and detail not shown on charts. The *Admiralty Sailing Directions* or *Pilots* embrace the world, there being 70 of them, and we were to use them in both the Atlantic and Pacific Oceans to good effect.

Today there is a plethora of *Pilots* of one sort or another, highly illustrated marine guide books for yachtspeople cruising in the more frequented areas, but we had only the Admiralty publications and they served us well. It is interesting to compare the styling of the volumes we were using compared to the modern versions. Ours were very conservative in presentation, in marked contrast to the glossy books emanating today from the United Kingdom Hydrographic Office. These are produced under the auspices of the national hydrographer, a civil servant as witness to the march of Whitehall bureaucracy. The 1950s sailing directions were 'published by order of the Lords Commissioners of the Admiralty' and produced under the care of the hydrographer of the navy, a rear admiral. Somewhat more imposing of stature. However, it must he said that the superlative quality of the content has not diminished. One feature that has changed has been the widespread use of aerial photographs as an aid to identification, whereas ours relied on sketches made by ships' officers, sometimes many years previously, but even so remarkably accurate. These pen-and-ink drawings are in themselves artistic gems.

24 September 1700 Sighted land ahead and it agrees perfectly with the description in the *Pilot*. It can only be Gran Canaria. What a tremendous relief and we settled back to enjoy a wonderful sail: little sea, fresh breeze from the NNW. On a broad reach under all plain sail with topsail and *Tern* going fast with the log whizzing round.

This leg from Lisbon, like the one down the Iberian Peninsular, had been trying, albeit blessing us much of the time with a fair wind. After leaving the coast at Cape St Vincent we had enjoyed a wind slowly veering from the south-westerly quadrant, ending up east of north and freshening as it went. We had entered the north-east trade wind belt. Although this meant cracking progress, it also meant more stressful sailing. With the wind dead astern, the risk of a heavy gybe was ever present, despite the boom preventer being permanently rigged. That risk was accentuated by our physical condition.

24 September The last few nights have been hell, it being almost physically painful to keep awake. It is a very great strain this running before a fresh breeze and biggish sea with the boom squared off. A moment's drowsiness and it is on top of one. Even with a light wind at night it is little better as the boom tends to fall in under its own great weight and scare the life out of us.

With the wind well aft we could not get the boat to sail herself and hold her course without attention. The watchkeeping system of four hours on and four hours off on the tiller was proving to be too much like a sentence of hard labour. We were glad to have arrived in the Canaries. Apart from the discomfort to which we had been subjected, it had not been the easiest of passages in a navigational sense. As an aspiring offshore navigator, struggling somewhat on occasion, I was, however, able to take some solace from the old adage:

It is better to be lost and know it than to be certain about where one is and not be there.

Chapter Four

The Atlantic Experience

Great seas of deep sapphire blue,
with here and there the intense
white of a breaking crest and
spindrift sparkling in the sun.

CLAUD WORTH

Las Palmas was to be where we organised ourselves for the crossing of the North Atlantic to the West Indies, Trinidad to be precise. Setting up dedicated downwind sailing arrangements would be at the centre of our attention, the imperative for this having been accentuated by our initial experience of trade wind conditions during the passage from Lisbon. This had taught us that the best place for the mainsail boom was down in its crutch, out of harm's way. However, the commencement of this programme was, by a unanimous decision, put on hold for a day whilst we 'took it easy' after the pressures we had been subjected to in dealing with our various visitors. This was not to mention the initial lack of sleep on our arrival, occasioned by keeping watches at anchor during the silent hours to safeguard ourselves against the attentions of marauding thieves, the 'Rats', as they were referred to locally. 'Lazy day with a very enjoyable swim on the other side of the isthmus. Visited in the evening by the crew of a small Dutch yawl, *De Zwarte Hebs*, out of Amsterdam and amateur steel built. The pair, whose English, of course, is good, are on their way to Curaçao for a "look see" before going any further.'

On our arrival we thought we had the anchorage to ourselves, not noticing another yacht tucked away in a corner of the harbour. The crew of the Dutchman, like us, had been worried about security, so it was agreed they would come alongside us, riding to our anchor with the cable veered to one shackle. They came on board in the evening and it subsequently became apparent that we 'did our guests [and ourselves] rather well'. As a consequence, serious work did not start next day; rather, after giving ourselves some time for recuperation, we confined ourselves to smartening up *Tern*'s appearance, her brightwork in particular. 'It is good to see some winking brass. White flannels and yachting caps the next cry.'

Anchored some way off, we were next to discover, was an ex-Grimsby trawler owned by a most pleasant young Englishman: an adventurer, ex-public school, cast in the empire-building mode. Hope-Vian could well have been in a John Buchan story, exemplifying his famous observation, 'It's a great life if you don't weaken.' Hope-Vian was on board us on several occasions and was welcome. He was congenial company. His plan was to take his vessel down to Liberia and indulge in coastal trading in the belief that there were good opportunities opening up for doing business on the west coast of Africa as it emerged from colonial days.

We were never to hear how his venture worked out, he still being in the anchorage when we left, but we admired his pluck and resourcefulness in undertaking what seemed to us a most daunting enterprise. He was very much on his own, with no one of his kind on board with whom he could communicate his thoughts, hopes and fears. The crew he had hired were all Spanish-speaking and of a totally different culture. His was a lonely existence and would explain the need for social contact away from his ship. We felt our presence helped to fill that need.

For our part we appreciated the company of the little group around us. We were not enjoying Las Palmas, despite the lauded beauty of its women and abundant fruit. The climate we found trying – so enervating – added to which was the constant threat of the Rats and a harbour so depressingly environmentally unfriendly. Unbeknownst to me, another naval officer, Victor Clark, was sailing in the area and had made an unscheduled stop in Las Palmas to effect some rigging repairs. He was also not enamoured with the place, writing later: '…the harbour was covered with oil, floating filth, garbage and dead dogs, leaving a black oily film on our clean side; our decks became progressively more soiled with dirt brought off shore on our shoes or blown on board by the breeze; and a constant watch had to be kept day and night against water thieves for which the port is notorious.'

Peter and I were as one. We wanted to get to sea again and get on with what lay ahead of us, the Atlantic crossing. Restraints delaying our departure included the essential requirement to get our downwind rig properly set up, and on a personal basis the wish to collect the mail that had been directed to Madeira. Getting hold of this in the Canaries was proving a painstaking exercise, not helped by the somewhat relaxed attitude of the staff in the British Consulate. We were assured they had been in touch with their counterparts in Funchal, who had confirmed they had been holding our mail and this would be on the weekly flying-boat service due the coming Sunday. It was not. The following weekend again our mail did not arrive, but this time neither did the flying boat. It had been delayed by bad weather. Virtually on the eve of our departure we got our letters, patience certainly being a virtue in those islands.

Of major importance to what lay ahead was the weather. The West Indies hurricane season begins each year at the end of May and extends through to the beginning of December, the worst months being August, September and October. The average frequency of winds of tropical storm force 12 or stronger quoted in the Admiralty publication *The Mariner's Handbook* is five in number over the season, which would probably mean more than once a month over the most dangerous period. Force 12 on the Beaufort Scale has a mean wind speed of 64 knots and over with exceptionally high waves, and we are told, 'The air is filled with foam and spray; sea completely white with driving spray; visibility seriously affected.' We were not keen to be part of this, our very survival in such conditions being in grave doubt.

Expecting a three to four week passage to Trinidad we did not want to leave too early in October. Because the southern regions of the Caribbean lie on the fringes of the hurricane belt we were comfortable with a mid-October departure from Las Palmas, which would mean arriving in November, but by that time the season would be well advanced.

On the boat preparation front it was taking more time and effort than I had expected – not uncommon with many undertakings in life – in getting the trade wind rig set up. *Tern II* had carried a squaresail all her life; a sail favoured by Claud Worth, spinnakers, it would seem, not being appropriate for cruising craft. He speaks approvingly of his squaresail in his *Yacht Cruising*:

'*Sunday Midnight* It was delightful sailing despite the rain. Besides keeping the vessel steady, there is a lift and drive in a big squaresail which imparts an eager buoyant feeling to both yacht and crew.'

As this sail, complete with its yard, was already on board, rather than change to a twin headsail rig I decided to stay with a square rig, but to give it more drive I had a sailmaker make for us a raffee before we left Plymouth. This triangular sail, hoisted to the masthead above the squaresail and sheeting to the ends of the square yard, was to prove most effective. We did not, however, adopt the Worth system of using the pole to take the weather clew of the squaresail out to one side, which in effect made it into a form of spinnaker. We had one of these as a separate light-weather sail and used it in the normal way.

As our squaresail rig would be engaged in the more serious occupation of taking us across the Atlantic, compared to the less demanding use to which the squaresail was put by Worth, its gear would inevitably be more elaborate. I wanted the yard to remain hoisted close up rather than lowering and hoisting it depending on wind conditions. To this end I fitted the sail with inhauls and outhauls on the yard so that the sail could be brailed into the mast and hauled out again to its full spread, everything being handled from the foot of the mast on deck. The sail was secured to the yard by parrels, sliding on wooden beads. Additionally there were blocks at the yardarms to take the raffee sheets. In the end the arrangements worked satisfactorily but they took time to get right.

The Atlantic crossing, because of the distance involved, would have to be by astronomical observation, which required the exact time to be known. It would have been feasible to have made the crossing the way it was done before accurate time could be measured. This was to find one's latitude by a meridian altitude of the sun and then, after getting onto the latitude of the desired landfall, sail along that parallel until the destination was reached. For this, accurate time is not necessary, a meridian altitude not being linked to knowing the exact time. This, however, is a somewhat blunt-instrument approach. If one wants to know at any moment where the boat actually is, precise time must be known, requiring, of course, a very accurate timepiece. In turn, this raised the question of the determination of our chronometer's 'rate'. All mechanical chronometers have an error but that is not important. What is important is to know how much the chronometer loses or gains each day: its rate of change. The chronometer error can be derived from astronomical observation, but much more readily from radio time signals. I had not been getting good reception on our portable radio receiver, but on passage to the Canaries I had spasmodically been able to get enough signals to establish the watch's rate. However, I was not sure what had happened to it since we had been in Las Palmas. The rate can change between sea and harbour conditions. Lying in the inner commercial harbour we could see a British tanker which we thought perhaps might be able, and moreover willing, to help.

Landing in the dinghy on the adjacent foreshore, and after a long walk round, I went on board and hesitantly asked for the second officer. In British ships this officer was usually the navigator. He emerged and met me on the gangway. He was only too happy to co-operate. At an appointed time that evening he would flash a light from the bridge on the exact second. However, something went awry with the arrangement and I missed the light. We went ashore that evening for a meal and, wondering what reception

I would get, I went round by taxi and once again accosted the second. There was no problem. He was quite relaxed about repeating the exercise at a new agreed time the following day. This time I was able to record that all had gone well. '0900 Time check: +1 min 13 sec'; the watch was fast. Satisfactory this, eventhough the result was rather unexpected: the sea rate, determined from earlier time checks, being less than that in harbour. Knowing the error at successive time checks and the number of days in between, it was straightforward to calculate the daily rate. Three days later I was successful in getting a time signal on the BBC West Africa Service. '2000 GMT + 1 min 13.5 sec.' I was now at peace with the watch. I knew what it was up to. It was gaining slowly.

The watch, being Admiralty pattern, was a good one and I endeavoured to give it the care and attention it needed. It was located centrally in the cabin, where the boat's motion was least, and housed in a padded box, complete with lid, to protect it from knocks and vibration as well as to insulate it against temperature variations. The routine for its winding was sacrosanct. This I would do every forenoon at 1100 and I developed a feel for the right number of turns of the key to maintain consistency of spring tension. The return on effort was good.

It was during this time that our social circle in the anchorage expanded markedly. In the small hours our old friend *Petula* came in and anchored near us, her complement not wasting too much time in coming on board to exchange greetings and have a drink. They had taken the same time as we had from Lisbon but appeared to have had a gentler passage. In the evening they returned hospitality by inviting us on board for supper. It was interesting to hear about their marine biological plans. They intended to start a slow sail across the Atlantic from Dakar, collecting data on the food chain in the ocean, involving scooping up and studying plankton. The three of them were a happy bunch and exuded good fellowship. They were looking forward to being at one with the sea and what it contained.

A couple of days later it was my birthday and the day was to be one of varying fortunes. I awoke to a recurrence of a stomach upset, but this time it was a real touch of the 'dog', courtesy of Las Palmas. Happily the frequency of attacks decreased as the day wore on, which was just as well as Peter had arranged a birthday party for me in the evening, inviting all hands from *Petula*, *De Zwarte Hebs* and Hope-Vian from the trawler for drinks. They completely filled our cabin and I forgot about my affliction. Although we were not to know it at the time, this was to be the last occasion when we would be in the company of people in small craft sailing under the red ensign. Henceforth, the few yachts we encountered anywhere would all be foreign.

A few days later *Petula* sailed, followed by the Dutchmen. The anchorage felt so empty and lonely without them. To help cope with a real sense of loss, Peter and I decided this was the time for a break from shipboard routine before we ourselves departed. A day's outing to the top of the island was mooted.

We made an early start, taking the dinghy ashore at 0730 and leaving it on the foreshore whilst we walked into town to catch the bus. The arrangement with our particular chapter of the Mafia was working well, enabling us to fulfil what seemed to us the not unreasonable wish to retain in our possession what was ours. We could leave the dinghy with the oars and gear in it in the full knowledge that nothing would be touched in our absence. Seemingly there were two arms to the waterfront thievery industry, one specializing in its practice and the other providing protection against it, the two having a close working relationship. Our man, Juan, an integral part of the latter body, had proved himself. He was completely unobtrusive but at the same time he was eager to do jobs around the boat. He was also a nice man. Everyone was happy with the system.

It was raining and cold when we set off on our excursion in the bus, and conditions got steadily worse as we climbed up the mountain. The bus was obviously not designed – if it had been designed at all, that is – to accommodate what we were enduring. We got steadily colder and wetter. However, our driver thoughtfully provided a diversionary service to his captive customers in that his style of driving tended to take our minds off our misery. We had to admire the supreme confidence and cheerful aplomb with which he swept at sickening speed round the bends on the hillside, spraying stones and pebbles out into space over the sheer drop into the valleys deep below. In the midst of all this, Peter suddenly developed toothache.

It had been an interesting journey, not without its moments, but we were not unhappy when it was over. We alighted to find a quite magnificent hotel giving the impression it was there just for our benefit. We saw no other guests. Having made a contribution to the bar profits we set off to walk back, partly because we were in need of exercise but also to avoid the thrills which were complementary to the bus ride. However, we were not to escape that easily. We were overhauled by the bus, which stopped beside us, and the driver, none other than the one who had put the fear of God into us on the trip up, made it clear he was fully expecting us to complete the experience with him. Despite Peter's considerable discomfort with his tooth, which he bore with commendable stoicism and which I was to learn was one of his characteristics, it had been a good break. The day had done a lot for our morale.

The bad weather we had lived with on the mountainside followed us down and out over the anchorage.

Blew up violently during the night from the SW and Petula *arrived back with her tail down. The Dutchman has gone and it would seem for good. I had not liked seeing the empty billets of these boats and I am all of a fidget to get away.*

Juan laid out the spare bower anchor on the 2 1/2 inch warp on his own in the dinghy and veered another 5 fathoms of chain on the main cable. She had apparently threatened to drag and there was a big lump of a schooner astern to us. I only woke up on hearing the cable being veered, a fine thing for the skipper! Went over to Petula *and shook them but they were quite safe, they said, as they knew their anchor was fouled and were quite prepared for the consequential complications later. Poor old* De Zwarte Hebs, *they must be having a bad time out there.*

The problem with Las Palmas Harbour is that it is wide open to the south, which is not normally a problem, the prevailing wind being the NE trades. However, gale force winds from a southerly quarter can occur, and when they do a bad surge comes into the harbour, adding to the difficulties resulting from the strength of the wind. This is what we were getting. We had known there was something brewing, as the fishing fleet had all come in. This was better than any weather forecast, which we did not have the means to obtain.

With the weather improving, *Petula* made another attempt, and with a feeling akin to sadness, we watched her clear the breakwater. We were not to see her again. Peter, now being able to get ashore in the dinghy, conditions in the harbour having bucked up, found a dentist and the offending molar was removed. We congratulated ourselves that the tooth had flared up when it did, as a week or so out to sea, life for him would have been near impossible. We would have been faced with the decision whether to endure the hard beat back against the trade wind or carry on downwind. In all likelihood, the prospects were for Peter to have had to endure a similar experience to that which befell a Victorian yachtsman of some standing, whilst on passage way out at sea. In his best-selling *Letters from High Latitudes*, the Marquis of Dufferin tells of an exercise in dentistry in his schooner-yacht, *Foam*.

'I requested the doctor to remove one of my teeth. This he did with the greatest ability – a wrench to starboard, another to port – and up it flew through the cabin skylight.'

However, there was a slight difference or two in our circumstances. In the first place Peter was not a marquis, or likely to be one in the immediate future, and hence not able to enjoy the privileged attention that had gone with that exalted rank. In the second I was not a doctor. Poor old Peter!

The dentist was a lucky find. He came on board a day later to check on Peter's mouth.

'*Bueno!* You can eat a proper meal. Señores, will you please dine with me tonight?'

This was the first time we had been in receipt of hospitality ashore. It was also to be the only time. The meal was thoroughly Spanish and quite delicious. He knew, of course, what to order, unlike the occasions when Peter and I had been eating out. Because of language difficulties we never knew quite what we would see on our plates. We fully appreciated the thoughtful gesture and graciousness of a charming man.

Before meeting our host for dinner we made a point of going ashore to the Club Nautico for a shower and smarten-up. In a small boat, keeping on top of the 'dhobeying' (clothes washing) and fulfilling the desirability of regular bodily immersion constituted something of a problem. The situation was generally not too acute for the ship's company as we were literally in the same boat, environmentally, with a high degree of mutual tolerance. At sea, there was the permanent problem of a shortage of fresh water, which we partially overcame by swimming over the side when feasible, or being towed on a line under the bowsprit. In harbour, laundering services and facilities for a shower or a bath were frequently hard to find. We did our best, but there were times when we could only trust that our special ambiance was not too evident to those in our immediate proximity. It had to be hoped that the purity of our souls shining through would be pre-eminent. In Las Palmas we were fortunate that the yacht club's amenities were excellent and we enjoyed them regularly. It was one of the few pluses the port had to offer.

Sunday 11 October Secured for sea in the hopes of getting away at noon but the wind very fresh from the S with a swell coming into the harbour giving unwanted life to the boat.

1800 Laid out the kedge anchor on its rode and suspecting the bottom would be foul with unimaginable rubbish took the precaution this time of buoying the anchor. The weather deteriorated during the day and conditions now most unpleasant in the anchorage. The rode on the spare bower chafed through and we are now faced with the problem of its recovery. We tried diving for it but it was a futile attempt in 4 fathoms. We have to hope we can get a professional diver to go down on the morrow.

The weather conditions steadily improved and the moment for sailing was on us, but what to do about the spare bower, a big fisherman type, lying on the bottom? I had no intention of leaving without it. We had many anchorages ahead of us. Juan went ashore and came back with a young lad who was prepared to make an attempt, oblivious seemingly of the uninviting state of the water around us. He also found it too deep. It was then that the indefatigable Juan, spotting a craft engaged in diving by a ship on the other side of the harbour, went over to solicit their assistance. His mission was successful, as shortly after the craft was alongside. Yes, they were prepared to send a diver down to search for and recover our anchor but, with the tide out in our peseta pool, the question arose of how we were going to pay for their services. Once again a bottle of Johnnie Walker Black Label came to the rescue and was agreed upon. The diving boat set off on its search and was soon back, complete with our anchor. I went below to get the bottle of liquid gold, but once again the recipient-to-be followed me down into the cabin. Like the harbourmaster before him, the diving boat's captain was keenly interested to see before his eyes a row of bottles lying in the grog locker. He indicated that two bottles would be an appropriate reward for their efforts. He and his crew were a tough-looking lot and I thought it would not be fruitful to argue the point that the agreement had been for one bottle. I had to admit it was still a pretty good deal.

Having earlier picked up our main bower anchor, all that was left now was to recover the kedge and say goodbye to Juan. The former undertaking proved easy, the latter hard. It had been apparent for a little while there was something on his mind. That something now came out. 'Señor, will you take me with you please to the West Indies? I can then get over to America where I want to work. It will be a better life and more money.' I hedged. 'But what about your family?' I knew he had a wife and several young ones. 'When I have saved enough I will send for them. They will be very happy.' This was one of the most difficult moments in my life. He was now more to us than just a paid watchman: he was virtually part of our world. Yes, we could take him with us to Trinidad, but what then? I could see all sorts of problems with the immigration authorities and I would be held responsible for him as he could well have been considered a member of the crew. We might be stuck with him for some time, or alternatively I might have to pay his return fare to Las Palmas. This I certainly could not afford. He seemed to accept my explanations, the conveying of which had not been easy, not helped by the language constraints, and left us. To what? We gave him our remaining pesetas and what dollars we could spare, but that was not what he wanted. It was very sad, leaving me with the gnawing doubt I had let him down. That feeling was to stay with me.

Monday 12 October 1400 Left Las Palmas under jib and mainsail with a light NNE breeze and in warm sunny weather. Feel very much the magnitude of the daunting task ahead of us but it is so good to be on our way, tackling at long last what is to us the Big One. We leave an anchorage devoid of yachts and think of Hope-Vian; now so very much alone. We can only hope it all works out well for him and so admire his courage.

We rounded the breakwater, heading to go north about around the top of Gran Canaria before altering course to sail south of west to pass under the heel of Tenerife. The Atlantic crossing was about to start.

The act of rounding the breakwater had an element of symbolism about it akin to rounding earlier the one at Plymouth. They both marked a significant change in a way of life from a secure established environment into the completely different unknown experience for Peter and me of deepwater sailing. An insecure world now lay ahead, of complete self-reliance and, moreover, a total dependence on mutual compatibility within the compass of that world.

There was a difference, though, between the two roundings. Clearing Las Palmas Harbour we were not seasick. Clearing Plymouth we had been; very much so. Passing that breakwater we had been met with brisk conditions in a fresh south-westerly wind, good English sailing weather, and an unpleasant head sea throwing itself over us. Doing his best to ignore the unpromising start to the way ahead, and acting on the suggestion it was time to put the kettle on, Peter vanished below, only to reappear almost immediately back in the cockpit. With a preoccupied look on his face he advanced at high speed to the lee rail and gave his all to the sea. The skipper, as he should, rose to the occasion. Expressing sympathy for his crew's condition, he went down into the galley to complete the tea-making operation. It was also to be a short-lived event. I joined Peter at the rail. We looked at each other. We had come all of 5 miles. We had a mere 14,000 to go.

We were, as it was to work out, not to be sick again, but I was reminded of the first and only time before that I had been in this condition. Seasickness is, of course, the enduring scourge of going out onto the sea. Many and varied are the remedies that have been advanced either to alleviate it or, at best, cure it. There is only one, however, I have found that always works.

My first experience of the affliction was during World War II in a frigate at sea in mid winter. We were providing anti-submarine protection for a light-aircraft carrier, bringing her round from Scapa Flow to the Clyde. On rounding Scotland's north-west corner, Cape Wrath, we encountered head-on a full south-westerly gale. Our charge was one of a class known as 'escort carriers'. A wartime phenomenon: starting out life as cargo ships, their upper works had been sliced off and a flight deck built on. I had a full view of our carrier making hard work of it. She would plunge her bows deep into the oncoming sea, the turbulent water welling up above the forecastle to flight deck level. Her stern high in the air, I could see along the full length of her rain-drenched and spray-streaked flight deck. Then her bows would lift, foaming water pouring off the foredeck, cascading over the anchors as the forefoot started to rise clear of the sea. Watching this performance I suddenly felt very ill indeed. As a midshipman, just on 20 years old, I had perhaps another 30 years or more of this. The thought depressed me profoundly. However, the navy has a cure. It does not recognize seasickness. Shortly afterwards I was on watch with no time to feel sick. Activity is the unfailing remedy. It always works.

13 October 1350 Wind W by N light. Sea calm. Barometer 29.96. On starboard tack, boat sailing herself. Put clocks back 45 minutes to SAT. Took noon sight for latitude. We had taken breakfast for the first time in the saloon, an event of more interest to us than the news items we had picked up on the BBC Home Service: of no importance to us. What is happening on the planet at large is irrelevant to us out here in the world of nature. All that matters in our little part of the globe is what is the wind going to do, the state of the sea and what we are going to have for supper. The sounds of a boat at sea encompass us, filling our senses. Voices hurling themselves at us on the radio are an unwelcome intrusion. A perfect morning after a calm night and following breakfast it had been 'hands to bathe'.

As we worked south and west the weather pattern became more established consequent on us coming clear of the influence of the Canaries Archipelago.

14 October Very fresh breeze during the night with the boat roaring along under reefed mainsail. The roller reefing gear is a treat to use now I am practised with it and I will never sail again without it. The drill seems to be to take the weight of the boom on the weather topping lift, slack up on the throat halyard; just a little on the peak and then roll in. If the peak halyard is not slacked up enough a very hard roll develops with great strain on the leech as well as the roller gear itself.

Over the last couple of days the wind had slowly worked its way round to the north and started to settle down. The NE Trades were not far off and we were on our way! These trade winds are the lifeblood of an east-west transit of the North Atlantic. They extend from the west coast of Africa over to the Caribbean. Apart from the occasional aberration, as we were to experience, they are remarkably constant from the north-easterly quarter, with a steady wind force on the Beaufort Scale of 3 or 4, perhaps 5, with the occasional incidence of 6. There is only a one per cent chance of being on the receiving end of a force 7. It is very calming on the soul not to have any real worries about gales. The direction of these friendly winds varies from NNE on the eastern side of the ocean to a little north of east over on the western side, or slightly south of east as one approaches Trinidad. However, although these variations in direction and strength are present, once embarked on the crossing one can look forward to day after day of downwind sailing, generally in benign conditions.

The normally rather pragmatic Admiralty publication *Ocean Passages for the World* tends to the lyrical: '.... fine, rainless weather, and a blue sky, over which characteristic "trade clouds" – small detached masses of cumulus – continually pass.' This book is a treasure chest of information containing a mass of detail about the world's ocean weather systems, winds and currents. Based on this data are recommendations on the 'navigating of the best and most economical routes between the various ports of the world', these having been 'laid down with special reference to the winds and currents that would be experienced on each particular passage'. Routes are shown separately for steamships, in particular for those which are 'low powered, or having a seagoing speed of less than 10 knots and sailing ships'. One notes with perhaps some disappointment that routes for 'steam or motor ships with auxiliary sail power' are omitted, an acceptance perhaps that modes of propulsion have moved on.

The edition which we used had been 'published by order of the Lords Commissioners of the Admiralty' in 1923, replacing the 1896 edition. Apart from its value as a maritime guide on ocean voyaging, it was in the 'nice to have' category as a collector's item. The expression 'Lords Commissioners of the Admiralty' has a ring about it evocative of Pepys, Nelson and the days when Britannia really did 'rule the waves', rather than just be a jingle at the Last Night of the Proms. Their Lordships have been replaced with a faceless, colourless bureaucracy lacking any sense of majesty – the prosaic Ministry of Defence.

The passage to Trinidad should benefit significantly from the North Equatorial Current, which starts out on life as the Canary Current, flowing through those islands at a good half knot, then to sweep SW across the Atlantic before being deflected NW as it approaches the West Indies, its flow rate increasing. It was of particular benefit to us on closing Tobago and Trinidad that the current flowed with some dependability at a full knot. The current as a whole, giving a lift to yachts of between 10 and 20 miles or even more per day, provides a big boost to their distances made good over the ground. A graphically detailed indication of what winds and currents can be expected each month is shown by wind roses and current flow lines on the Admiralty sheet, *Routeing Chart – North Atlantic*. Such charts, covering all oceans, are of considerable value in making a passage plan, but as we were to find out, nature does not always obediently follow what man thinks it should do.

The 'feeling in the air' about the trades being around was correct. The wind continued its steady clockwise perambulation round the compass, and by the following evening it was 'sea rough, wind NE fresh'. We hove to, handed the mainsail and got under way again under a twin headsail rig, which I had spent some time in Las Palmas getting set up as an alternative to a square rig. It comprised the working staysail, which had its own integral boom, set out to starboard with a fore guy leading to the end of the bowsprit. On the port side was a spare staysail boomed out on a pole, also with a fore guy. This arrangement was complemented with the mizzen and the trysail sheeted well in to help in providing lateral stability. 'Ship going fast and apart from some rolling is very comfortable.' We now had the pleasure of the company of the north-east trade winds, which we would enjoy for the best part of the next 2,000 miles. With the prospect of a permanently fair wind we were aware of a decidedly feel-good factor.

Not being content to leave well alone, and feeling we could do even better, we dismantled after a few days the twin staysail rig, albeit it was effective, and replaced it with the squaresail, but this was to bring in its train another problem – chafe. The squaresail pulled us along well, but with the wind falling light and the boat rolling heavily the yard sawed across the forward side of the mast like Menuhin playing his violin. The jackstay being close into the mast, and with the inevitable flexing of the wire, it was unable to restrain the yard enough to keep it off the mast. The whole assembly was just not rigid enough. However, against this: 'Ship steers wonderfully easily, it being a relief to have the mainsail down and our old friend, its boom, safely stowed.' We were also making faster time than under the twins. We never completely solved the chafe problem but we were able to alleviate it to a considerable degree by pressing into service a variety of materials, including sacrificing a couple of blankets, plus frequent applications of tallow. It became a routine practice for me each forenoon to go aloft up to the crosstrees to administer the appropriate care and attention. This, however, was not too much of a chore, as standing high up there on the spreaders my horizons were now literally wider, and I could take in the magnificent beauty of the ocean in motion around us, the contrast so outstanding between the intense blue of the sea and the stark whiteness of the crests foaming across it in ever changing patterns. What was apparent from my elevated viewpoint was the surprising unevenness of the wave formations. They had been under the influence of strong winds from a steady direction for hundreds of miles, and it might have been supposed that there would have been a high degree of symmetry to them, but not so. Criss-crossing them, as though obeying some theory about the law of chaos, were separate wave fronts, all at different angles, which helped to explain why, when running before them, we were so prone to rolling.

What was also evident is that trade wind sailing is very much a one-way street, east to west, unless one is a masochist or circumstances dictate otherwise. Trying to work to windward against those big, steep waves, with their breaking crests, would have been wet, almost impossibly hard work for us, with little progress to be seen for it. It put the discomfort of rolling downwind into perspective.

I had been aware of the rolling problem, endemic to sailing in the trades, before we had set out. It featured in many of the writings of transatlantic voyagers making the passage in the more traditional type of ocean-cruising yachts. Such boats tended to be relatively narrow of beam, with all their ballast externally hung on the keel. *Tern* was no exception. She would roll first one rail under and then the other, scooping up a sidedeck of water, and throw it into the cockpit and over the unfortunate helmsman, soaking him from the waist down. A wet backside became a permanent way of life. Oilskins often were not an option because of the heat of the sun. Foul-weather gear in my case comprised an ex-navy standard oilskin coat and no waterproof trousers, Peter being no better placed. Neither of us had sea boots, finding, in the main, bare feet quite adequate. They adjusted to the temperature and did not mind getting wet. As a result of a constantly wet backside and the sliding to and fro on the cockpit seat, induced by the boat's motion, we developed a rash akin to bedsores or nappy rash. For us, the discomfort was, as for those other sufferers, alleviated by that marvel of modern times, Johnson's Baby Powder. Its soothing softness was bliss. We brought the trade wind a little on the quarter, and setting the trysail helped to dampen the cycle, but there was always an uncomfortable lurching motion.

Having settled the squaresail down and persuaded it to draw properly, we then played our trump card. We set the raffee. What a difference it made! Set above the squaresail and high up, it gave life to the boat. Under squaresail only our progress, although satisfactory, had been somewhat pedestrian, but now we were achieving days' runs by log of 145 miles, noticing that with the lift in speed through the water she was tending to sail more upright with less rolling. It was unfortunate that I had not acquired a copy of Worth's book, *Yacht Navigation and Voyaging*, before we had sailed, as in it he reveals, rather as a confessional, the lessons learned in *Tern II*. In the book he expresses again his love affair with square rig. 'On an ocean cruise the squaresail is generally the most useful sail in the vessel,' going on to describe in some detail the improvements he had effected in *Tern IV*.

A week out from Las Palmas we were settling into our ocean routine, comfortable with each other and our boat, at peace with our environment: 'Developed into a pleasant night, the ship sailing along the path of a setting moon, practically steering herself, with a warm, soft breeze comfortably on the quarter. I seem to have overcome the awful agony of eyes trying to close all the time.' Eric Hiscock's similar experience of being at one with the boat could be appreciated: 'All that afternoon we ran happily on our course; the 9 ton yawl *Tern II* was revelling in the breeze: with mainsail, topsail, mizzen and squaresail bellying out in firm curves, she logged 6 knots hour after hour, lifting her shapely counter gently to the following sea, and running steady and true with a light helm.'

The day had seen the demise of the Las Palmas bread, the last loaf being riddled with mildew, but the day was also particularly noteworthy in that Peter baked his first loaf of bread. Thereafter he was to bake regularly. Two loaves at a time, and what heaven they were too! Fresh bread straight out of the oven in a small boat in mid ocean is a gift from the gods, represented on Earth in the form of Peter, unrelated to the one on high.

Although the old boat with her long keel and easy sections would hold her course for lengthy periods, with little needed in the way of helm corrections, a guiding hand had always to be near. With a watch-and-watch routine, sleep, or rather the lack of it, was a major factor in our lives. We tried various combinations of watch-keeping systems, aimed at giving the watch below the maximum sleep time but without overextending the time the watch on deck could hope to stay alive and alert. Having experimented with periods on the tiller between a two hour and a six hour watch, we finally fell back on the centuries-old four on and four off. We had reinvented the wheel. We elected not to break the day up with 'dog watches', ie 1600 to 1800 followed by an 1800 to 2000 stint, the system used from time immemorial to avoid the same person keeping the same watch day after day. Our day began at 0700 when Peter called me and I relieved him on the helm and he prepared breakfast, usually from a selection of porridge, figs or prunes, eggs, tea and toast. The rest of the forenoon was devoted to work about the boat, taking of astronomical sights for longitude and, every other day, Peter baking bread. After the midday meridian sight for latitude, lunch was prepared (soup, cold tinned meat, a vegetable of some kind, tinned fruit after the fresh had gone, bread and jam plus lime juice and a vitamin pill). Peter then enjoyed a two hour sleep in mid afternoon followed by tea, which we invariably had together as something of a ritual, with cake or biscuits and a mug of tea. Whoever's turn it was would prepare the evening meal. This was the big event of the day and we took a lot of trouble over it, every move closely watched by the face at the helm, peering down through the entrance to the doghouse. The menu was varied. Curries, rissoles, fish pies, stews, potatoes and vegetables, followed by a selection of desserts – fruit and custard, rice pudding, suet pudding, sponge pudding and jam roly-poly etc – and finally coffee. I would then have my two hours sleep before relieving the helm at 2300. Showing no mercy, I would call Peter just before 0300 for me to turn in until 0700, when the day's routine started all over again.

Porridge was a much looked-forward-to feature of our daily diet, and although appreciating its widely known health-giving qualities, we were not overtly aware of the full extent of its benefits to mankind. I was subsequently to read an authoritative statement that the humble oatmeal enhances one's libido. Desirable as this may be, it can, however, be argued that libido enhancement may not be all that relevant in a boat way out in mid ocean with an all-male crew, 1,000 miles from shoreside delights.

We lived well, kept healthy and fit, and looked forward with relish to our meals. Two factors contributed to this happy state: widespread use of the pressure cooker and Peter's guiding hand. Due to him, my cooking skills, from a very low starting point, developed considerably. He set a high standard, and in doing so constituted a challenge. I had to measure up. We each developed our own pet dishes, and in my case, in the pursuit of inspiration, I turned to a little book, *Yacht Cookery and Hints to Small Boat Sailors*. Written in 1935 by a gentleman called JF Marsden, it was a gem. In it I discovered the secrets of spotted dick and roly-poly and learned, amongst other things, that steamed pudding was essentially no more than flour, sugar and margarine, and as such, with the aid of the pressure cooker, within even my capabilities. Peter, being on a different plane, did not resort to a cookbook, perfecting a series of dishes of his own. He enjoyed cooking, to which he brought innovative practices. I had noticed that as he finished a tin of tobacco, being a pipe smoker, he made a point of retaining the tin and then proceeding to wash it out meticulously before putting it away in a locker. I wondered vaguely about this somewhat odd behaviour, but all came clear when in due course he produced for supper little apple pies baked to perfection in his tins. They were quite delicious, and it was not a case of hungry men at sea just eating anything.

Tern, following standard design for cruising yachts at the time of her birth, had her galley in the forecastle, an arrangement which, like the curate's egg, could be good or bad. In trade wind conditions, being right up forward, the cook and his apparatus, although having to function in hot conditions, were out of the way of wind and rain blowing in from astern through the doghouse. Moreover, the motion being a rolling one and not pitching, being positioned up in the bows was not an inconvenience to the cook in going about his business. It was a different story when on the wind, with the boat dipping her bows into head seas, when the motion could at times border on the violent. The galley could then be untenable. This had not been a problem in her early days, as of course, gentlemen then 'did not go to windward', or if they were forced to, no doubt the paid hand would be despatched forward into the galley. To enable us to continue with the cooking business on all points of sailing, I had installed an arrangement whereby a single-burner Primus stove could be hung in gimbals at the after end of the saloon. In the South Pacific we were to find this of some considerable benefit in maintaining a supply of hot food without making ourselves ill in the process.

More and more, as we progressed into the passage, I was to give thanks for my choice of companion. It could have been otherwise, as had been observed by a yachtsman of some distinction in the early 30s. Prior to the Second World War, AGH Macpherson had cruised extensively, with ocean passages spread over the North Atlantic, Baltic, Mediterranean and Indian Ocean. These had been conducted principally in his 32 foot *Driac II*, with a mixed bag for crew of paid hands and friends. 'This matter of stable companions on a long voyage is almost more important than that of the boat; for whereas a reasonably designed hooker, providing she is sound and strong, will hump round the world in her own sweet time, the gent who doesn't fit with the surroundings may easily wreck the whole outfit.' In our old hooker this dire circumstance did not arise.

Everyone who has sailed long distances, living within the confines of a small craft, would agree with Macpherson's sentiments. One of the problems, it would seem, is created by overcrewing. Too many people on board means there is not enough action to engage fully each individual's interest. Boredom that comes with inactivity and the excessive time spent in idleness inevitably leads to an overcritical awareness of others' foibles and faults, be they real or just perceived. Active dislike ensues, the team spirit breaks down and the cruise is ruined. Near magical marvels of modern technology, in the shape of super-efficient aids to navigation and boat management, have supplanted much of the time-consuming effort demanded of the earlier breed of ocean-going yachtspeople. In doing so, the problem related to crew underdeployment has become exacerbated.

In *Tern*, being totally devoid of such aids and, moreover, short-handed, the opposite situation pertained. For us, the day was not long enough to cope with what was required to work the boat and at the same time get the sleep demanded by our bodies to offset the tendency towards permanent tiredness. Working watch and watch, we did not have enough unutilised time together to run a critical eye over the others' mannerisms and behavioural peccadilloes. On the contrary, we valued our periods of 'togetherness'. Whenever possible, weather permitting, we would eat down below together at the table, but almost regardless of the circumstances we also made a big point of having the shared afternoon teatime, the off-watch man joining the helmsman in the cockpit. It was an invaluable 'bonding exercise', in today's 'speak', much looked forward to each day. A chat over a 'cuppa' provided an opportunity to learn more about each other, our interests and importantly our likes and dislikes. We seized every opportunity that presented itself, or if needs be, ones we fabricated, for bonding frequently over a measure of rum.

One such occasion was Trafalgar Night, 21 October. Celebrating Nelson's great victory with a tot of neat rum raised to toast the 'immortal memory' was an essential part of being in the navy. On this particular occasion, for us at sea the day also marked the birthday of Peter's sister. What could be more appropriate for celebrating two such significant events than the issue of a double tot of Nelson's Blood to all hands?

Macpherson's name for his boat, *Driac*, is fairly readily discernible as Caird spelt backwards, and therein lies its own story. He seems to have had two principal purposes for living. One was cruising in small sailing craft and the other collecting pictorial representations of Britain's maritime history. This latter pursuit spanned his years working in the days of the

Raj in India, having been born there, and subsequently in England on retirement. The Macpherson Collection became well known, being described in the words of an associate as '…that collection of pictures and prints of old sailing ships, yachts, steamships, naval ships, naval actions, portraits, seaports, 12,000 in all, now the property of the nation and housed in the National Maritime Museum at Greenwich'.

Macpherson spent so much of his money on his obsession with collecting that he became financially embarrassed but did not want to break up the collection by selling it off piecemeal. He felt it should be presented to the nation, it being quite unique, but before this could occur there was the small matter of settling his debts with clamouring dealers at his heels. Sir James Caird, a wealthy, influential Scottish philanthropist, who also happened to be a friend of Winston Churchill's, came to the rescue and made it all take place. It is the same gentleman who is immortalized in *James Caird*, the name of *Endurance*'s boat that Shackleton sailed from Elephant Island in Antarctica to South Georgia, one of the greatest of all open-boat passages. Caird had also been one of Shackleton's benefactors.

Strong rain-laden squalls are a permanent feature of the trade wind phenomenon. Under the distinctive cloud effect of enormous towers of soft cumulus rising up into the vivid blue of the sky, often there could be seen, at random round the horizon, localised, dense, black clouds from which a curtain of heavy rain would be falling. Most of the time these would be far enough off to one side of our track to pass us by harmlessly. However, when we could see one building up from astern the warning had to be heeded. If the squall looked particularly threatening, and often it could look downright dangerous, the usual practice was to let the raffee halyard go, and with the downhaul pull the sail down into the lee of the squaresail, handing the mizzen for good measure. The helmsman then had the choice of either trying to keep dry by donning his oilskin coat, putting up with the heat inside it, or enjoying a most welcome freshwater shower. 'Enjoy', however, is not quite the right word, as the rain precipitating from some height was bitterly cold on a warm, naked body. The invariable decision was to forego the shower. The option preferred by the watch below was to remain in the dry, putting up with the discomfort of the hot, humid air, all cabin openings being shut off.

The squall seemed to take an agonisingly long time in arriving, but when it did it soon made its presence felt. The boat took off with a high, foaming bow wave rising to deck level. The intense rain flattened the sea such that the boat stopped rolling and roared along, bolt upright, under the double blast of wind and rain. Then it was all over. The squall passed on ahead, the sun came out again, the sea resumed its disorder and the rolling recommenced. The helmsman, feeling like a human hothouse, divested himself of his oilskin, and the watch below emerged from his own hothouse to reset the raffee and mizzen. The crew as one man, now sweating worse than ever, vowed that next time they would not deny themselves the opportunity for a refreshing cleansing douche. It never happened. We always chickened out.

For our ablutionary needs we were well catered. Spoilt for choice, in fact. From the heavens above there was a full-flow shower, albeit with an unadjustable cold tap, and from the Earth below a bath of quite some size, also with cold-water supply only, unfortunately with a choice confined to salt water, but nevertheless in unlimited quantities.

Tuesday 2 November 1230 Observed position 12° 16′N 56° 24′W. 'Hands to bathe'; dunking from the bowsprit end on a line around our waists. IT WAS MARVELLOUS.

Surfing ahead of the bows was exhilarating in boisterous conditions with the boat going fast, but so was bathing a couple of days later equally pleasurable in more leisurely conditions.

Swam from the boat, both of us in the water at the same time in a long, lazy swell, with the helm lashed hard down, the squaresail brailed into the mast and the head of the raffee let go. She looked very much the deep-sea cruiser, with her chafing gear on shrouds and backstays and the squaresail yard aloft. We had a unique view of her, admiring her shapely form as she slowly and gracefully rolled, showing her red, antifouled underbody, then rolled back towards us, revealing the gentle sweep of her deck.

On reflection, it may not have been too smart for both of us to have been in the water together away from the boat. If the wind had got up suddenly, although the helm was hard down such that she would not have sailed off on a steady course, nevertheless she may have blown bodily downwind faster than we could have swum, particularly as we would have been tiring rapidly. Also there was the consideration of sharks, even though we had not seen any. However, we worried not, because, as is well known, the young are immortal.

We had been at sea long enough now with no contact with other human beings, by sight or sound, to feel the world we were in was ours, special and personal to us. The impression was later destroyed with an unexpected encounter with a ship late one night. I had only just settled into my watch, and having finished sipping my hot chocolate drink, the usual semi-coma-like state associated with a night watch began to envelop me. As I sank in the warm embrace of the darkness, close ahead, very fine on the starboard bow, there appeared as if from nowhere a ship's lights. In the words of the ColRegs, the Collision Regulations, she was a 'power-driven vessel under way' and, moreover, heading straight for us; on a collision course if ever there was one. Her two masthead steaming lights were dead in line and making a perfect isosceles triangle with her port and starboard side lights. In other words, she was about to run over us. We, of course, did not have any navigation lights of our own on display; why should we when we were in our private playground? For us, when night fell it was not just a matter of flicking a switch and on came bright electric lights. Ours being oil lamps, it was a case on each occasion before use of checking they were topped up, wicks trimmed and glass clean. Then the lamps had to be lighted, out of the draught, in their stowage position in the forepeak, to be carried carefully on deck, the bearer braving the weather conditions and a jumping deck to clamp them in the light boards on the shrouds. Most of the time it was all too much effort, but I was now regretting my laziness.

As the situation seemed to suggest, it would not be too rewarding to invoke Rule 18 (a) of the Regulations: 'A power-driven vessel under way shall keep out of the way of a sailing vessel.' All I could do was shine my torch on the leading face of the squaresail and try to get out of the way, a somewhat forlorn hope in the dying breeze and the rapidly closing distance between us. Our visitor from outer space was almost immediately revealed as a large, deeply laden tanker, probably out of Venezuela, in full view as she passed close down our starboard side. Too close! How she had missed us I know not. She appeared to have altered course, but of this I could not be too sure. Judging the relative movements of vessels in close proximity is far from easy and very much prone to human error, as countless Courts of Enquiry into collisions at sea have found.

The intruder into our privacy, black and menacing, slid silently past, this being in the days before thumping great diesels, and rapidly vanished astern to merge with the night. It was as though she had never existed, apart from bequeathing severe palpitations to the helmsman, me, and engendering a sense of bemusement in the crew, peremptorily wrenched out of deep slumber. Peter offered no comment on what had transpired, and I was to observe on similar occasions when he was the victim of a circumstance not of his making how he was able to say so much without saying anything. With the palpitations subsiding and sleep reclaiming Peter, now once more alone we reverted to our erstwhile routine and reconnected with the ambient natural world, devoid of other alien human beings. We played a part, if perhaps one that was not too significant, in the ocean's marine life, with us constituting a linkage to the food chain, putting something into it by way of our edible rubbish and taking something out in the form of flying fish. Neither Peter nor I were fishermen by natural inclination, and neither of us would unwittingly kill bird or beast just for the sake of killing, but we were more than happy to enjoy flying fish when they landed on our doorstep, as it were. We certainly would not throw them back if still alive. Frequently in the morning we would find one or more, or even several, of these curious creatures lying in the scuppers, soon to be in the frying pan. We told ourselves they tasted like trout. It was a common sight during the day to see the surface of the sea suddenly erupt with a large flight of the fish taking to the air to escape some, unseen by us, predator. During their long flights they would change direction several times, no doubt to outwit their pursuers, but they never landed on us, presumably being aware of the presence of the boat. At night this was not the case.

Our other friends were dolphins: delightful companions and so beautiful to watch with their graciousness and perfection of movement. They would suddenly appear alongside in some numbers in complete harmonization with each other, swimming at times close by us, then diving under the keel to reappear just clear of the bows. We spent many an hour sitting on the bowsprit trying to capture them on film as they played under us and ahead of the boat, but with little success. They were just too quick. We were subsequently able to identify them as probably being the 'short-snouted spinner dolphin', occurring mainly offshore in the deep water of the Atlantic, but unfortunately for them also in the Caribbean, where sadly they are hunted. According to Mark Carwardine in his informative book *Whales, Dolphins and Porpoises*, they see with sound. 'Whales, dolphins and porpoises have a remarkable sensory system, called "echolocation", which enables them to build up a "picture" of their underwater surroundings with the help of sound. The basic principle of the echolocation system used by cetaceans is quite simple: they transmit ultrasonic clicks into the water, and then monitor and interpret any echoes that bounce back.' This would explain how our dolphins knew we were there. Although we were aware that the ocean, on top of which we were perched, was an enormous battlefield of predators and prey, we saw little sign of the protagonists – partly, I suppose, because we did not set out to catch any of them.

Similarly there was only limited bird life on show, with one particular disappointment being the non-sighting of the boatswain-bird, officially identified as the red-billed tropicbird or *phaeton aethereus*, well known to mariners of old as the 'bosun bird' because of its white, long tail feathers resembling marlin spikes. Also, the call it makes is reminiscent of the sound from the boatswain's 'call', that is his whistle. We were possibly a shade too far north, as subsequently I have seen these most attractive, nearly all-white birds, with their strikingly distinctive tail streamers, a little further south in the North Atlantic. However, there was still hope we would later spot them in the southern regions of the Caribbean, as they are known to frequent the coast of Venezuela along to the Panama Isthmus.

As we got into the western part of the ocean the trade wind became less reliable and started to play up, varying in strength from fresh to very light, but more unfortunately hauling further south, ending up SSE. The Log laments:

A beautiful day but not for sailing although the breeze picked up slightly during the afternoon. The wind being very much in the southerly quarter means the yard is hard on the starboard shrouds and the weather clew tacked down inboard to the foredeck.

Peter baked again this morning and two goodly loaves they were too!

We were now approaching the outer West Indies, and on the horizon, crossing our bows, was what appeared to be a local trading schooner under a full spread of sail heading south, but seemingly towards nowhere when I checked the chart. This threw me a little, and why she was on that course had to remain a mystery. Apart from this encounter and the near miss with the tanker, we had not had another sighting of anything man-made other than an airliner passing directly overhead when we were in mid ocean, on more or less a similar course to ourselves. I had wondered idly at the time what navigational system its pilot had been using. I could only speculate that this would have been with a bubble sextant and his lot made easier with the newfangled air navigation tables.

Then it all happened!

Thursday 5 November Noon Observed position 11º 40′N 59º 27′W. Wind: Fresh SSE Bright and sunny. Sea: rather rough on the beam but the boat going fast.

1700 Sighted Tobago fine on the starboard bow.

This was a great thrill for me. I had earlier told Peter, after the noon fix, that we would pick up ahead the northern tip of Tobago Island at 1700. This confident prediction had been made, I must admit, with some degree of bravado, but there it now was, just where it should have been and right on time. We had been 24 days at sea. Peter said 'well done' and I indulged in an orgy of self-congratulation. The happy state of euphoria was not to last long.

Chapter Five

Caribbean Odyssey

*A good landfall always puts a
navigator in a fine humour.*

THOMAS FLEMING DAY

*Any landfall will do for me, after so
much water.*

CHARLES DICKENS

'A ll's well. The light on the shore on our port beam is clear and
bright.'

'Light? Can't be! There's no light on this coast of Tobago!'

It was 2300. I had come up to take over the watch from Peter and was
still basking in the feel-good factor. This happy state of mind was suddenly
shattered. He was right, there being no gainsaying the evidence before our
eyes. Embedded in the blackness of the shoreline there was a flash of light
every ten seconds; it had to be a lighthouse, an indisputable fact I had to
accept, despite a last ditch, forlorn attempt to convince myself it was a
bright light in someone's bathroom, frequent users of the facilities raising
and lowering the blind. The chart showed no light of any kind on the north-
west facing coast of Tobago Island. I had been so confident earlier on in the
day and now I had lost all that certainty. Peter wasn't saying anything, and
whether this was because he still had faith in his navigator, or was coming
to terms with the revelation of the fact that that same navigator had feet of
clay, was not clear. Up till this moment it had seemed that fortune had for
us been certainly favouring the brave. During the afternoon, when we had
been approaching the land, it had been obscured by sea mist, which had
then lifted for half an hour to give us a glimpse of the top of Tobago, or what
we thought was that island. Visibility had then reduced again, but we had
seen what we wanted to see: land!

I reworked my sights and could find no error. A possibility perhaps was
that the light had been installed after we had left Plymouth, or alternatively
the chart was incorrect. However, to attribute a navigational uncertainty to
a chart imperfection is not generally considered a good idea. We decided

to play for time, reducing sail to the number 2 jib, and await daylight. Hopefully then the visible topography and land contours shown on the chart would confirm that what we thought was Tobago was in fact Tobago. A casting vote could be expected from the *Pilot*, with its general description of the coast and sketches of the land as seen from seaward. We had settled for going down the west-facing coast that night, this being the leeward side of the island, but this action was to add to our woes. As the log complains, we 'ran into an area of much confused sea with short, breaking waves, caused no doubt by the strong currents, throwing the boat about in a most infuriating manner'.

It was, as I confided to my journal, 'a thoughtful, uncomfortable and worried night', but at daybreak the fears of the night vanished, it being evident we were undoubtedly off Tobago, the shape of the land fitting the chart contours and also agreeing with what the *Pilot* had to say. My sights had been correct after all. The sense of relief that flowed over me was palpable. Of course, amongst the first things I did on arrival in Port of Spain was to check on that 'wretched light', and sure enough it had only recently been installed. Suddenly all was well again with the world and we 'had a grand sail down but looks like an early morning arrival at Port of Spain'.

There were some delightful, inviting-looking spots along the shoreline of Tobago, with very much a ring of Harry Belafonte about it all.

It was tempting to consider indulging ourselves, anchoring for a night or two of relaxation in a palm-fringed bay with a jungle backdrop. The island was not at that time suffering from being a tourist attraction but did have one or two claims to fame. One was that it had provided a background setting relating to Defoe's great story, so much so that it was known widely as Robinson Crusoe's Island, rather than its official name on maps and on our chart. Presumably Chile would have other views on the subject, they having changed the name of one of their islands also to that of the same gentleman. The other point of interest, attracting international attention, was that the island, whatever its name, had become a holiday retreat for Princess Margaret. To help her enjoy more fully her stay, there had been in attendance, it was reported, a young male companion, something which had not been overlooked by the media. We were disappointed not to have seen them as we sailed by close inshore.

Trinidad Island, lying off the north coast of Venezuela, is separated from the mainland of South America by the Gulf of Paria, in the north-eastern corner of which is tucked Port of Spain, the capital. Guarding the northern entrance to the gulf is the imaginatively named Dragon's Mouth, so called perhaps because within its jaws are several boldly outlined islands and rocks which could be construed as teeth. For us the dragon was sleeping as we ventured between its fangs, the wind dying and the sea calm in the dark of the night. Falling back on the engine we headed over the billiard table smoothness of the inky water in the direction of where we knew lay the town. No lights were to be seen and the land was invisible. It thus came as a shock to find suddenly, close under our bows, a large open boat containing several agitated men. Much shouting ensued as they scraped down our side to pass clear astern and be lost to view in the pitch black of the night, still positively registering their alarm. It had been a shared experience, not only with Peter and I joining in the chorus with our own contribution to the shouting, but possibly with common guilt over neither of us displaying any lights. It would seem in both cases that slavish adherence to the International Collision Regulations was not at the top of the agenda.

0500 Anchored in Port of Spain harbour in 2½ fathoms off the customs shed in company with a handful of trading schooners, all silent as graves.

Everywhere was totally still, this being broken only by the sound of our anchor cable rattling out, the absolute silence of the night settling over us again. We sank into our bunks, comfortable with the thought we had put the Atlantic behind us. It felt good.

The long, deep sleep-in, which we had been looking forward to enjoying and which we felt we had earned, was to be short-lived. After what seemed only a matter of minutes under the covers we were rudely woken by a heavy bump alongside and a loud voice demanding our attention. '*Tern II*!' The port authority had arrived. Selecting a spot for anchoring adjacent to the customs shed would appear to have been an error of judgement.

Our visitors wanted to know in some detail our movements to date and where we planned to go next. It was evident that wandering small-boat sailors were of some interest to the authorities, yachts arriving from overseas being so infrequent, particularly from across the Atlantic. 'Last port of call?' On being told this had been Las Palmas the next question was not unexpected. 'May we see your clearance from there, please?' They took some convincing that the port administration in the Canaries was not as tidy as their own, in that such details were not considered of any great moment. It was then pointed out that even if this were the case I should have known better. After delivering their stern admonition they were friendly and helpful. Included was a strong recommendation that on our way to the Canal Zone we went nowhere near Venezuela, keeping that coast, from the time we cleared Golfo de Paria, below the horizon at all times. Piracy was rampant, particularly directed at small craft, and we were regaled with disturbing accounts of boatloads of armed men intercepting boats along the coast, ransacking them and murdering the crews. No one would ever know what had happened to us, should this be our fate.

Shortly after this interlude there was another bump and customs were on board, we having scrambled up Flag Papa in the meantime. Their visit was short and to the point, leaving us free to do what we wished, having gathered from them that there was no security risk in leaving the boat lying unattended at anchor whilst we went ashore. This was after all, as they said stiffly, a British-administered port. The contrast with our last stopover experience was strikingly apparent.

On stepping ashore into the thronged streets we were immediately aware of the ethnic mix that made up the lifeblood of Port of Spain. We were also made forcibly aware of the overarching poverty. We could not move without a throng around us of louts and touts, all clamouring with loud voices for our attention and a share of the money which they assumed was in our pockets. Wherever we went our followers were there, waiting for us to emerge from each stop we made, whether it be at the bank for money and to collect our mail or the barber's shop for a badly needed shearing. We stopped off for lunch, and when we came out the throng had not moved; if anything it had multiplied. We gave in, handing a two dollar US note to a very black and very muscular young man. It had an immediate effect. 'Mah name, man, is Johnson and ah will take care of this trash.' And he did, making it clear in language which they understood, but with which we had difficulty, that any money that could be expected from us was now in his pocket. The crowd melted away. To do Johnson credit he stayed with us until we went back to the dinghy to return on board. He demanded no more money and seemed happy just to keep us company with that enormous, white-toothed grin, maintaining constant chatter. In staying with us I think he knew what was coming. The dinghy was not where we had left it and was now a few yards along the jetty. With it was an individual, of West African origin, who indicated he had saved it from certain destruction. It had, he informed us in graphic detail, been on the verge of being crushed by an island trading vessel berthing alongside with no regard for our boat. However, its saviour had just in the nick of time moved it out of the way. He gave us the impression that a thank you on our part in the form of some cash would not be inappropriate. Johnson took care of the situation in a few seconds flat; then, patting us on the shoulder, he disappeared.

An integral feature of Trinidad's history, and so evident in its mix of society today, is slavery. No one really knows the full extent of the Caribbean slave trade and how many West Africans were to fall victim to it. Estimates vary widely between 30 and 50 million over the centuries, dating from 1498 when Columbus claimed Trinidad for Spain, triggering the interest in the West Indies by the Europeans and the development of the vastly lucrative sugar plantations. The insatiable demand for low-cost, virtually no-cost, labour to work these plantations continued until the early 19th century when the introduction of sugar beet in Europe changed the scene entirely. The bottom falling out of plantation profitability saw the resultant fall off in demand for slave labour, the seeds being sown for a natural wind-down in the slave trade. Well-intentioned souls in Britain hastened the process, with the axe falling on slavery in 1838.

Commercial pressures being what they are, it is arguable that Wilberforce and the like would have faced almost impossible odds in winning their cause if profits from growing sugar had remained at their peak. The newly emancipated slaves left the plantations in droves, and their replacements, in the form of indentured labour, recruited from elsewhere, added to the racial mix. This had originated when Indian tribes migrated to the West Indies from South America, to be followed in turn by Spanish, French and finally British colonists after seizure of the island by Britain in 1797. Sir Walter Raleigh, that archetypal colonist, would have been delighted, it being 200 years since he had visited the island and laid waste to the Spanish colony. Over the intervening period Trinidad has become progressively more multicultural, bringing remarkable colour and richness to its existence, all brought about by change from a plantation-based economy to one dependent on oil and latterly tourism. The change has seen East Indians supplanting African labour, with Chinese workers arriving, to be followed by migrants from the Americas, Europe and elsewhere. This hotchpotch was all round us as we walked the crowded streets.

Music is at the centre of life in the Caribbean, and nowhere more so than in Trinidad. Here was invented in the slavery days a way of getting around slave owners' attempts to inhibit discourse between slaves and hence the fostering of insurrection. The slaves were, however, allowed to sing, and so calypso came into being as a way of communicating amongst themselves through the lyrics. Originating on the island, it has spread and is now a feature of the region, its popularity fostered no doubt by the demand for entertainment by the increasing floods of tourists.

It is fashionable today to pour opprobrium on the European colonists, but it is worthy of note that they were not the first of the land-grabbing sinners. Over the centuries, prior to Columbus, successive tribes of American Indians arrived in the Caribbean to push out the incumbents. The last to arrive were the warlike Caribs, who gave their name to the region. It was then the turn of the Europeans.

During our stay, which was an enjoyable experience, the island was still under colonial rule, with British presence very evident, none more so than in the yacht club, a centre of social activity amongst the white community. We called on the secretary, who extended a warm welcome, but were ignored by the throng of members in the bar, dominated, it seemed to us, by screeching females, a phenomenon not altogether unknown in expatriate circles. We were, however, to be the recipients of a full measure of kindness and hospitality elsewhere in the community. John Hale, who together with his son represented the Heinz company in Trinidad, knew all about us and had been awaiting our arrival. Before leaving England I had, with some hesitation, approached Heinz with an outline of the plan to sail out to New Zealand, wondering if this would be of any value to them as a public relations exercise. Bearing in mind the size of such an operation and the calls it must have from hopefuls looking for sponsorship, somewhat to my surprise I received an almost immediate response to the effect that they certainly were interested. Their proposal was that they would donate a quantity of their special self-heating tins of a variety of soups, in return for which I would send them progress reports from our ports of call on our experiences. They would use these ongoing accounts in their house journal as a special feature.

I, of course, was happy about this arrangement, and a quite considerable consignment of these tins was delivered on board in Plymouth. The product was an interesting one. It had been developed during the war for use on those occasions when the ability to provide hot nourishment was difficult. Let into the top of the tin was a small heating element, set off by simply pulling a tab. Instant hot food in a boat in bad weather had to be a good idea and so it proved. I had duly sent off a report from the Canaries, which the Hales had read and so knew we were on our way.

Both the Hales went out of their way to look after us, helping to make life easy for us, particularly with stores purchasing. They lived well, and dining with the senior Hales was a special treat in their house overlooking the golf course, with a magnificent view down a long valley and out to sea. Sitting on the veranda in the cool of the evening, sipping a sundowner, was an experience we did not find hard to endure. Fortunately for us, the days of the British Raj were not yet over.

It was the younger Hale who introduced us to calypso. We were taken out for dinner to a large hotel to witness it being performed. It was folk music with its own special flavour of melody, humour, gossip and satirical, social commentary. The lyrics, the core of calypso, are largely improvised on the spot at each performance by the singer, the theme being topical or satirical, often bitingly so. Unbeknownst to us, one of our party had briefed the singer on our voyage, and somewhat to our embarrassment he, accompanied by a steel band, treated the hotel guests at large to a wildly inaccurate but colourful account of our exploits, fulsome praise of these fearless English sailors not being in short supply. Although our egos did not suffer from the attention, we were glad when it was over.

Traditionally, we were told, calypso has guitar backing, but dating from the last war the steel band has come to the fore, resulting perhaps from the number of discarded empty 40 gallon oil drums left lying around. The sound from these drums is solid rhythm, enough to fire up even the most phlegmatic of listeners. Victor Clark, who also visited Trinidad, gives an informed account of what a steel band is all about in his book *On the Wind of a Dream*.

'The drums which provide this fascinating metallic music are 44 gallon oil drums, or rather half drums. A band will normally have drums of five different tones – first pan, second pan, trump pan, tenor boom and bass – the tone being obtained by cutting off the drum at different levels from the top. The flat end is then heated and sectioned by tapping indentations with a punch – any number from four in the case of the bass to a dozen or so on the first pan. These sections are then beaten out until each provides the requisite note when drummed with a stick. The only other instruments in the steel band are the maracas, which consist of a couple of calabashes with large dried seeds inside them, making a most effective rattle. It will, perhaps, be a 12-piece band in action, the players colourfully dressed in yellow shirts, red trousers and a blue sash, and carefully groomed with the hair grown long and brushed forward with an upward sweep in front – a coiffure, in fact, as original as the instruments played.'

The essentiality of music to the black races, and not least to African sailors, is highlighted by the deep-sea sailing ship narrator Basil Lubbock in his 1902 book *Round the Horn before the Mast*. 'It was our forenoon watch on deck and we chantied the topsails up in fine form. The thing to hear is a nigger crew chantying. They sing most beautifully, with splendid minor and half notes; they cannot do the least bit of work without chantying.'

In the field of human endeavour, Trinidad, in addition to introducing such unique and quite fascinating features like calypso, 'pan' music and the steel band, has made a significant contribution to the gin-drinking world in the form of Angostura bitters. Port of Spain is home to this very special product, even though, as the label tells us, the name comes from a place called Angostura in Venezuela where it was first created. It has nothing to do with the widespread belief that it comes from crushed beetles but rather is gentian based. Bitters are, of course, the essential ingredient of the once ubiquitous pink gin, just a few drops turning an uninteresting glass of gin and water into something much more exciting. It is one of the tragedies of modern life that this beverage has been largely supplanted by the rather dull gin and tonic. In 'my day' in the navy the pink gin was the predominant drink, the bitters bottle occupying a central position on the shelf at the back of the wardroom bar. It used to be the practice on Christmas Day for the chief petty officers to be invited to the wardroom to partake of good cheer before their Christmas dinner. On one occasion a chief, on spying the bitters bottle, something new to him, asked to try it. Removing the cap, he poured himself a generous measure and sank it. After recovering he was heard to comment, 'Cor! That's why pigs is pigs,' the term used with variable degrees of affection for officers. Angostura Ltd describes its product as an aromatic preparation with 44.7% alcohol by volume.

Our stay in Trinidad was drawing to a close: the need to press on to the west was now looming large in our minds. Our impressions of this outpost on the southern flank of the West Indies chain of islands were pleasurable, and the memory that was to remain with us was one of the colour, vibrancy and warmth of its people, with their broad grins and powerful music.

Tuesday 17 November 1145 Weighed anchor and got under way under jib and mainsail. Set all plain sail. In the afternoon saw our first waterspouts and very impressed. They were enormous and looked forbiddingly dangerous. Fortunately not appearing to be heading our way. If one had passed over us it would have been catastrophic.

1600 Cleared Gulf of Paria via Bocas Navios at the entrance. Moderate NE wind bringing up a choppy sea in the open water outside.

Set course NW ½ W for Islas Testigos. Streamed log. We are on our way.

The danger from waterspouts had receded and on this we congratulated ourselves. We had been witness to nature laying on a dramatic performance in the form of a tall, thin, rapidly twisting dark column of water reaching up, like a stalagmite, from an upwelling hump pulled from the surface of the sea. This had joined up with a fearsome, black cumulonimbus cloud hanging over it, the trunk of the spout swinging to and fro as it all advanced downwind, with the fallout of rain akin to the density of a plunging waterfall. Study of the phenomenon indicates that wind speeds inside the column of water can exceed 150 knots, far in excess of those of the usual hurricane. If a waterspout arrives on board, it would appear 'neither craft nor crew would have much chance of surviving the experience', according to an informed opinion on the subject.

The passage plan was simple and straightforward. Leave South America to port and keep it well out of sight. We had every intention of making it a straight run to the Canal Zone, but the first night at sea confirmed once again the old adage about harbours rotting ships and men. The last ten-day stopover, with every night and all night in our bunks, had softened us up such that now, with the land dropping away astern, we found 'we had got out of our sea routine in a big way, with neither Peter nor I having any appetite, or will, to do anything serious in the cooking line'. A brief discussion ensued:

'Ten days or so to Colón, but with Curaçao getting in the way halfway there. What do you think?' 'Good idea.'

In the event, we were to enjoy, in fact, the brief passage of four days, the log containing happy references to 'under spinnaker in perfect weather', and again the next day: 'Wind SSE. Light. Delightful day's sail with balloon foresail lifting her along'. What was also encouraging our feeling of well-being was the knowledge that the west-going current was helping us along to the tune of 20 or even 30 miles per day.

All too quickly came the evening, when we sighted on the starboard bow the easternmost island of the group of three islands that form what are known as the ABC Islands, consisting of Aruba, Bonaire and Curaçao in the Netherlands Antilles. Bonaire had little to offer, and after skirting its southern flank we enjoyed a quite magnificent run under spinnaker up the south-western coast of Curaçao to its capital, Willemstad. The entrance to the harbour constituted something of a problem, in that it had across it a road bridge floating on pontoons, the whole assembly being hauled out of the way to allow shipping to move in and out of the port. As we drew near we could see the boom was firmly in place, blocking our entrance, leaving us with the question of what had to be done to persuade someone to open it for us. The problem was solved by a freighter, MV *Araby*, which overhauled us and headed for the bridge. Our concern was that whoever was responsible for working the bridge would let *Araby* through and then close it again before we had time also to get through. It could safely be assumed no one would be too interested in opening the bridge, thereby disrupting traffic across it, to accommodate a solitary, small sailing craft. We could see ourselves left outside to endure another night at sea. We had been under easy sail in our approach to the bridge to give ourselves time to think, but now we set everything we had to catch up with *Araby*, she having slowed down whilst the bridge was being towed out of the way. Catch her we did, to our great relief, and went through the opening, tucked under her stern, to sweep into the inner harbour under full sail. This was an occasion when a powerful auxiliary engine would have been useful, our little contraption being of no use, as we needed to sail in excess of the best speed it could manage.

We planned to sail up further into Santa Anna Bay, where we thought we might be more secure from inquisitive/acquisitive fingers in more peaceful surroundings, but we had been spotted by the harbour authorities. Their launch caught up with us to haul *Tern* back and deposit us alongside the quay, which also did duty as a main thoroughfare, a mere stone's throw from the town's centre. We found we were opposite the harbourmaster's impressive-looking building. Whether this was coincidental or by design was not evident. Small boats appearing in South American waters from nowhere were the focus of some attention by the authorities. The harbour authority's representative was promptly on board, followed closely by customs and immigration. The trinity were very relaxed, asked a few questions, conducted a cursory check on our papers, had a chat and climbed back onto the quay. When we wanted to sail, 'Just go,' they said. The immigration man, however, did not seem in any great hurry to leave and kindly thought it could be useful to tell us something about Willemstad in general terms, but more specifically to inform us about the whorehouse, situated a little out of town but 'not too far', he hastened to reassure us. 'Well worth a visit!' he said, almost with an air of civic pride. The Dutch are more comfortable with accepting this useful, time-honoured activity in their midst than the British, the window displays in Amsterdam coming to mind.

Perhaps this is what the chantyman also had in mind as he tried to boost the flagging spirits of a tired crew as they ground round the capstan, leading them into flights of fancy with:

Mark well what I do say
In Amsterdam there dwelt a maid

The easy, informal attitude of the bureaucracy we experienced in Willemstad was so different to that we had gone through in our last port of call. It is something of a mystery as to why the British are such sticklers for following to the letter what any regulation demands. Every box on every page of every form must be ticked within a regime of inflexible discipline. Ever since we had left Plymouth we had noticed how at variance the British were with everyone else when it came to obeying the rules. The French were so easy-going in Brest, and the Spanish even more so in the Canaries. Admittedly it was a different story in Lisbon, but the circumstances of being under virtually a police state probably resulted in behaviour at variance with the natural inclinations of the Portuguese race. This contrast in national characteristics was so evident when comparing our departure from Port of Spain with that from Willemstad. In the former place, on the day of our departure we went through a time-consuming, tedious performance, strictly in accordance with the rule book. In the latter we just sailed off.

We found Willemstad an attractive little town, warmly presenting itself with the building fronts in lightly toned variegated colours facing the waterfront, all on full display from our berth. The scene would be described in guide books as possessing an 'old-world charm'. Being alongside the waterfront, the Handelskade had its pluses and minuses. To meet our daily needs and replenish ship's stores meant just a few paces into the shopping area, but by our proximity we were of some interest to the locals, whereby we attracted all too much attention from those strolling by. They were kindly disposed towards us, however, and it would have been churlish not to have responded to the steady flow of questions, eventhough the constant repetition became somewhat tedious. Amongst the strollers were two young men who gave the impression their mission in life was to make us feel welcome and, in achieving this, to provide what help they could. It appeared they had read about us in the *Trinidad Guardian*, the daily newspaper, which included the Netherlands Antilles in its circulation. 'What could they do?' Well, for a start we needed the spinnaker repairing. This was no problem to our new friends, Birt and Albert, who took it away with them on the spot to return it that evening, all neat and tidy, adamant there was nothing to pay. With the sail they brought a large container of ice, to us of more value than a bag of gold. Later in the evening they were back to take us out to dinner, and on the way introduced us to the management of a hotel to enjoy the rare luxury of a shower. How does one acknowledge such displays of kindness? To finish off the evening we invited them back on board for drinks, a somewhat protracted session, as it turned out, which included, as my journal recalls, 'an exchange of presents'.

During the course of the day we had been moved off the quay to make room for a steamer and put alongside a fish barge lying ahead of us, fortunately it not being too apparent that this was its role in life. In command of this vessel was a happy-looking local who, with good cheer and chatter, took our lines and helped us secure. At 0600 next morning we were woken, but had some difficulty in coming to life out of deep slumber, a state which no doubt owed something to the night before. Our neighbour informed us there was a road water tanker alongside on the quay. 'I stopped it for you, boss,' he said, having assumed correctly we would need to top up our tanks. He refused our offer of some US dollars. He was his own man. It could well have been that his genealogy dated back to the start of commercial operations on the island in the mid 1600s when the Dutch set up a merchandise-trading centre. This functioned in conjunction with the establishment of the principal slave market for the Caribbean. Having no natural resources to fall back onto, the abolition of slavery dealt the economy a devastating blow, the region's future looking bleak until the fortuitous discovery of oil in nearby Venezuela in the early 1900s. The establishment of an oil-refining industry saved the day for Curaçao. Over the period there has been one commercial enterprise which has brought a modest income to the island, the sticky liqueur of that name being produced over the centuries in a distillery in the outskirts of the capital. Made from the skins of small green oranges, it has been an imaginative utilisation of natural resources. We eschewed it, neither of us being fans of rather cloying drinks of this nature, but many no doubt are, including tourists making the mandatory visit to the distillery. In recent times, happily after the time of our visit, tourism has become another step in the evolutionary development of the group of islands, making big changes in particular to Willemstad and its rather special Handelskade. We were spared – although we did not know our good fortune then – the impact of that horror of the modern day, the cruise ship. We enjoyed the place the way it was. 'Went for a stroll in the evening but it was only a temporary respite from the heat. The boat is hot and there is an all-pervading smell of oil fuel, but I haven't regretted calling in here; it is a pleasant little place with pleasant people in it.'

Just before we were due to make our departure, the inseparables, Birt and Albert, appeared with a present of a US Navy Oceanographic Office wind and current chart, which confirmed our expectations of the difficulties that lay ahead. I had given the couple in return, as a memento, our Admiralty Routeing chart for November, which had largely served its purpose – adding to this my copy of that gem *Clochemerle*, a best-seller in its day and a plot which only the French could have dreamed up. Accompanying the chart from our friends was a thermos flask full of ice. This warm, helpful pair had added much to our stay.

24 November 1400 Slipped under jib and full mainsail. Cleared the harbour entrance whilst the bridge was open for a ship. Set course to pass south of Aruba Island.

Next stop would definitely be the Canal, and we disciplined ourselves not to indulge in any more unscheduled deviations off the straight and narrow. However, we were to find sailing conditions not as benign and enjoyable as the passage from Port of Spain. On that leg we had benefited to quite some degree from the favourable current carrying us along at up to 1½ knots. Now, however, as we turned down into the Gulf of Darien, leading to the Panamanian shores, we had the current reversing to a north-easterly direction, which put it against the wind, and furthermore was backing northward and freshening. The seas became short and so did our tempers. With the run of the sea no longer easy, life became somewhat tedious and uncomfortable, accompanied by the decks washing down, an existence that had gone out of our memory. 'Water on the decks continuously and often in the cockpit, with steering very hard and difficult.'

With the coast of Columbia close aboard we were entering historic waters – Drake's waters. Close on our port quarter lay Cartagena – just another prosaic, undistinguished port today handling petroleum products, not to mention drugs, but once central to the wealth, power and glory that was Spain in the 16th century. Here had been transhipped the treasure purloined from the civilisations in the western regions of South America and then brought across the isthmus of Panama by mule train. The fortified port of Cartagena had been at the hub of Spain's transatlantic commerce, and being pivotal to the movement of silver and gold bullion and precious stones, it had been a lodestone attracting frenetic attention from Elizabeth's licensed pirates, spearheaded by the likes of Sir John Hawkins and his protégé, the hyperactive Sir Francis Drake. Frustrated in his attempts to lay hands on what he considered a rightful share of all this wealth, badly needed to refill Elizabeth's coffers and his own, Drake had gone so far as to sack the town and hold its elders to ransom. It was for us to speculate whether the present-day residents had much knowledge of its exotic and romantic past.

Gybing before a brisk ENE wind and bringing the lights of Cartagena astern, we laid off a course for Colón. Arriving off the Panamanian coast we were abreast the site of Nombre de Dios, the Caribbean terminus of the Spanish mule teams. In its role as a treasure transit location it was another irresistible attraction for Drake, and what was to be a fatal one. He and a swathe of his men contracted dysentery. Disaster, which had progressively become the dominant feature of his Caribbean adventures, was now finally to claim him. With little treasure in his holds to show for all his efforts, and consumed by bitter disappointment, he moved his ships along the coast to Puerto Bello, where the great navigator lost the will to live: 'The dying admiral of a fleet filled with dying men.' It was 1595. Dressed in his full armour, encased in a lead coffin, he was lowered into the waters of the bay, a league offshore, to the appropriate thunder of guns and roll of drums.

> *Monday 30 November* 1600 Entered Colón harbour under jib and mainsail. Boarded by customs and port authorities.
> 1700 Came to anchor in 7½ fathoms off Cristobal oiling wharf.

We had seen the last of the Atlantic, enjoying to the full the rewarding achievement of one of our main objectives. Ahead lay the broad sweep of the Silver Sea – the Pacific – and thence through the South Seas to home, but before that we had facing us the challenge of negotiating the Canal.

Tern II. *All dressed up with some way to go.*

My two homes. Eagle *comes out to wish her sister well.*
INSET: Tern's *crew. Peter and I face the press.*

Traditional seamanship. I make Baggywrinkles at Mashford's Boatyard, Plymouth.

LEFT: *My Nazi sextant. Courtesy of a U-boat.*

RIGHT: *The start of it all. A press boat sees us off at Plymouth Sound.*

Trade wind nasty – a North Atlantic tropical squall.

INSET ABOVE: *Our trade wind powerhouse – squaresail and raffee pull us along.*

INSET RIGHT: *Morning bath. Bowsprit dunking makes us nicer to know.*

Colón. What the pilot saw; expecting us all ready to go.

BELOW: *Gatun Lake. The team that got us through the Panama canal.*

Galápagos. Wreck Bay high street in the rush hour.

BELOW: *Marquesas. Nuku Hiva city centre on early closing day.*

Pao Pao Bay today. Every tourist and yachty's favourite.

INSET: *Pao Pao Bay, Moorea as we knew it. All to ourselves.*

*Moorea to Auckland.
Oh for some wind!
Peter lives in hope.*

BELOW: *South Pacific.
We get our wind and
plenty of it.*

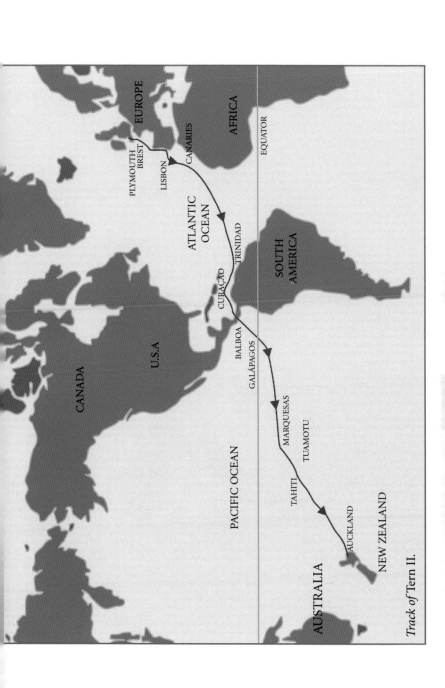

Track of Tern II.

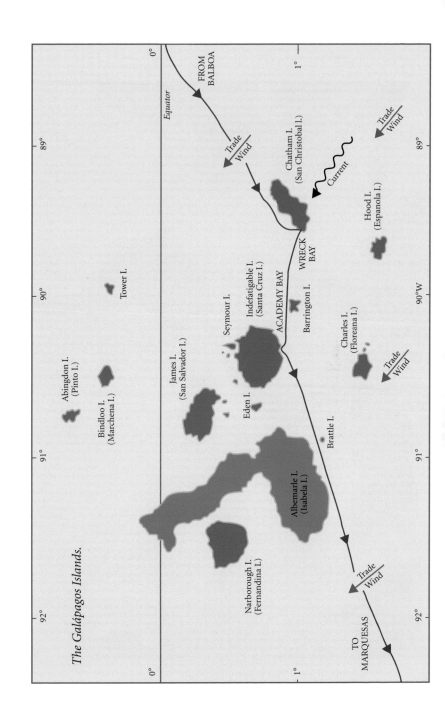

The Galápagos Islands.

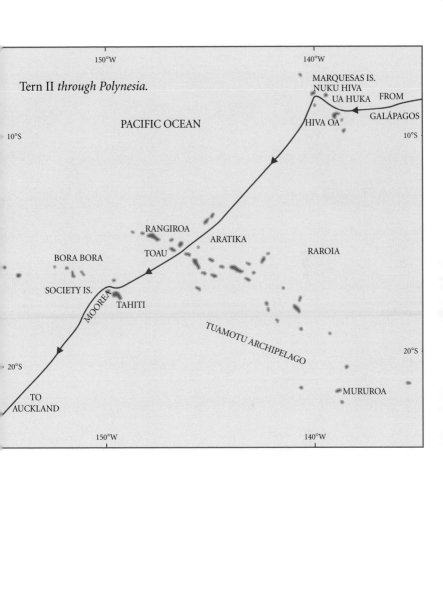

Tern II *through Polynesia.*

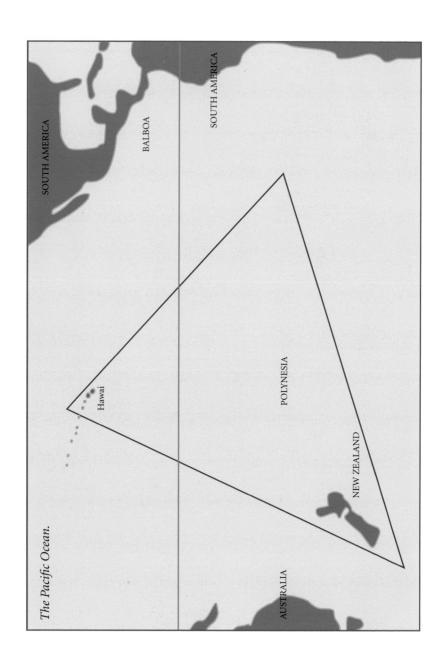

The Pacific Ocean.

SOUTH AMERICA

BALBOA

SOUTH AMERICA

Hawai

POLYNESIA

NEW ZEALAND

AUSTRALIA

Chapter Six

To the Silver Sea

*Besought Almighty God of his
goodness to give him life and leave
to sail once in an English ship
in that sea.*

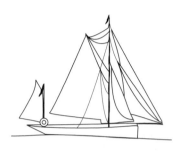

DRAKE'S PRAYER ON FIRST SIGHTING,
IN 1572, THE PACIFIC OCEAN FROM A
HILL ON THE ISTHMUS OF PANAMA.

'Jeez! This is the first time we had this happen with guys like you.'
So said the harbour authority man on being presented with a full set of entry documents, already completed and signed. Unprecedented in his experience, it would appear.

Almost as though they had been there waiting especially for us, as soon as we passed through the jaws of the breakwater entrance into Limon Bay a large launch, its decks crowded with men, came alongside to deposit on our decks an impressive force of what turned out to be customs and port officials, the latter issuing precise instruction on where we had to anchor. This information was, for us, very much in the 'need to know' domain if we were to entertain any hope of a night of sweet dreams in our bunks. The bay was the waiting area anchorage for the never ceasing flow of ships coming through the breakwater and certainly not geared for accommodating one small yacht. Despite the fact we were still under way, heading for our designated anchoring spot, the legion got down to work, the first task being to run a tape measure over us. They weren't prepared to accept my word on our dimensions. Their rule book said otherwise on such matters. Recognizing that we were about to anchor, and that that activity was fully occupying our attention, they suspended operations whilst their boat cast off and stood clear. It was apparent they were accepting that they were having to adjust from dealing with big ships to the dictates of a small craft. Once we had anchored and stowed the sails it was back to business. It was not evident whether we were an irritation to them or they were enjoying the change to their normal routine. The latter was to prove the case. Their boat came back alongside to deposit even more uniformed officials. Following us down below, the cabin was filled to overflowing with a large group of large men, all Americans and very polite. Those that could not squeeze into the cabin jammed the entrance, effectively shutting off the flow of air. Adding to the throng in the front row of the stalls, the cabin, were the principal actors: the harbourmaster's man, who did much of the talking, a doctor, a customs man and a policeman, the last named individual short on words but not on height.

Additionally, there was a supporting cast whose exact function was not entirely clear, apart from ensuring all available space down below was fully utilised. They all wore rimless glasses and crew cuts, speaking in deep, powerful voices, usually all at the same time. However, proceedings were to get off to a good start, occasioned by my producing the pre-completed sheaf of documents. This was to prove a good move, a very good move, and was to help significantly in giving us a fair wind through the Canal bureaucracy. Before we left England I had contacted the US Embassy in London to enquire about the formalities involved in making the Canal transit. They had been friendly, as are most Americans in my experience, forthcoming with general advice and sending me as well a full set of the documentation that would be needed on our arrival. These would normally be filled out by the ship's master on being boarded, for completion of formalities before entering the Canal. In procedural terms we were being treated by officialdom as any ship, regardless of size. On seating himself at the saloon table, the spokesman for the group extracted from his briefcase the formidable pack of papers.

'Captain, you gotta complete this lot!'

It was then I had played my winning card. When in reply I produced an identical set already filled out and signed, he expressed his surprise and was evidently favourably impressed. What's more he was also much relieved, as were his companions, that the time to complete formalities would be appreciably shortened. Although the cool of the evening should have been making an impact, it was soon unbearably hot in the overcrowded cabin; shirts were sticking to backs and foreheads running sweat. Putting both sets of papers back in his case, he took time to give a résumé of what going through the Canal was all about, adding what were to prove valuable tips on what we should do to make the transit as easy as possible for ourselves. The rest of the party chipped in to contribute to the dissemination of advice and information. The show was now all over. The doctor was of the opinion we were healthy, and in view of the ambient temperature in the cabin did not want to dwell too much on the subject. Customs were equally relaxed and the policeman comfortable that we were not a threat to law and order. Leaving behind a present of a thermos of ice, they filed up the cabin steps, over the side and back onto their boat. Amid expressions of mutual goodwill they vanished into the night. They had plenty of work in front of them, judging by the frequency of vessels passing between the breakwater ends into the holding anchorage.

Peter put together one of his inimitable concoctions for an early supper and we turned in to sleep 'the sleep of the just'. A journal entry says it all: 'What a tremendous change to have a boat come out to meet us and tell us exactly what to do!' The Canal was in American hands and was to remain so until the millennium. One can only surmise how our treatment would compare with today, with the Canal under Panamanian control.

Launching the dinghy early in the following forenoon, we went ashore to the Colón Yacht Club, encountering a friendly reception from the crews of a handful of yachts lying close by, both local and from overseas, plus a particularly warm reception from the club's secretary. A berth on the club's pontoon was offered us and we gratefully accepted the kind gesture.

1400 Moved into the yacht club 'trot' with bows between piles, the bower anchor out ahead and our stern to the catwalk. The best billet we have had so far.

This operation was not as straightforward as it would seem, nor, it had to be conceded, was it executed with impeccable seamanship. With her self-folding propeller, *Tern*'s astern power was not a force to be reckoned with, manoeuvres of this complexity demanding liberal use of bad language, warps and the willing, tolerant involvement of shoreside helpers. Success finally crowned our efforts. We could now step ashore at will. The shore party dispersing, we had our first visitor. A large Afro-American, dressed somewhat informally, presented himself off our stern, having waited judiciously until the berthing activity had subsided, and with it the demand for manpower.

'Anythin' fer me, baas?'

Presumably he meant cash, a commodity also greatly cherished by Peter and myself. I cast around for a substitute offering, as apart from any charitable feelings we felt it a good idea to keep onside with waterfront loungers. I remembered a half-empty stoneware jar of '*vino tinto*' which we had acquired in Las Palmas. It had not travelled well. Holding up the jar with both hands, head tilted back, our new-found friend allowed the next best alternative to vinegar to pour down his throat. We waited with interest for the reaction. Wiping the back of his hand across his mouth, he pronounced complete satisfaction with the sampling.

'Ma-a-an, thet wus good!'

At which he took himself off, clutching the jar to his chest. We were never to see him again, hopefully not because of any dire repercussions occasioned by the imbibition of our gift.

Acting on the helpful hints to young sailors given us the day before in the briefing by our boarding party, I was soon around to the Canal's operations room. There it was evident our friends had wasted no time. We had been checked in and were now 'in the loop'. Covering the whole of one wall was a floor-to-ceiling board on which were shown the names of the vessels scheduled over the days ahead to pass through the Canal. There at the bottom was *Tern II*. Countdown had started. As each day's locking was completed we were to move up the ladder, and as the day of our own locking got nearer, the name of the unfortunate pilot allocated to us was added. No regard seemed to be taken in the order of locking through of vessels' size or type. We just took our turn. There was no indication whether we were a full-blown large tanker or just a little yacht. The authorities just took it in their stride, or so it appeared. Personal, off-the-record discussion with the movement controllers suggested otherwise. They were, in fact, not relaxed about having the responsibility for the safe transit of a small, fragile wooden vessel through a waterway system just not designed to accommodate the likes of us. However, they put a brave face on it, advising we would be required to take a pilot just as for any other vessel. The 'anointed one' would come on board early on the day and would take complete charge of operations. Our responsibility was to do as we were told and crucially provide lines from the four corners of the boat, long enough to reach to the top of the cavernous locks and strong enough to hold us in position in the middle of the lock against the swirling, mad rush of water. This frantic water movement, we were told, would occur as the locks emptied and filled, being worse when fresh water from the lake, located in the middle of the canal system, mixed with sea water. For good measure, we were warned of particularly violent disturbance from the wash of the propeller as the ship with which we would share the lock turned her engine. This effect could be dramatic, we were gloomily informed. It was beholden on us to provide the necessary manpower or, as it turned out, also womanpower, to tend the controlling lines throughout the performance.

The graphic description of what lay ahead left me somewhat apprehensive, and as we were to learn later, this feeling was shared by our pilot designate when the news was broken to him that he had been allocated to us. For his services there would be no charge. It was now a case of checking on our ascent up the movement's board and being organised when the call came.

During our 12 day stay in Colón we became members of a little sailing fraternity and benefited accordingly. The Colón experience was typical of similar 'social cells', unique to blue water cruising and no doubt carrying through to the present day, occurring in scattered locations throughout the world wherever ocean voyagers meet. Membership, which included some locals, of these very informal 'clubs' is constantly changing as boats arrive from across the oceans and then move on, their place being taken by new arrivals. Seldom do 'members' meet again but the memories are retained. The time together is not only one of enjoyable companionship but mutually beneficial. The exchange of seafaring information and opinions based on lessons learned the hard way is invaluable. Equally important is the common spirit of willingness to help each other in practical ways through gifts or loan of gear and assistance with tasks on board one another's boats. It is a very different ethos to that which generally exists in inshore waters cruising, which has ready access to shoreside facilities and professional assistance, mutual dependence not being of any particular significance.

Our introduction to the Colón cell had occurred on our first day when we had been helped with our berthing, to be followed up later when we went ashore for dinner at the yacht club. Outside the club we met James, who introduced himself as being off a large American schooner, *Windjammer*, which we had noticed lying on the hammerhead at the end of our pontoon. He was quite loquacious and seemed to want to prolong the conversation. It transpired he was the vessel's navigator and we gathered he had a problem. About this we were to learn more in due course.

Next morning our circle widened when I was invited aboard another American yacht also sharing our pontoon. Her owner, Blennerhassett, had his contacts in the Canal Zone and was only too happy to be helpful. He took me around to the US Hydrographic Office and I was introduced to staff members. I had been aware of some gaps in our chart library and welcomed being able to procure more charts for the Galápagos Archipelago, as well as additional wind or 'pilot' charts for the Pacific, all published by the US Navy. These were certainly valuable as planning guides but I had learned not to treat such charts as the undisputed word of God. Like all prognostications on the weather they had a degree of fallibility.

Berthed next to Blennerhassett was an interesting little boat, *Atom*, which was in the process of a single-handed 'slow boat to China' world circumnavigation. Her owner, Jean Gau, was a disciple of fellow Frenchman, Alain Gerbault, who had also been something of an inspiration to me, his pre-war book *The Flight of the Firecrest*, making for useful and entertaining reading. We were to see quite a lot of Jean, and like his hero, Gerbault, he proved a rather fascinating character. On our first encounter he invited me on board for a chronometer time check, his radio reception being much more rewarding than was forthcoming from our limited-performance receiver.

Following up on a warm invitation from James, we went aboard *Windjammer*, a lovely, sleek, black, near-on 50 footer, a typical American eastern-seaboard schooner with a centreplate. We were welcomed on board by her owner, in her own way something of a unique personality. Peggy, in her 30s, had been a journalist working for a New York newspaper as its correspondent in Europe covering the last war. Like so many others in its immediate aftermath, she was unsettled and could not face returning to what now seemed the dull way of life of a city desk in peacetime. She had bought *Windjammer* and, complete with large black Labrador, planned to sail round the world, ultimately to write a book about it all as seen through the eyes of the dog. She was already an experienced sailboat sailor but lacked confidence in her ability to navigate offshore. This was strange, as she gave the impression of being an assured, confident woman. Enter James. Also in his early 30s, he had been an oil tanker captain for some years, despite his relative youth. Such individuals were much in demand in the post-war years and had been earning good money. But like Peggy he was looking for something more exciting and romantic. When his path crossed that of Peggy's it seemed they 'were made for each other'. Holding a US master's ticket he was an experienced, competent navigator and would fill nicely the gap in Peggy's life. Moreover, he was presentable in appearance. Together they had got as far as Colón but, as we were to be duly enlightened, all was not well.

We liked Peggy and we liked her boat, both attractive creatures. The latter was well appointed and comfortably furnished. Later in the day Peggy in turn visited us and, knowing we were shortly to make the Canal transit, suggested she and James came with us to act as line handlers, gaining at the same time for them first-hand, invaluable experience before their own transit. This seemed to us a good idea, meeting the essential requirement for extra hands on board for line tending and without whom a transit could not be made. Quite apart from that, their company would be welcome.

A path was being worn between *Windjammer* and *Tern*, as shortly after Peggy had gone, on board appeared James. We had a general chat over coffee about what was going on around the pontoon, but it was evident he was not on board just to exchange gossip or for a chat about the weather. He unburdened himself.

'I can't take much more of living on board with Peggy. It's wearing me down. Would you be interested in taking me on with you as a third hand?'

Peter and I looked at each other and hedged our bets.

'This is pretty unexpected, James. We would need to talk about it between ourselves. Can we come back to you?'

I think he had sensed what would be our decision. I was clear in my mind but I needed Peter's reaction. Having bitten the bullet, James felt free to reveal all. Peggy was, he said, a very demanding woman and he was finding it all too much. He needed some respite, he declared. It was quite apparent she was very much a full-blooded woman and no 'shrinking violet'. After he left, Peter and I discussed his proposition. Changing from a two- to a three-watch system would transform our lives at sea and, moreover, another crewmember with James's professional qualifications, combined with his small-boat experience, would be a valuable addition to *Tern*'s complement. However, despite his seductive suggestion, I thought it would be too disruptive to our now well-settled way of life to introduce a third person into it. In fact, there was no debate. Peter agreed with me, as my journal duly observed: 'The upset, we thought, would be too great. Besides, he seems to be rather chatty, which could become a trifle wearing over time.' Neither Peter nor I were especially given to loquacity.

The situation fortunately resolved itself, as in short order James was back on board to inform us he had patched things up with Peggy and they had found common ground for agreement. We were pleased for them. It was just as well they were as one again, as their participation as our line handlers might have been compromised, Peggy also perhaps drawing the conclusion we had tried to do the dirty on her and gone behind her back.

How it all worked out between them we were never to know. We were shocked to read later in a Pacific Island news journal that *Windjammer* had landed up on a reef, becoming a total loss. Whatever the reason for the loss, it was sad that such a beautiful creation was no more. The write-up did not say what had happened to her complement or the dog. This informative journal, more accurately described as an expanded news-sheet, was published monthly and distributed amongst the eastern group of islands and helped to keep expatriates informed on events. Included was information on movements of voyaging yachts. The numbers were sufficiently small for the news-sheet to accommodate this. In it we were able to follow *Tern II*'s progress as reported to the world through the eyes of the editor. Of particular note, in one edition I read that Humphrey Barton, of *Vertue XXXV* fame, was inviting interest from blue water yachtsmen and women in the forming of an ocean cruising club 'in order that a record may be kept of long-distance voyages in small craft'. I wrote to him concurring with the concept and in due course became a founding member. The Ocean Cruising Club has remained a success story to the present day.

We were enjoying our Colón life despite the uncertain climatic conditions. 'Rather trying weather, hot and humid, every movement being an effort. Our existence at the moment is really very easy here, with fresh water at the back door and two minutes from a shower.'

Our pontoon socialising continued with another visit to Jean in his *Atom*. 'The boat is the cleanest, neatest and tidiest we have seen for some time.' He was happy to see us and talk about his adventures, a characteristic of single-handers. He showed us a folio of water colours he had painted of a passage in the 40 foot schooner *Onda II* from New York to Cadiz where she was wrecked. They were first class and would be incorporated in a book he was writing which had promise of some appeal with good sales potential. I subsequently learned he completed his solo globe circling in 1957. In doing so he could be included amongst the pioneers, being just the eighth after the great Joshua Slocum to accomplish this feat. Of these, half were Frenchmen.

Single-handers are unique and a strange tribe, not conforming to the old axiom that 'no man is an island unto himself'. It is not easy to avoid being judgemental. They contravene the most important rule in the *International Regulations for Preventing Collisions at Sea*. Rule 5 states unequivocally: 'Every vessel shall at all times maintain a proper lookout by sight and hearing … so as to make a full appraisal of the risk of collision.' Note 'at all times'. The need for sleep, even if only taken in catnaps, negates a fundamental tenet of centuries-old sea lore of constant vigilance at all times. In our own experience with the tanker in our Atlantic crossing we could well have been run down if there had not been an eye open in our cockpit.

Our time for departure was drawing near. *Tern* was getting near the top of the board and we now needed to attend to domestic matters such as topping up general stores and provisions. This would be much more easily accomplished here alongside a pontoon than 'on the other side' out on a buoy in Balboa. In this exercise we were again the beneficiaries of American generosity. Captain Russell, a retired US Navy officer, in his ketch, *Uruguay*, was another member of the 'pontoon lot'. As host, as he saw it, to a visitor to his country, he was anxious to assist with practical demonstrations of hospitality. He was set up for this, having the use of a car in which he took me shopping, carrying with us several jerrycans which he had generously donated to our cause. These we filled with petrol and kerosene, ie paraffin, at the Canal Zone Commissary, as well as procuring the essentials for our provisions' last top-up. 'What a tantalizing place this is: full of good things at quite reasonable prices. Oh for more dollars!' The commissary, stocking most consumer products, and as such akin to the supermarket concept of today, was very much an American institution, set up to serve the needs of Canal Zone expatriate employees. In this regard we were privileged to have access to what it provided. The commissary no doubt went with the Americans when the Panamanians took over the Canal but that would not have been the only change. When Captain Russell took me shopping, Colón was quite a safe and reasonable place to roam around in – the Americans saw to that – but now, after their exit, it is all quite different, apparently. A fellow Ocean Cruising Club member recently making the Canal transit wrote: 'Colón was as poor, stinking, filthy and dangerous as we'd been led to expect.' Included in my shopping list, which had been compiled by Peter with a high thought input, and also with an input from me, were toilet rolls, a commodity not demanding, one would think, of particular thought, but subsequent events were to prove this assumption incorrect.

The day marked the eve of our impending Canal adventure. *Tern* finally had reached the top of the ship movements ladder.

'Brought the dinghy on board in the evening and sorted out our fenders, included being a pile of old motor tyres which had been given us by another well-wisher, and we laid out the warps for the morrow. *Windjammer* has been very kind in lending us a 20 fathom coil of 2 inch manila rope. Indeed a self-sacrificing gesture, as we all know the positioning lines we will be deploying in the locks are going to take a beating.' This they were to do with a vengeance.

All that was left now were the farewells to our fellow voyagers, a rather sad moment as we knew we would never see any of them again, then goodbyes to the yacht club staff and in particular to the secretary, who had been so helpful. A last meal in the club, the standard of fare remaining determinedly unimproved, a shower and we were then ready for an early night under the stars in our beds made up on the sidedecks. We were ready and anxious now to be off. We had settled our accounts and paid our dues. The total cost including berthing and Canal fees had been all of US$2.80. I believe that now, for a yacht of our size, the fee is US$500, plus a deposit of $600 or more. An outlay of $1,100 is a lot of cash to find. We had been treated so well. It had been a happy experience. We dropped off to sleep, with the expectancy that the pilot would be on board at 0630 next morning. We wanted to be refreshed, relaxed and ready for him. We were not, however, to enjoy to the full that happy state.

Friday 11 December 0545 Pilot appeared on board, followed shortly by Peggy and James.

0615 Started engine, flat calm. Got under way for Gatun Lock.

A simple enough operation when put that way in writing, but in fact the occasion was not to be without its moments.

Something had been intruding into my dreams as I lay in my blankets. As consciousness flooded over me I realized that 'something' was our pilot. Standing on the pontoon at our stern, it was evident he was not too pleased. Although he was there three quarters of an hour early, he had expected us to have been up and about, ready to go. 0630 meant to him 'get moving', not just thinking about being on our way. As we were to learn soon, he was a worried man. With guilt-ridden alacrity, Peter and I deposited our bedding down in the cabin and set about unmooring. This operation was expedited with the help of our loyal support team from *Windjammer*, who fortuitously had also arrived early. What was concerning the pilot was the need for us to arrive at Gatun Lock, at the Atlantic entrance to the Canal, in time for the first locking through of the day. This was when the waters would be at their quietest before they got churned up with successive ship movements and the turbulence that would build up as locking operations proceeded. Neatly attired in well-pressed, light tropical suit with a little bow tie and under a trilby hat, he seated himself at the tiller and, with Gladstone bag close beside him, took charge. He was to remain glued to that tiller and only rarely did he relax throughout the transit. It was to emerge in due course that he had seemingly made a private arrangement with a colleague who would be piloting the ship expected to be in the first locking with us. The objective, as was to be revealed, was to make our lot easier and, more importantly, safer. This was an added reason for the sense of urgency he was conveying.

Although it had not been the best of starts to the day, we were nevertheless now on our way. Things were now, I thought, beginning to pick up. The engine had started more or less on the first swing, and watching the bubbles flowing past our waterline I was pleased with the engine's performance, as we could never be sure how it would feel about things when demands were placed upon it. Looking at those bubbles, it was conceivable we were approaching our maximum speed of nearly 3 knots, which was quite something.

'Engine going well this morning, Peter!'

'Yes. Certainly seems fine at the moment.'

Close on the heels of this interchange came the voice of the pilot.

'OK, Skipper, you can put her full ahead now.'

This was something of a personal affront, I felt.

'But she is going full ahead!'

A look of total disbelief, mixed with something akin to horror, crossed the pilot's features. He restricted himself to the briefest of commentaries.

'Jesus Christ!'

Having digested this piece of information, he proceeded to make it clear that we were not going to make that crucial first locking. Something had to be done. Passing us was a banana boat which responded to the pilot's call for help and sent over a towline. In the words immortalised in *My Fair Lady*, she 'got us there on time'. But only just: the ship that was to be our locking companion was already in the lock.

Gatun Lock has two parallel sets of locks, each with three flights, which raise ships 85 feet up from the Atlantic. It is the first step in the enormously impressive Canal operation. Locks had not, as it happened, been considered in the original design proposals, which were to be a straight cut through the isthmus from one ocean to the other. This was not, after all, a new idea, but one which had been thought about as far back as the early *Conquistadores*, who saw, or thought they saw, an easy way to get the spoils of their conquests from the Pacific over to Spain. In recent times the straight-cut concept was changed to one of using locks when it was realised how much spoil would have to be dug out and equally importantly disposed of. There was, as well, the need to cope with a 20 foot difference in tidal range between the oceans.

We squeezed into the first of the locks close under the stern of our ship, a large cargo vessel, light and looming high over us, with her propeller half out of the water. Immediately behind us the great gates silently and smoothly closed, slowly shutting off our last view of the Atlantic Ocean, which had been so much part of our lives. The old had given way to a new phase now about to unfold, and we had to wonder what that would bring to us. However, we did not wonder too long, as the action started in a big way.

The pilot, I think, had been hoping we could have secured alongside our friendly banana boat, but she evidently was not going through at that time. These robustly built boats, with their heavy fenders, can take being bashed about in the locks and could provide an ideal cushion for the likes of us. However, this was not to be, and we had to face up to being on our own, astern of our freighter, held in the middle of the lock by our four lines, one from each bow and the other two from the quarters aft. These had to be tended continuously as we rose up the canyon of the lock, the secret to survival being to keep these lines taut under full tension at all times. Without Peggy and James we would have had no hope of coping. Around us surged the frightening chaos of the rushing, swirling water as the lock filled. Looming over us was that awesome propeller, so close we could almost reach out ahead and touch it. There were moments of near panic during the ascent as *Tern* came alarmingly close to taking charge and ramming the rough concrete walls crowding above us. It was all we could do to keep enough tension on the warps to arrest those wild charges and then haul ourselves back to somewhere in mid basin. How Peggy managed was a wonder, but she was that kind of girl.

The maelstrom slowly subsided and the gates ahead opened, ready for us to move out into the second flight. It was now that the arrangements made beforehand by our pilot became apparent. The ship waited for us to move ahead of her, clear of her bows, before she started her engine. With that great propeller thrashing round, it probably would not have been possible for us to have retained control. The wash would have been too much.

At the next locking we were anticipating an easier ride, as under our pilot's auspices we secured alongside a Canal Authority tug, *Culebra*, but even so we came close to disaster, as halfway through the flooding she sheared violently over to one side, pulling a cleat off our deck and fracturing a bulwark stanchion. With the final flight now ahead of us, the pilot, anticipatory and enterprising as ever, was able to negotiate a slightly more restrained flooding, with the result that there was just that little less drama. He was a senior pilot and knew everyone. In turn, all the staff knew him and he was obviously well regarded.

With aching arms and overstrained nerves we finally emerged, with Gatun Lake stretching out before us. *Culebra* was still alongside, and dialogue ensued between her captain and our pilot. Against company rules, the tug captain, with great sympathetic understanding, kindly agreed to tow us the 20-odd miles through the lake to Gamboa, which lies in the approaches to the next set of locks ahead of us, Pedro Miguel. Without the tow there was no way we could have made the 50 mile Canal transit in one day. Ships usually make the crossing from one ocean to the other in about nine hours. It would have taken us the best part of that time just to have traversed Gatun Lake alone. Anchoring was frowned upon and the booking programme, including the services of our pilot, did not have accommodation built in for a second day en route.

Whilst we were under tow our pilot took a breather and allowed himself the relaxation of some non-operational conversation. I offered him a whisky as he looked as though he could do with one, but he resolutely declined, as he was consistently to do when offered one from time to time during the remainder of the crossing. He would, however, like a cup of tea. This gave a clue to his background. Captain Roberts was English, although his appearance and accent suggested a true-bred American. He had been born and raised in the Midlands, and life after that had given him no cause to regret changing citizenship. He enjoyed being of the US. It had been good to him. He told us of his concern on being assigned to us and could not refrain from drawing a comparison between his present lot and his previous charge. The day before, he had been on the bridge of the liner *Gothic*, bearing our new queen, Elizabeth, accompanied by Prince Philip for the royal tour of New Zealand. The thought of him on one day standing on the bridge of a fully powered ocean-going liner and the next seated in our little cockpit was faintly ludicrous. Attempting not to give offence, he made it clear which position was his preferred choice. Perhaps somewhat irrelevantly, we assured him we were not at all miffed about not having been invited on board his first choice to meet the royal couple as a mark of recognition on their part of our role as the only British occupants of the yacht basin.

Approaching Gamboa we were nearing the end of our tow, and I spoke to Captain Roberts seeking his advice on what would be an appropriate gesture on our part to thank the tug captain for his invaluable help.

'Don't worry about it, Skipper. We all help each other in this business, but I don't think he would turn down a bottle of rum.'

As we let the towline go at Gamboa, I passed over one such bottle. It was little enough but the captain seemed surprised and pleased.

The tow through the lake had meant far more than just a convenient way to cover distance. It had enabled us to relax and even enjoy ourselves. We could take coffee over a chat – or tea in the case of the pilot – and have lunch, but also we were able to take in the significance of this largely man-made stretch of water, literally the centrepiece of the Canal system.

Originally it had been just a swamp in the rainforest fed by the River Chagres which, cutting across the isthmus of Panama to exit on the shores of the Caribbean, almost separates North from South America. Rio Chagres has a romantic if brutal place in history, playing a major role in the early days of the Spanish exploitation of the region. Close by the river ran the route of the mule teams bringing treasure across the isthmus. The river was useful to the Spanish colony as a commercial waterway, and along the banks had been located warehouses and trading posts fulfilling, as well, the function of 'lay-bys' for the mule trains. The river was also of interest to French privateers who had explored its potential as a way to gaining access to the treasure supply lines. When Drake arrived on the scene, they formed a business association with him and passed on the results of their research, including their findings that the river could be navigated for some distance inland from its Atlantic mouth. Drake built this information into his own grand plan. He sent his brother, John, to explore the river and check out on the French intelligence. He concluded that, following three days rowing upstream, a pinnace would reach Venta Cruces, where the mule trail from

Panama on the Camino Real, the Royal Road, came down to the river, and where a wharf and storehouse were situated. We understood at the time of our Canal transit that what was left of that road could still be seen.

Based on John's survey, Drake hatched his plan of action to make his fortune, and that of his followers, not to mention restoring the health of the finances of Good Queen Bess. The big picture was an attack on Panama itself, but an interim tactical plan for immediate financial gain was to knock off a mule train. As well as working with the French, he had established a close relationship with a band of *Cimarrones*. These were escaped black slaves who not unnaturally were unfavourably disposed towards their former masters. In fact, their dedicated mission was harassment of the colonists and to kill as many Spaniards as possible. The *Cimarrones* were a valuable conduit for information on Spanish bullion movements, but they had a problem concerning gold. They were at a loss to understand the Europeans' fixation with what the *Cimarrones* considered to be a completely useless material. Nothing could be done with it, unlike iron which could be turned into tools and weapons. To the black men, an iron nail was worth more than all the gold and silver in Christendom. To this end, Drake was a useful provider of what they needed, as well as being a valuable ally with his men and weaponry in the *Cimarrones*' attacks on the Spanish and seizure of goods from the colonists.

Drake was now ready to launch Plan A. With 12 *Cimarrones* and 18 of his own men, he marched overland to within a few miles of Panama, where he was able to glean information that a mule team was due to leave for Nombre de Dios that night. Falling back to near Venta Cruces he prepared an ambush. With his men wearing white shirts to enable them to keep track in the dark of each man's whereabouts, as well as to distinguish friend from foe, they hid themselves in the undergrowth beside the trail. With ears pressed to the ground, they were in due course rewarded with hearing the thud of hooves. It was at this moment that the excitement of the occasion proved too much for a young seaman, Robert Pike, who leapt to his feet and, brandishing his musket, rushed, wild of eye and shouting at the top of his voice, towards the mule team. He had been drinking brandy to keep his courage up but had taken one swig too many. The overwhelming advantage Drake held of surprise had been blown. The Spanish troops escorting the train had time to marshal their defences and, outnumbering Drake's force, he had no option but to withdraw, leaving behind a fortune that could so easily have been his, and one almost within his grasp. Fortunately, it is not on detailed record what punishment was afforded young Pike by Drake and his frustrated shipmates. The sole reason why they were there at all with Drake was to make their fortunes.

It was some time later that Drake made another attempt, destined to be his last, to lay hands on Spanish wealth. Plan B, involving the Chagres river, came into being. With Drake was an army officer, Thomas Baskerville, who was to land with 800 men, march along the mule track to Panama and take it. Drake, with the rest of his forces, would proceed in boats up the Chagres. The isthmus would then be in his hands. It all went awry. It was the wrong time of the year and the troops, under Baskerville, were ill-equipped. Exhausted, worn out by their labours, slipping and sliding on the sodden tracks, they were in no shape to confront the town's defenders and were thrown back. Defeated, famished and totally demoralised, they straggled back to their ships. Drake, who was about to start up the Chagres in his boats, gave up on the whole idea and died. He was an old man of 56.

Fast-forward two centuries and Rio Chagres is once more in the frame. In the course of the canal's construction the river was damned, flooding the rainforest and thereby creating the Gatun Lake shipping waterway. As we progressed along the well-marked channel stumps of old, dead trees could still be seen projecting above the surface. Encompassing it were dense, rainforested banks and hills. Close by was what is now the Parque Nacional Soberanía, a magnet for birdwatchers and home to sloth monkeys, tarantulas and the wildlife which had made conditions near to impossible for the contractors forcing through the cuts for the mammoth project. In the park's intricate *canales*, the natural waterways, as a travel writer put it: 'You could be in the remotest corners of the Amazon until you turn a corner to meet a huge car transporter in the main channel.'

The tow so generously provided by *Culebra* had been a big boost to our spirits, but more than that it had meant real progress, in easy mode, such that we would now make the transit in the day. It was 8 miles to Pedro Miguel, a lock which has only a single flight and was thus expected to be just that little easier on crew and gear, not to mention the strain on Captain Robert's equanimity. The run through the Culebra Cut, after which our tug had been named, revealed just how stupendous had been this marvel of civil engineering. The cost of driving this cutting, otherwise known as Gaillard, through the spine of the isthmus, the appropriately named Continental Divide, involving the removal of enormous quantities of rock and soil, was a major reason for the bankruptcy of the original contractor, de Lesseps of Suez Canal fame, in 1888. The unstable ground and frequent rockfalls were still causing problems at the time when we went through. The Canal was not finally completed by the Americans, who had taken over its construction and the cost as well, until 1914. The total cost in both dollars and human lives had been staggering. 25,000 men, at one time at a rate of 40 per day, had died, mainly in the process of hacking through the mosquito-ridden jungle. As if malaria was not enough, yellow fever and cholera contributed to the death toll. The final bill to the US taxpayer was US$639 million.

For us in *Tern* it was so far so good in our progress through the Canal, but another big test lay in negotiating Miraflores Lock, with its two flights handling the transition from the waters of Gatun to the Pacific. We were told that something over 50 million gallons of water from the lake are used per ship throughout the system. The mixing of the lake's fresh water and the salt of the ocean exacerbates dramatically the inherent turbulence occurring when the locks are flooded. Our pilot was particularly concerned about what lay before us in Miraflores, so much so that he obtained the services of a Canal company launch to take us through. He was right, as we were to see, to be concerned. The flow in the lock, combined with the swirling madhouse associated with the meeting of the different salinities of the two waters, was nothing short of horrendous, certainly as seen from our perspective. On our own, even with an army of line handlers on board, we could well have been out of control. As it was it was almost too much even for our high-powered launch, as with wild charges we repeatedly tried to ram the wall.

Then it was all over. It had been a profound experience, commencing with the last glimpse of the Atlantic as those great doors of Gatun Lock had slowly closed, to the culmination with the Pacific appearing before us as the gates of Miraflores swung open. Framed in the opening was the pink glow of a tropical sunset heralding our soon-to-be venture out onto the great sweep of the Silver Sea.

The launch put us alongside the pontoon of the Balboa Yacht Club, where we were to drop off our pilot and our support team. It was 1600. Without the services of *Culebra* and the launch we could only guess at what time it would have been when we finally arrived, even assuming we would have arrived at all. I paid off the launch and gave the skipper a parting gift of what was now becoming standard practice, a bottle of rum. It was well received. He, like the captain of *Culebra*, had done us well, but unlike that vessel there was a cost, amounting to US$21. This was an outlay we could ill afford but we had no cause to complain. Without that launch we might well not have survived Miraflores. I preferred not to dwell on the damage we could have incurred, not least being the breaking off of the bowsprit.

Seated in the cabin, Captain Roberts was in no hurry to leave.

'Skipper! Where's that bottle of Scotch? I need it!'

Before our admiring eyes we witnessed a remarkably efficient demolition of a whisky bottle. If anyone had earned it, he had.

Chapter Seven

In Pursuit of Darwin

The journey is the reward.

OLD CHINESE SAYING

'Ben, will you do something for me when you get to New Zealand?' Caution is always needed when confronted with loaded requests like this.

'Certainly I will, Sandy, if I can.'

The setting for this conversation was the Galápagos Islands, Sandy and I standing on the foreshore of one of the few inhabited islands. Sandy was quite distressed.

'In the mail you brought from Balboa there was a letter from New Zealand. My mother is dead and my father wants to know when I am returning home. I am not. I can't ever leave here and he will never be able to understand why. What I am asking, Ben, is that you speak to my father and explain, to try to make him understand. I could give you a letter to take with you but I can't put down in writing what it's all about. You have seen my world here and understand the way of life. Only you can explain to my father the meaning of it all.' I understood.

The visit to the Galápagos had been one of the most rewarding experiences in my life. It was the fulfilment of a great wish, fostered by the writings of the pioneering small-boat ocean voyagers, to see for myself these fascinating, strange, lonely islands. Now I was here and did not want to leave. I could empathise with my companion.

Sandy epitomised the type of person who chose to be here, essentially individuals, very private to themselves, who wanted to lead their lives the way they wanted to lead them, subject only to nature and not to the dictates of interfering officialdom. Many books could have been written, too late now, about the hotchpotch of the islands' inhabitants of various nationalities, beliefs and characteristics, but all with a single common feature. They were escapists from conventional society.

As if he needed to justify even more his decision to remain in the Galápagos, isolated from the world, Sandy had gone on to tell me how terrified he was at the thought of coping with everyday life should he return to New Zealand.

'I wouldn't know how to deal with the things that don't exist here, like tax returns, life insurance, bank accounts and the rest of that stuff. All so complicated! Too difficult. I don't have a clue about such things and don't want to have to learn.'

Sandy Sanderson was a New Zealander, the complete adventurer, his own man and a total misfit in the world that the rest of us inhabit and understand. During our stay I spent quite some time with him. There was an affinity between us. We were fellow countrymen in a strange land, but more than that we were both living an adventure, even if in the pursuit of that he was a full-time participant, whereas for me, as adventurers go, I was acting out a temporary role and was something of a tyro at that. He told me about his background. He had gone to sea before the war, and when that arrived he volunteered his services as a soldier in the New Zealand Division in North Africa. A 'Desert Rat', he found himself as a driver in what was loosely referred to as the Long Range Desert Group, comprising a collection of individuals who were characterised by being highly independent, tough and adept at 'living rough off the land'. If there was a rule book they had never lifted its covers. They would set off in jeeps and lightly armoured vehicles, loaded with weapons, ammunition, jerrycans of water and basic rations to drive long distances and harass the German forces under Field Marshal Rommel. Sandy had found his niche.

Unfortunately for him the war finished, and like many of his kind he was left high and dry with no personal compass. Wandering to no particular point, he met up with an English couple, an ex-army officer and his wife, planning like so many hopefuls before them to find Captain Kidd's fabled treasure, supposedly buried on a coral island in the British protectorate comprising the Cocos Islands. If ever there was a quest entered into more in hope than with facts, this was it. Kidd, a Scottish pirate, albeit operating with a commission from the king to suppress others of the kind, had strayed a little from the straight and narrow. On his return from the Indian Ocean to what was then the colonial town of Boston in America, he was arrested, tried and executed in England, taking his secrets to the scaffold with him. Sandy and his new-found friends ended up being wrecked on one of the uninhabited islands. A fishing boat in due course took off the colonel and spouse, but Sandy, tiring of their company, elected to stay. Being himself something of a latter-day Alexander Selkirk, this was a character to whom he could relate. Sometime later, however, he did accept a lift from another fishing boat which happened to pass by. He was dropped off at Academy Bay. Sandy had come home.

Balboa was only a few hundred miles from the Galápagos but the gap felt like thousands. They were so contrasting, the one pragmatically functional and the other exotic. Balboa had, however, in its own way been an interesting and enjoyable necessary pause in our westward progression. We needed a little time there to adjust, mentally and emotionally, to launching ourselves onto the largest expanse of water on the planet, the Pacific Ocean, with its people and their ways so different to what we were about to leave behind, the Western world.

Overall, things went well in Balboa, the stresses and strains of the Canal behind us. Our team from *Windjammer* took their departure with kisses and shakes of the hand, stepping on to the pontoon to return to Colón, their work done. Despite assertions of keeping in touch, we knew we would never see either of them again. Sad in its own way. They had been good company and of great value to us. We were moving on but they were left with their human relationship problems. They were followed shortly afterwards by Captain Roberts. A very pleasant man, and we felt privileged to have had such a rock-like character to look after us.

We were not to be left alone on board for long, as appearing on the pontoon was Mr Hart, a senior member of the Balboa Yacht Club, on behalf of which he extended a cordial invitation to call it our home. Reminiscent of the warm reception we had received at the Colón club, we were urged to use the facilities at any time. We would be their guests as regards berthing charges. With him on board we slipped from the pontoon and, under his guidance, moved out into the harbour to secure to a buoy. On Hart's departure ashore we suddenly felt very tired. Peter prepared one of his simple but tasty meals and we took to our bunks. The events of the day were, though, still pressing in on me. As I finally dropped off to sleep I made a promise to myself.

Never again will I have a boat with a bowsprit: the punishment ours took today was awful. Still, we are through and now on the last lap in the Pacific.

The ten days lying off Balboa were to go past all too quickly, with work on the boat to repair the ravages of the Canal transit and the time-consuming performance in obtaining visas for the Galápagos and French Polynesia. Interspersed with ship's business, we could enjoy the serious business of socialising. Close on the footsteps of David Hart came Captain Baverstock, senior citizen amongst Canal pilots, yachtsman, raconteur, part-time practical joker and Galápagos historian. One of his more important roles was as self-appointed 'agent' for the expatriate community on the islands. He was hugely knowledgeable and intensely interested in the archipelago, cruising down there at least once a year in his yacht. He arrived on board to extend an invitation to dinner that night at his home. He and his wife, Sissy, proved a generous and entertaining host and hostess, full of information about the archipelago, including revelations about some of its darker secrets. Our interest in visiting the islands was further titillated, not that we needed any encouragement.

Baverstock had heard, possibly through the pilots' network, that we were bound for the islands and wanted to ask of us a favour.

'I have been building up a pile of mail for the expatriate residents, most of whom live on one island, Indefatigable, scattered around the only decent anchorage at Academy Bay. You have to go there. There is another family of Germans living on Floreana, but more about that later. Would you be kind enough to take this pile of mailbags with you? The only way I can get them their mail is to ask boats like you passing through. The Ecuadorians get their mail via a steamer that arrives periodically from the mainland. They can look after themselves.'

There was, of course, only one answer to such a request.

The Galápagos, their official name being the Archipiélago de Colón, have always had an aura of mystery associated with them following their discovery – the one most acceptable to history – in 1535 by the Bishop of Panama, Fray Tomás de Berlanga, who was driven off course whilst on his way to administer to the spiritual needs of his parishioners, Spanish and 'converts', down the coast of South America. Apparently he was not overimpressed with what he had stumbled upon. Subsequent visitors shared a common problem, first in locating them and then in actually reaching their shores, beset by strong currents, fickle winds and the frequent risk of murky weather. Due to their elusiveness and their proclivity to do a disappearing act in the mists, they seemed bewitched, acquiring the name *Las Encantadas*, meaning just that. The reputation for mystery and positional uncertainty was fostered by pirates, mainly English, who were on the scene from the 17th century onwards, in order to preserve the exclusivity of the islands. They were too important as safe havens to the *boucaniers*, and also as convenient bases for mounting forays against shipping on the nearby mainland coast to open them up to all-comers.

Amongst the early pirates, one of the most notorious was John Cook who, in 1684, whilst on his way to the South Seas, took an unlikely prize – and for him and his crew a happy one. They captured a Danish slave ship with 60 black slave girls on board. Cook changed ships and renamed his prize *Bachelor's Delight*. He could not believe his luck. He had gained a better ship, and additionally the retention of the other acquisitions that had gone with the change had met with a considerable measure of approbation from all hands. With Cook was the colourful William Dampier, who divided his time between privateer, straightforward pirate and Royal Navy officer. He compiled a detailed description of the islands in his best-selling *A New Voyage Round the World*, which until quite recent times was still in print.

Also on board was William Ambrose Cowley, an English mathematician who had been conned by Cook into accepting the position of navigator on a world cruise, unaware of Cook's true vocation, or so he said. Cowley put his time in the waters of the Galápagos to good purpose by charting the islands, the first man to do so. Although an academic, he was also something of an adventurer in his own right. In due course he parted company with Cook and joined another English buccaneering ship, wherein he enjoyed some financial success. Eventually tiring of the life of a pirate and, one can surmise, a certain lack of intellectual stimulation coming from his shipmates, he joined a Dutch ship in Batavia, taking her home as pilot without event to Britain. A few years later he had published an account of his circumnavigation and life as a pirate, but perhaps wisely he did this under a pseudonym, 'An Ingenious Englishman'.

Dampier reappeared in the archipelago in 1709 as navigator of a ship under the command of Woodes Rogers, another privateer and a successful one at that. On their way to the Galápagos they had stopped at the island of Juan Fernández, off the coast of Chile, where they took off Alexander Selkirk, the original Robinson Crusoe, he having been marooned there four years before from a ship whose navigator had been the same William Dampier. Woodes Rogers was subsequently appointed governor of the Bahamas, with the specific charge of stamping out piracy, the assumption being that having been good at it he would be equally good at putting it down. It would appear this was the right thinking as he was appointed for a second term, dying out there.

The cult of mystery enshrouding the islands persisted, with one of the greatest of them all occurring in the last century. It was one which was to attract worldwide attention, largely through the publication of a book describing the lurid, bizarre happenings on Charles Island, known now as Floreana Island. For many years most of the islands have enjoyed two names, English and Spanish, the ones in English being bestowed upon them by the early pirates, often taking the names of English kings. Their Spanish names were acquired when Ecuador annexed the archipelago in the 19th century, in 1832. When we were there in *Tern* our charts used the English names with Spanish subtitles. This practice will no doubt have been reversed today, Admiralty charts no longer holding their dominant position in the world.

I had heard of the 'Galápagos Affair' through the writings of yachtsmen visiting the islands between the wars, and I was aware of this intriguing story, or as much of it as was ever to be known. Further details of the saga, the interest value of which had been enhanced by the salacious connotations, were furnished by Baverstock, who had done considerable research on the weird case history.

In 1929, a somewhat deranged, not-of-this-world German doctor, Friedrich Ritter, harbouring pretensions of being a mystic and accompanied by his devoted and completely subservient mistress, Dore, settled on Charles Island. They were in search of their Eden. They just managed to eke out an existence, mastication of what they had grown being facilitated by a common set of stainless steel dentures. Ritter was not well pleased when, three years later serpents invaded Eden in the guise of another set of Germans, Heinz and Margret Wittmer plus son. Although the two groups lived in relatively close proximity to each other there was virtually no contact, which helps to explain why the tragedy about to unfold was never fully explained.

Hot on the heels of the serpents there was yet another and even more unwelcome intrusion into the now rather battered Eden, by a mad Austrian woman, styling herself baroness, who was in possession of one or two other interesting personality traits, such as megalomania and nymphomania. Accompanying her was a retinue of two lovers. Furthermore, she carried a six-shooter, which she was only too ready to deploy. It was certainly helpful on one occasion in persuading a passing fisherman to come ashore on a temporary assignment to ease the load on her in-house lovers.

Two years later matters took a turn for the worse – fatally so. The baroness and one of her lovers disappeared. No one knew anything about anything. The Wittmers claimed later that they thought at the time the couple had gone off in a passing yacht, but it was strange the baroness had left her clothes behind. The second lover confirmed the yacht story but he himself seemed suddenly desperate to get off the island. This he did in yet another fishing boat, containing a Norwegian, but did not get very far, their bodies being found later on an island nearby. Dore was to claim in subsequent years that she had heard a protracted scream followed by total silence. She did not investigate but was informed by Ritter, with a surprising degree of conviction:

'The baroness has gone for good. She won't be back!' Ritter then promptly died.

No one ever saw her or her lover again. Dore eventually got back to Germany, and although she had a book published about her existence on the island, she did not reveal anything worthwhile about what had actually happened. The Wittmers stayed on, now the sole occupants of Eden, and the family grew, enjoying the life they had wanted in the first place until the tourists changed it all for them.

Miles Smeeton, who had been in the region with Beryl in *Tzu Hang* a year before us, related an anecdote about Baverstock's involvement in the mystery. Possibly becoming fed up with loose 'scuttlebutt' gossip in the yacht club bar and the marked interest amongst overseas visitors about the baroness's fate, he had taken a couple down to Floreana in his yacht, with Sissy also onboard. The two visitors were keen to do their own investigatory work. In the course of digging around in the cave, to which they had been directed by Baverstock, they unearthed a set of dentures. Returning triumphantly on board in a state of great excitement they were greeted by a furious Sissy, minus teeth. Baverstock admitted 'to having been a little naughty' in taking them when she was asleep, to sneak ashore and plant them in the cave. I do not recall Baverstock telling us this story, but that may not have been too surprising as in all likelihood this would have had to have been in front of Sissy. However, I can accept it as being near enough true.

A year or so after I arrived in New Zealand in *Tern*, I met Victor Clark, who had arrived in Auckland in the course of his circumnavigation in his ketch, *Solace*. We spent some time swapping notes about the Galápagos, particularly as he had visited different islands to us. He had called at Floreana and had met the Wittmers but, not wanting to press the issue, had learned nothing new. Heinz was still alive then but was to predecease Margaret by many years. She went on to die at 92, taking with her the answer to the riddle of Floreana.

On the other side of the island lies the equally well known Post Office Bay, home to the famous barrel used as a letter transfer receptacle. It had been originally erected by whalers in the 19th century, the practice being to deposit letters in it, to be collected by the next homeward-bound vessel. The barrel is central to the history of the archipelago, symbolic of an environmental disaster that was to overtake the islands, barrels being used for holding oil, whale oil. Whalers in ever growing numbers decimated the sperm whale population that had proliferated around the Galápagos. In the process they also wreaked havoc amongst the tortoises roaming the islands. Hundreds of thousands were slaughtered as a much sought-after source of fresh meat, wiping the breed out on some of the islands, Floreana being one not to escape the carnage. The whalers comprised the first wave of human beings to create disaster for the wildlife, to be followed in more recent times by a second wave in the form of tourists, fortunately these being under more control than their whaler predecessors.

On our buoy in Balboa we still had the Galápagos experience ahead of us. An early task had been to climb over the hurdle of officialdom to complete the formalities for entry into both the Galápagos and French Polynesia, noting at the time:

'The Ecuadorian business was achieved in much less time than expected, although outrageously expensive – US$28. After obtaining a bill of health from the port captain, the whole performance took just over half an hour. My visa for Tahiti had, in the meantime, come through at a cost of US$1.40, a much more reasonable proposition.' However, although I felt we had been fleeced by the Ecuadorian Consul, at least he did it with words of good cheer. He could afford to. '*Hasta la vista! Buen viaje.*' So long! Have a good journey.

As it was to transpire, we need not have concerned ourselves too much over the Galápagos, no one there being particularly interested in checking our entry permits. It was, however, to be a different story in Tahiti, where we would be once more subservient to bureaucracy.

We had come to the conclusion we were actually enjoying our stay in Balboa, largely because we had made some good friends and had been made to feel welcome. The Baverstocks had gone out of their way to be helpful. Warm and hospitable evenings dining with them had been what we needed, a break from the confines of life in a boat. Hart, likewise, had contributed to making our stay pleasurable. A gesture which we appreciated was the time he devoted to giving us a guided and well-informed tour of old Panama, taking in the sights of this historic town with its long, romantic, if infamous background. The tour included a stop for refreshments at the city's top hotel, El Panamá, luxurious as measured by the standards of the day, and a visit to the alligator hide factory, where the animal came in one end and emerged out the other as a pair of shoes and a handbag.

This, in fact, was not my first visit to Panama: I had been there 11 years before, almost to the day in 1942, during the war. Having joined the Navy I found myself in a passenger liner, SS *Ruahine*, commandeered to convey members of the armed forces from New Zealand to England. The ship was of personal interest as she had carried my mother in the opposite direction after the Great War. She was to live in New Zealand for the rest of her life but never came fully to accept it and always referred to England as 'home'. She was just a little emotional about her old ship, *Ruahine*, now taking her son 'home'. After leaving Wellington, we had crossed the South Pacific via a somewhat circuitous route in the hopes of avoiding German surface raiders, arriving eventually at anchor off Balboa, not too far from where *Tern* lay on her buoy. *Ruahine* not being due to lock through the Canal until the morrow, we were allowed ashore that night. The backstreets of Panama were an eye-opener to me; so wide, in fact, that those eyes were in danger of falling out. On display was raw sex. Every window, doorway and balcony along those streets, and there were quite a few of them, had on full display women of varying shapes and ages exhibiting their all, cajoling, enticing and beckoning. The effect on a young man, just turned 18 and straight from home, was devastating. Fortunately, there were two strong, controlling factors: one, fear, and the other, lack of cash. Recent photographic views of Panama City show the dreary, monotonous high-rise skyline of a modern city, a tourist trap devoid of individuality. Could be anywhere. It was not always thus, as I had discovered in my youth. Perhaps behind that rampart of graceless, tall buildings, the hallmark of modern construction, there still lurks some of old Panama.

With the demands of forthcoming officialdom met and refitting work on the boat well in hand, we could take more notice of what was around us. There was one small craft that had come in after us and on an adjacent buoy. We started to see quite a lot of her crew, Leo Topolowski and Boris. We soon found, however, that all was not sweetness and light on board. *La Polonaise* was a very small boat indeed, and both skipper and crew large. They were encroaching on each other's space. Going on board for our first visit we were greeted by Leo in the cockpit. Boris was up in the bows and stayed there. Leo felt some explanation was in order.

'Boris and I are in the middle of a stand-off. It happens from time to time. When we feel the need for relief from each other, Boris takes over the forward half of the boat and I remain in what's left. At the moment Boris is in a huff and not communicating.'

We saw what he meant. Leo was the epitome of the small-boat ocean roamer with no ties to anyone or anywhere. Essentially a loner. Boris was big and black, of uncertain lineage, but could possibly have laid claim to membership of the Labrador extended family. He certainly bore a resemblance to Peggy's Labrador in *Windjammer* but without the same measure of blue blood. He did, however, greet us with a perfunctory wag of his tail but continued to ignore Leo.

They had come down from California and, after the usual windless struggle along the coast of Central America, had reached Balboa. They had no plan on where to go next, nor was it clear what they did for money. However, their outgoings would have been small. *La Polonaise* had the simplest of rigs and sail plan, no gadgets, no frills and no engine. They were still there when we left, and we could only hope that like Peggy and James they would, before too long, patch things up between them. Perhaps for Boris a run ashore to do what dogs do would have made all the difference. Leo would not appear to have had the same imperative. At either end of the Canal were two similar characters. Leo in the Pacific in his little *La Polonaise*, and at the Atlantic end Jean in his equally small *Atom*. They were very alike in their approach to life, and although 'kindred souls' in attitude and approach to life, there would be little communion of those souls when their paths crossed. Both were sociable, even gregarious in company, but neither welcomed intrusion into their lives. Alone but content.

Our own time to move on had arrived. The last morning was spent in preparing for sea and receiving visitors. Baverstock and Sissy came on board, bringing the Galápagos mail. It was rather a daunting pile of mailbags, large packets and parcels, which we managed to stow down below in the forepeak and heads compartment, leaving just enough space for essential operations – use of stove, washbasin and toilet. For us, the Baverstocks had brought bags of home-made biscuits and a stack of freshly baked French bread. With deep regret we watched them step over our rail into their boat and depart our lives.

Soon after they had gone, David Hart sailed alongside in his Star Class boat to say his farewells. We would miss him too, and the warm reception we had received from his club. We were leaving on a good note, but the programme of visits had not yet run its course. A young New Zealand doctor with wife and daughter came out to wish us Godspeed. They deposited on board a great pile of cans of fruit juice. A thoughtful and much appreciated gesture. It now was really time to go.

Sunday 20 December 1615 Slipped the mooring. Got under way under all plain sail. Wind dropped completely. Started engine. Sea like proverbial sheet of glass.

We were off. Next stop the Galápagos. It was not to be, however.

That evening, our first at sea, when we came to light the cabin lamps they refused to oblige. They would feebly flicker and die. All our domestic paraffin was contaminated. What would appear to have happened was that whilst in Colón to boost our stocks I had acquired an empty, supposedly clean 10 gallon oil drum. It obviously wasn't.

There was no option but to turn back. We could have got by without the navigation lights and, with difficulty, the one for the compass, but neither of us was prepared to put up with no cabin lights, torches, we felt, being an inadequate substitute. Morale was not good. To cap it all, the weather was not helping as we altered course back to Taboga Island, which we had just recently passed. The log laments:

'Most uncomfortable night with wind varying from very strong on the port quarter to next to nothing from ahead, accompanied throughout by TORRENTIAL downpours.'

Taboga was a pleasant little town, and being there made us feel better, the contrast to the squalor of Cristóbal and Panama being most marked. A smiling, welcoming lad in a boat came off and took us ashore to the local store for a fresh supply of paraffin. We could not but notice how spotlessly clean was the store, giving us the confidence we needed on the state of the new drum we had bought and the fuel that went into it. It would have been fun to have spent some time on the island but the evening saw us on our way again. Morale was on the rise once more.

But facing us now were the best part of 900 miles, on a rhumb line, of tedium and frustration in waters not intended by the gods to be sailed over unless equipped with a large, powerful engine, a luxury we could only dream about. The ordeal commences first with trying to get out of the Gulf of Panama. Flat calm over lengthy periods, breezes, when they come, all over the place, and squalls with rain of the solid variety making a mockery of oilskins.

Having finally struggled out of the gulf, one enters the grandly entitled 'Inter Tropical Convergence Zone', known to the more simple sailor as the Doldrums. These, in December and January, extend down to 2° or 3° north of the Equator; that is, down as far as the northern islands of the Galápagos group. In other words, the whole wearisome way. If it was any consolation, we knew that those before us had put up with much of the same. One such was William Albert Robinson who, in his enduring classic, *Deep Water and Shoal*, says it all when referring to his passage in 1928 from Balboa to the Galápagos.

'The *Pilot* book was no place to go for encouragement, for it said: "The navigation in this region becomes one of the most tedious, uncertain and vexatious undertakings known to the seaman.

A great river of cool water from the South Pacific – the Peruvian (Humboldt) Current – follows the west coast of South America northward and meets the Mexican and the Pacific countercurrents in the bight of Panama. The meeting of these three powerful ocean currents of contrasting temperatures causes variable weather, squalls, calms and uncertain local currents. The Doldrums, and the fact that whatever wind there might be would be south-west, putting the Galápagos dead to windward, precludes sailing a direct course".'

Our log is a litany of accounts of widely varying weather conditions and equally varying mental states, from the benign to the not so benign.

The forenoon was particularly uncomfortable with a short, choppy head sea causing her to pitch violently, throwing water over the foredeck continuously to rush down the side decks and end up in the cockpit. The plunging bows smash the bowsprit down to immerse it up to the gammon iron in the sea and bring *Tern* almost to a dead stop.

But then again:

Had supper together down in the saloon with the table set as though in harbour. This is the flattest calm I think I have ever known with almost no movement on the boat whatsoever.

2000 Breeze came in from the west and we are making progress again.

Bad habits crept into our sea routine. During the dark hours, with no wind, the practice was to flatten in all sheets to keep the sails quiet, and at such times during my watch I would sneak down into the saloon for a little doze, propped up in the corner of the unoccupied settee. I was to be caught out. In accordance with this highly undesirable procedure, on the next windless night I had, after a good look round, retired below to the cabin. In doing so I felt relaxed. Earlier in the day we had been overtaken by what looked like a tuna boat heading for the Galápagos, and sometime later a large schooner under full sail, presumably motorsailing, had crossed well ahead of us. We had seen nothing else, and as a consequence I had been seduced into believing the sea was ours and ours alone.

Waking from a little doze, and with a faint twinge of guilt, I crept silently up into the cockpit to reassure myself. The ensuing shock hit me like a physical blow. Ahead was the dreaded perfect geometric arrangement of navigation lights, masthead white steaming lights exactly in line, and below them, equally spaced along the base of the isosceles triangle, were the red and green side lights. It was a replay of the incident with the tanker in the Atlantic, except that this time there was no possibility of a near miss. The ship ahead was going to hit us. We, of course, had no navigation lights displayed, and also, of course, no radar reflector up the mast. Such a thing did not exist in those days. Even if her bridge was fully manned, and there would be a big 'if' about that, they could not have been expected to have seen us, visually or on the radar scan. It was a dark night, and being an all-wood boat our radar reflectivity was not good. Our hope lay in our own hands, or more specifically in our engine. There was still not a breath of wind. The sound of me clambering down the ladder in the cabin to get at the engine cranking handle brought Peter to the surface of a deep sleep, where he had been '50 fathoms down'.

'What's going on?'

'What's going on is we are about to have company. I've got to get the engine running. I hope to God the b***** thing starts!'

My prayer was that I had not allowed the engine to stop when we had last used it without changing back to petrol. If it had been left on paraffin it would not start.

Having put the fear of God into me, that authority on high now relented and came to our aid. The engine started first swing. Rushing back into the cockpit I slammed the gear lever into ahead, kicked the throttle wide open and, with the tiller hard over, hoped for the best. The mast headlights started to open.

Being thrown all over the place, we took the full wash of our nearly-to-be visitor as she passed, her propeller half out of the water, with the great blades thrashing down into the sea. As on the previous occasion, Peter revealed nothing of his inner thoughts and climbed back into his bunk to leave me with my guilt.

It was during one of those all too frequent calms, with the sea smooth and remarkably flat, that we had another visitor bearing down upon us, but this one we were happy to receive. The wind had gone, leaving not even a memory or sign it had ever been there. On the sea surface there was no movement, a mirror reflecting the sky, and even the usual slow rise and fall of the underlying swell was not to be felt. We were totally motionless and all around us was still, but then the spell up till then of being in a world devoid of animation was broken. Over towards the eastern horizon where lay South America there was movement. Indistinct in the heat haze could be seen a small, dark object, or at least it appeared small in the distance, swimming strongly towards us. It arrived alongside and looked us in the eye. A turtle of quite substantial size. We took a flipper each and managed to get it over the guardrail to lie it on its back on the sidedeck.

'Fancy a turtle steak?'

'Sounds a good idea. I will keep an eye on our friend here, Peter, whilst you get the big kitchen knife.'

'Well, actually I thought you might be better at this than I am'.

Pause. The eyes were still looking at us.

Taking again a flipper each we eased our guest back over the side. Without looking back it set off with considerable energy for the same spot on the horizon from which it had come. The ripples on that flat tabletop of a sea spread out and died.

The waters we were struggling through teemed with marine life, most of which was invisible to us but which we knew must be there, judging by the shoals of small fish about us, mackerel and the like, combined with the frequent appearance of predators, sharks swimming effortlessly and menacing around and under us. Dolphins and whales shared this prolific breeding ground. At times the emergence of the marine underworld could be quite dramatic. In the midst of yet another flat calm and billiard tabletop of a sea, we were startled to see the surface erupt as a giant ray became airborne to a height of five or six feet, then 'fly' for a short distance before falling back flat onto the sea with a great splash. Whether it was hunting, being hunted, or perhaps just shaking off parasitic irritants we, of course, knew not, but here was an inhabitant of the hidden world below us suddenly joining ours and then returning to its own. It was so big that if it had landed on us we could well have ended up joining it down in its domain. It would appear we had been witness to a spinetail mobula ray, which frequents the waters of Mexico and Ecuador, and enjoying other more exotic names like 'devil ray'.

It was to take us 17 days to reach the Galápagos after leaving Taboga, the wind with which we were blessed being persistently in the south-to-west quadrant – the direction we wanted to go. At times we were driven near to despair. All too frequently there was no wind, and when it came it was invariably nearer to south-west than in the south, which would have allowed us to lay the course, and usually coupled with rain squalls, the deluge completely flattening the sea. Arching overhead were leaden skies and it was cold, the effect of the Humboldt stream of polar water up from the south. Multilayers of thick jerseys and oilskins were the rig of the day, leading Peter to remark:

'Reminds me of home. Could be a summer's day in the Channel.'

Log entries reflect our mood:

Oh God! Are we tired of this endless beating to windward. A miserable morning with the wind in the same old quarter and raining steadily. The day's run for the last 24 hours a bare 25 miles. This kind of sailing is painful in the extreme and never have I looked forward more to anywhere as those islands ahead.

But life went on and Christmas Day was upon us.

Friday 25 December A quiet day with the ship sailing herself and reasonably steady, such that we could eat down below together. Peter prepared our festive dinner which was very successful. Tomato juice, curry and rice and Christmas pudding with rum sauce, well washed down with red wine.

During the afternoon we were treated to a magnificent display of bottlenose dolphins completely surrounding the boat in large numbers, living up to their universal reputation of the 'friendly dolphin'. We welcomed their company on this special day.

The dolphin act was followed a day or two later with a *pas de deux* by a pair of humpback whales. One could be clearly seen heading for us on our starboard beam on a collision course, which caused us some concern – a lot, in fact – but it cleared our bows with little to spare and proceeded on its way. We then saw what was presumably its mate coming up fast from dead astern directly in line with us. If there had been room for doubt about the first one colliding with us, there was none about this one. It was going to strike us. We had a dangerous situation on our hands. Stories abound of boats being attacked and destroyed by whales, a famous example being the sinking of Dougal Robertson's *Lucette* 200 miles west of the Galápagos, in waters not too far from where we were being threatened. He described it all too vividly in his widely read book, *Survive the Savage Sea*, and subsequently the incident was relived by his son Douglas in *The Last Voyage of the Lucette*. As we watched helplessly whilst that great animal closed us, it suddenly for no known reason sounded, its great fluked tail lifting up clear of the sea with foam-streaked water streaming off it. Talking about it afterwards we surmised that what might have happened was that its skin had brushed against the rotating log line, which was always towing astern to tell us our distance run, alarming the whale such that it dived. Whatever the reason it had been a frightening moment: the Robertsons' whales were orcas, known widely as killer whales. The humpbacks, in contrast, are a species more popularly known for their apparent playfulness than aggression, Herman Melville referring to them as being 'the most gamesome and light-hearted of all whales'. Perhaps our whales just wanted to be friendly but it did not seem quite like that to us.

A feature of all this agony in working to windward was frequent sail changing to help the boat's performance. To this effect we used the jib topsail to fill in the fore triangle above the working jib, but more frequently we set the Yankee jib. With its luff reaching from bowsprit end to masthead it gave a significant boost to boat speed. The downside was that the boat would not point quite as high into the wind. This posed a dilemma. We relied on 'gut feel' and the 'feel-good factor'. If the bubbles going past our sides broke out of their lethargy under the Yankee, we would leave it set to keep on doing its bit.

Despite our painfully slow progress, with the feeling at times we would never get there, we finally got within striking distance of those bewitched, elusive islands, but we were harbouring a nagging uncertainty. We could miss them altogether. The problem was the strong current, the Humboldt, sweeping across the archipelago with its general drift north-west. If we got too far to the north and west it would be a difficult task indeed, if not impossible, to sail back against a knot and a half, at least, of current and the light south-east trade wind combined. Our little engine would not have been man enough to make the difference. If we had found ourselves in such a predicament it would not have been too disastrous, just so disappointing, as we had set our hearts on experiencing the Galápagos. It would have meant putting the helm up, freeing sheets and embarking on the 3,000 mile run to the Marquesas Islands.

The other principal cause for concern was: where were we exactly? For the past few days the heavenly bodies as well as the horizon had been indistinct with haze, inhibiting the taking of reliable sextant sun or star sights. It had been a case of grabbing each opportunity as it presented itself to snatch an observation. However, as it transpired, all was well.

Thursday 7 January Position 0° 12′S 88° 45′W. Obtained a good position, the sun behaving for once and expect to pick up land from midday onwards. We have crossed the Equator with islands of the archipelago now safely down to leeward, albeit way out of sight. The horizon once again hazy I had given up hope of seeing anything when I saw a lump of land right where Chatham Island should have been. A relieved navigator.

Despite this being a first time crossing of the line for Peter, we had decided against inviting King Neptune on board for us to pay due homage. He can be a little hard to take when afforded the full ceremony. The wind, remaining true to form, with no hint of a land breeze coming in, failed during the night. With the sea also reverting to glass-like mode we were visited at first light by a sea lion. They are renowned for their inquisitiveness, particularly the females and the young, the bulls tending to display machismo and being more stand-offish. We took it our friend was a female and obviously extremely curious about us, coming right alongside to find out more. There was no fear.

Our long-awaited objective now lay before us. The name *Galápagos*, Spanish for tortoises, had been bestowed on the islanders by a Flemish cartographer in 1574 when they first featured on any map. He had picked up reference to tortoises abounding on the islands in the writings of Tomás, Bishop of Panama, the first man to land on the group. Also dating back from those early days was the other competing name of *Las Encantadas*, which means either 'bewitched' or 'enchanted'. Both descriptions we were to find relevant.

Before a capricious breeze we worked down the coast, the stark bareness of the land revealing its volcanic origins. It appeared sterile and unsupportive of any life. We were now in hot pursuit of Charles Darwin. This was the first island he visited in the archipelago, and with a pen more descriptive than mine he gives his impressions:

17 September 1835 In the morning we landed on Chatham Island, which, like the others, rises with a tame and rounded outline, broken here and there by scattered hillocks, the remains of former craters. Nothing could be less inviting than the first appearance. A broken field of black basaltic lava, thrown into the most rugged waves and crossed by great fissures, is everywhere covered by stunted, sunburnt brushwood, which shows little signs of life.

In the nigh on 120 years that had elapsed between the visits of HMS *Beagle* and SV *Tern II* there had been no change. For us it was Friday 8 January 1954.

1200 Position Wreck Bay bearing 190° Distance 10 miles. Wind light SW.
1700 Anchored in 4½ fathoms in Wreck Bay. Veered 22 fathoms of cable.

We had arrived in Las Encantadas, for me an occasion of particular significance. A deep-seated wish from boyhood had been fulfilled.

Wreck Bay, no doubt enjoying the stature associated with being the port of entry for the Archipiélago de Colón, was in reality a funny little place. It boasted a couple of shops in what constituted the main street, this being the beach. Also in the main street was a bar which additionally served food of the more basic kind, with no claims to *haute cuisine*. Illumination was provided by a crude system of electric lighting from a generator somewhere, some dubious-looking wires hanging in festoons between the buildings. We understood the place had 'come on' as a result of World War II when the US

Navy had taken an interest in the islands. The Americans had been concerned that enemy forces would use the islands as a base from which to threaten the Pacific end of the Panama Canal and the shipping using it. Another legacy of those days was that the 'town' did have running water via a pipeline running down from the hills behind, ending up along the rather rickety and not quite straight wooden jetty jutting out from the beach, the high street, the only one.

We couldn't help but notice, as we had come in to anchor, the highly visible Ecuadorian flag of impressive dimensions flying from a particularly tall flagpole. It seems to be universally a common feature of officialdom in more remote places that the size of the national flag on display is in inverse proportion to the size of the location. This particular national flag was certainly important to Wreck Bay bureaucracy, as we were soon to find out. Almost as soon as our anchor went down we were visited by that bureaucracy, who came off in a small powerboat with the Ecuadorian ensign prominently waving at the stern. The three men in this particular boat were the port captain, customs officer and the health official. They were not interested in such boring things as entry visas, what, if anything, we had to declare, or the state of our health. What they were interested to know was why we were insulting their country by not displaying an Ecuadorian courtesy flag. We found it hard to come up with an answer that did not make matters worse. It had simply not occurred to me to have one, not thinking it relevant in such an out-of-the-way spot. To have admitted this would have been tantamount to saying they were not important. We had to do some grovelling to placate them, the process of ingratiating ourselves being not a little helped by several glasses of rum. Rum, we were finding, was frequently the preferred choice over whisky. With the trio's honour now once more intact we parted on the best of terms, with an invitation from the port captain, alias resident naval officer, to have refreshments with him and his wife next day in the naval base. Until he pointed out its whereabouts further along the front, we had not been aware of its existence.

We were ashore that evening, strolling, or rather stumbling, along the main street, the sand soft under our feet, until we found the bar. At first we couldn't see anything, the interior being so dim, but as our eyes adjusted, what was revealed was a small room with a few tables occupied with what were evidently local men. No women. We took the one remaining free table, ordered wine and absorbed the scene. It was then we noticed that at a table against the back wall there was, in fact, one woman. With her was a group of pretty tough-looking men. They looked like what we thought gauchos would look like, and that was more or less what they were, as it transpired. The woman was white and quite heavily made up, middle-aged, good-looking and slightly plumpish. She was smartly dressed in a white shirt, riding breeches and tall boots and looked totally out of place in that rough spot; but she wasn't. In fact, she was completely at home. This was the legendary Karin, known, admired and loved by the small-boat voyagers who had called at Chatham Island over the last 25 years. I had first read about her in *Deep Water and Shoal*. Robinson was amongst the first to have fallen under her spell, and she was another reason why I had so wanted to come to the Galápagos. She beckoned us over to join her table. It was a memorable evening with a remarkable woman. I was not much older than Robinson when he had known her, and although she had moved on a generation or so I could share his feelings. Her English was good, still with her Norwegian accent, and she wanted to talk, the conservation flowing about her life in this strange, lonely, isolated and largely unknown part of the world. With the talk flowed the wine. She invited us to visit her in her home in the family-run settlement of Progresso, 5 miles away up in the hills behind Wreck Bay. She was only down for the night and would be returning next day on horseback with her escort of rough, tough and devoted *hombres*. It had been such a stroke of luck that our visits had coincided.

Robinson has left us a very human record of Karin, with whom it is evident a close relationship had developed. It would have been surprising if this had been otherwise. She was an attractive girl of 20 and he a personable young man of 28.

'Everyone who has visited the Galápagos during the last few years has come away with a vision. That vision is Karin. I fell in love with Karin – but so have others of our fortunate few.

Karin is one of the Norwegian pioneers who came in 1926 to form a colony on San Cristóbal. Theirs is the tragic story of a little group who emigrated with their all, in the treacherous 1,000-ton concrete boat which they called *Albemarle*, from their native land to the far-off Galápagos. They failed, through lack of co-operation and the necessary money, to hold out for the four or five years necessary to get things on a paying basis.

There were 80 of them, 56 men and the rest women and children. They brought with them all their possessions, furniture, farming implements, fishing material and even a Ford tractor and wagons.

Only a few of the cream stayed when the others gave up. The *Albemarle* was sold in Panama to a Colombian by a party that cheated them out of a goodly part of the money received for it. The other things were sold to Ecuadorians, also at great loss. When *Svaap* arrived at San Cristóbal there were only 14 of them left. Four of these left on the Cobos schooner a few days later, and by now I think only Karin and her family remain.

Karin lives in a neat little board shack miles back in the mountains. There, high in the hills above Progresso, with only a mysterious hermit nearby, the girl Karin tills the land with a handful of cut-throat peons and ex-convicts. She rides among them, unafraid of their great knives and machetes, with a tiny gun in her pocket. They obey her every order.

What mixture of bloods can have produced such a person – completely and utterly feminine – is hard to imagine. She is not brave – the word is futile – she is heroic.'

San Cristóbal started its inhabited life as an Ecuadorian penal colony. The governor, Cobos by name, a particularly cruel individual, ended up by being hacked to death by those in his charge. The Ecuadorian government abandoned the settlement idea and gave the island to the son, Manuel, who continued to rule it under a totalitarian, feudal system. Such was the setting when Robinson visited the Cobos family seat in Progresso, staying there as the guest of Manuel, during which time he met Karin. She subsequently married into the family, and when Peter and I met her she was Karin Cobos, with her own family of three sons and two daughters. There was something of a mystery about her husband's whereabouts. He was apparently on another island engaged on government business, but when later we visited Indefatigable Island, his name was not mentioned. To our knowledge, the only other inhabited island was Floreana, on which dwelt the Wittmers. Whatever the situation, Karin was, single-handedly, running the property, farming the land, battling with the dubious hand of the bureaucracy and held undisputed authority over her workers. We could see that for ourselves when we were with them in the bar.

We followed up on the invitation of Commandante Northia and took tea, or the next best equivalent to that ritual, in his residence in the naval base, which had been constructed in wartime years by the US Navy. We noted the enduring American legacy, the few Ecuadorian Navy sailors around wearing US-style uniforms, albeit with a somewhat more relaxed dress code. There was a general air of informality throughout the base, with the faint suggestion of a stage setting for HMS *Pinafore*. There was, however, one outstanding feature to which our attention had been drawn with something akin to pride.

'Señores, you must look at Charlie Darwin! He is over there.'

The great man was still on the scene where he had first begun to think seriously about our origins. It was in this weird region, populated by dragon-like creatures and species of life within which there were so many variations, that suspicion first entered his mind that what he had been brought up to believe as the indisputable truth about creation was perhaps not true. There he was, a weathering bust residing on a cracked concrete plinth. The near godless scientist Darwin and the near goddess Diana, Princess of Wales, must be the two English persons most widely known on this planet.

We were warmly received by the *commandante* and his spouse. In the course of conversation it emerged they had a small household problem. Could we help out with a 'loan'? Peter and I looked at each other. Not in money terms, they hastened to assure us, but in victuals. For ongoing supplies of food produce not grown on the island they were dependent on the rather infrequent steamer service from Guayaquil, away on the mainland. Normally this was not a problem, but at the moment they were running a little short of staple items such as coffee, sugar and the like. Could we assist? Yes we could. We were well stocked. On returning on board we pulled out what they wanted from the stock stowed in the forepeak, and now under the pile of mailbags, the commodities having been packed in large sealed biscuit tins when we had stored in Plymouth. When later these were delivered ashore, the consignment was accompanied by our dirty laundry, which our hostess had insisted on washing and ironing.

Our plan for the following day had been a visit to Progresso, a pilgrimage in effect following in the steps of our predecessors to that shrine. However, that was not to be. Peter was overtaken with the first really bad attack of asthma. There was, of course, no complaining by him but he was in some considerable distress. There was no way he could have made that trip *arriba*. This Spanish word, meaning 'above', was, we were to find, to be the term universally used when referring to the upper reaches of the islands. These being on the higher slopes, they were much of the time lying in mist and cloud, as a result of which they were greener and more fertile than the lower sun-baked slopes with their sparse growth. Although it was not much more than 5 miles to where Karin lived, it was, we gathered, 5 miles of hard going. Both the Smeetons and Victor Clark made the trek, and from their observations it had either to be on foot or preferably on the back of a horse, this being the way Karin herself did it. We would have made hard work of that journey had we tackled it.

It was, for me, a cause for lingering regret that I had not met Karin again and seen where she had carved out such a unique and extraordinary lifestyle under almost impossible circumstances.

The enforced rest enabled Peter to shake off his disability, which caused him so much debilitation on the occasions when it struck him, and it was now time for us to leave, but not before a last drink in the pub. We were joined by a local barfly. He said his name was Fred. Despite this, we had a language problem but gathered he was frustrated at the life, or rather lack of it, in Wreck Bay. He had heard of Tahiti and the delights on offer there. He was keen to experience these. We pieced together what he was saying to us.

'Señores, take me, *por favor*. I want better *vida*.' Life in Wreck Bay was *no bueno*.

This was a replay of what we had experienced with Juan in Las Palmas, but we were infinitely more sympathetic to Juan, who had been seeking satisfaction in other ways in wanting to go to America. It was much more difficult to get the message across to Fred.

Next morning at 0700 we weighed for Academy Bay. The passage across to Indefatigable Island was leisurely and relaxed, notwithstanding the fact that the warm south-east trade wind was somewhat fickle and uncertain. It was gentle sailing under spinnaker until late evening when the breeze took itself elsewhere, leaving us totally becalmed, lasting until the early hours of the next morning. Lowering the mainsail to stop it jerking and snatching at its boom lacing and worrying at the hoops on the mast, the crew of *Tern* turned in. The lightest of winds putting in a reappearance at breakfast time, and with the mainsail reset, we edged towards the land. Our slow progress was obviously under close observation, as come mid-morning a small powerboat came out and took us in tow for us to anchor at lunchtime in Academy Bay. Our 'rescuer' was Gus Angermeyer, one of the leading lights, as we were to find out, in the settlement's community. It was our good fortune to see a lot of him and his charismatic elder brother, Carl, during our stay.

That evening was open house. The Angermeyer brothers and Sandy Sanderson came on board, soon to be joined by a fleet of small boats secured astern. The mail boat was in! It was a red-letter day. It was particularly gratifying for us to see the very evident pleasure evinced by those around us in re-establishing contact with their families and connections in places so far away. It made us feel good.

A little earlier we had received another visitor.

Met on arrival by the port captain, who came off in a rowing boat; cursorily looked at our papers but seemed more interested in acquiring magazines which we had been given in Balboa and Wreck Bay. What an absurdity sporting such a man in a place like this!

Our time in the community was happy, with fulfilling days and the stay far too short. We were warmly welcomed and rapidly came under the spell of the island's magic, to harmonise with the inhabitants' philosophy which saw no point in struggling in the outside world with all its social problems, pressures and insecurities. Why should one, they said, when it was so easy to live a satisfying self-made life with an excellent climate and plenty of food? We talked, ate and drank with the locals, ashore and aboard *Tern*, fished, trekked up into the mists and greenery of *arriba*, mixing with Darwin's 'reptilian zoology' of fearless iguanas, swam and relaxed in the sun, with the temptation getting stronger of wanting to stay for ever. However, we were still able to see there could be flaws in this existence, such as the situation where one of our hostesses, we were quite openly told, had of necessity, due to a woman shortage, been obliged, or perhaps coerced, to circulate within a group as wife to each unattached male in turn. We had been accepted into the community to the extent that we were made privy to the local gossip.

It has to be accepted, as in all collections of human beings, that there is a serpent in Eden. A woman on her own confided in us she was having an ongoing problem with her next-door neighbour, a single male. A voyeur, it would appear. He was given to peering through her bathroom on inappropriate occasions. Her protestations were ignored. She seemed to be seeking our assistance in helping with this matter, even to the extent of suggesting a demonstration to illustrate her cause for complaint. As interesting as this might have been, we felt it perhaps better that we did not become too closely involved.

The Angermeyers were 'top table', the royal family of Indefatigable Island, talented, charming, interesting and sociable. Carl, the 'elder' in the family, good-looking with considerable popular appeal, such that he could have been something of a film celebrity, certainly conveyed the impression of being matinee idol material. In fact, such status, we were to learn, might well have happened. Shortly after the end of the war he had made a brief visit to America via a vessel that had called at Academy Bay. Whilst in the States he was induced to undergo a film test which had, it seemed, gone well enough for the prospect of an offer likely to be forthcoming. However, it appeared he did not want to live in a world of tinsel, preferring the company of the iguanas of Las Encantadas to the lounge lizards of Hollywood.

Originally there had been five brothers who, fearing for their future, had fled Nazi Germany in the mid 1930s, sailing off in a big, heavy ketch, not quite sure where to go. They knew vaguely of the Galápagos and finally ended up there, in the pot into which flowed others like them who did not know where their niche in life lay. On their way to freedom, as they saw it, they had suffered near shipwreck off the Cornish coast but eventually were dumped on the lonely foreshore of Academy Bay. There Carl, Gus and Fritz had stayed, one brother having returned home and the other dying, a little before we arrived.

Carl was married to Marga, and the exoticism, a feature of the Angermeyers, did not stop there. She had been married before and her daughter from the previous relationship had married Fritz. Miles Smeeton, visiting Academy Bay in *Tzu Hang* just before us, had also been intrigued by the unusual affairs of an unusual family.

'The relationship between Carl and Franz [Fritz] was rather intricate, as Carl had married a European woman from Academy Bay, and Fritz had married her daughter, so that Carl was the father-in-law of his younger brother.'

Both Carl and Gus were married and lived 'up the hill' on Angermeyer Point, off which we were anchored, in somewhat basic shacks which they had built themselves. We were invited to Carl's for tea, served by a gracious hostess in a rudimentary setting. It was an unreal experience. On the table was a lace tablecloth with a fine bone china tea set, with elegant teapot, milk jug, sugar bowl and all that goes with a formal afternoon tea occasion. On side plates little cakes were served. It was a 'genteel' occasion in such unlikely surroundings. We had been very honoured.

Carl was in the process of 'redecorating' and earlier in the day he had rowed out to raise with us a difficulty he was having with painting the outside of the dwelling.

'My old paintbrush has given up. I am having to use one I made from the end of my donkey's tail. It is hard to get a good finish with it. Could you help by selling me a paintbrush if you have one to spare?' We were only too happy to present him with a new large brush from our ship's stores.

We were so enjoying the companionship and friendship extended to us. Gus, a warm, friendly man, took us lobster fishing and he knew what he was about. We gathered in two dozen, which we salted down under his direction. The principal source of income, if not the only one, for the Angermeyers and many of the others in the community was catching fish, drying it and exporting through Wreck Bay to the mainland of Ecuador. Apparently, the customers were church bodies who used it on religious occasions. He was keen to introduce us to sea turtle hunting, which we assumed they normally did purely for food. The result was the capture of a large one. Even though the meat would have been welcome in the family larder, Gus was in total accord that we could not kill it in cold blood. We put it back on its feet and away it went at high speed, reminiscent of the performance turned in by its brother – or was it sister? – on our previous encounter at sea on our way down from Balboa.

Around in the next bay from Angermeyer Point lived an American couple, the Divines. Hot on the heels of our arrival in the anchorage, Bud came on board for a chat and to invite us to lunch with him and his attractive wife. Their house was very pleasant and so were they. Practical but bookish, they seemed to us to be just a little out of setting in the environment in which they had chosen to hide themselves away. However, that was one of the charms of the place, its inhabitants being of such differing backgrounds, combining varying degrees of culture and sophistication with beachcombing.

With Sandy there were frequent visit exchanges, and with him we swapped books, freshening up our respective libraries. We did this throughout the trip and certainly did not arrive in New Zealand with any of the books we had on board when we left England. He obviously welcomed our company and many hours were spent just talking. His was a lonely existence but he was not lonely. That was the way he wanted to live his life. The days slipped past and I did not want our stay to end. I recorded the sentiment:

It is a very lovely place and filled with warm, charming people.

Our pursuit of Darwin was nearing its completion. Around us, almost within arm's reach and still completely tame, were the same species of the animal world which had so fascinated him. Having been witness to what he had seen, it would seem not inappropriate to quote from his diary an observation made of the tortoise, or rather turtle, which had given its name to the Galápagos Islands.

'We will now return to the order of reptiles, which gives the most striking character to the zoology of these islands. The species are not numerous, but the numbers of individuals of each species are extraordinarily great.

I will describe first the habits of the tortoise. These animals are found, I believe, on all the islands of the archipelago; certainly on the greater number. They frequent in preference the high, damp parts, but they likewise live in the lower and arid districts. I have shown how very numerous they must be. Some grow to an immense size: Mr Lawson, an Englishman, and vice-governor of the colony, told us that he had seen several so large that it required six or eight men to lift them from the ground; and that some had afforded as much as two pounds of meat.'

The observations he made of the wildlife peculiar to the Galápagos were, of course, to lead to the tortuous intellectual path which culminated in the *Theory of Organic Evolution*. The fact, as he pointed out, that life exists in enormously different varieties, each of which has adapted to its particular environment, was proof, claimed the evolutionists, that there had not been a vast number of separate, immutable creations at the beginning of time, but a process of gradual change or, in other words, evolution. Not so, said the creationists. The theory did not explain the origin of all this life in the very beginning. It must have come from somewhere in the first place. It had to have been created. This could only have been done by a superior being. Here were Peter and I, in the birthplace of the ensuing titanic struggle between the two factions, which continues through to the present day.

It all centred on a humble little bird. Darwin noticed something special about finches in the Galápagos, and study of them revealed the inescapable fact that there were different kinds on different islands, and it was evident they had adapted to suit the environment peculiar to each island. All 13 species he saw had, it appeared, descended from the original species but now differed from it, particularly their beaks, which were, as Darwin wrote, 'modified for different ends.' In other words, the finch variants had evolved to further their survival on their particular island and had not been created. The Book of Genesis had to be wrong! It took Darwin some time to accept this, but his erstwhile captain and friend, FitzRoy, never did, his ensuing life being one of torment whilst he wrestled with the conflict between what his intellect was telling him and the anchor that was his faith. Peace in the end was only to come with death. Tragically this was self-induced. When Darwin had embarked in *Beagle* he, like most of his contemporaries, believed in the 'immutability of the species', and Genesis was the unassailable, universal truth. It was likewise for FitzRoy, and his distress could well have been exemplified by the observation of John K Galbraith: 'It is a far, far better thing to have a firm anchor in nonsense than to put out on the troubled seas of thought.' However, notwithstanding all this, like Darwin, we had to move on. He had wanted to get home, and now so, of necessity, did we.

There had been quite a change in the boat's internal arrangement during our stay. The forecastle, which on our arrival had been full of parcels and mailbags, was now once more full, this time with bread, fruit and vegetables, much of it donated. On the forthcoming passage to the Marquesas we were to eat 'bananas and pineapples till we looked like them'. All had been brought down from *arriba*, the produce from which was so abundant as to be growing almost out of control. It was all so good.

Sunday 17 January Forenoon spent in preparing for sea.

Gus, Carl and Sandy came out to say their farewells. A great empathy has built up between us.

1400 Weighed and got under way under jib, staysail, main and topsail. Wind light SSE. Bright and sunny.

God how I hate leaving this place! It is with very real regret that I see each house, which became so well known in such a short time, one by one disappear from view behind the point. I can never come back!

The fame of the islands was founded upon one thing: they were infinitely strange, unlike any other islands in the world. No one who ever went there ever forgot them.

HERMAN MELVILLE

Chapter Eight

Into the South Seas

*Eight degrees south and the day two hours
a-coming. The interval was passed on deck
in the silence of expectation, the customary
thrill of landfall heightened by the strangeness
of the shores that were now approaching.
Slowly the Marquesas took shape.*

ROBERT LOUIS STEVENSON

'How's our little friend this morning?'
'Hasn't moved and I am rather worried about him. Still won't take
any nourishment. Tried him with some different crumbs this time, and a
little water, but not interested. Just sat close to me when I went up forward
to be with him.'

A few days out from Academy Bay our visitor had, literally out of
the blue, made a landing on our foredeck, quite unafraid and seemingly
exhausted. Over the next few days it became part of our world and the
focus of our attention. We wished we could have done something for it
but recognized nature was having its way with one of its own. There was
no place for us in that world, apart from providing a place of rest. To our
unesoteric eye it could have been a member of the finch genus, a land bird,
in which case the longer-term prognosis was not good. If our identification
was correct, the little bird had been blown downwind on the trade wind,
against which it would not have had the strength to get back home again.
The nearest attainable refuge lay in the Marquesas over 2,000 miles away
down to leeward. Too far for any chance of survival, we feared.

Then one morning came the inevitable announcement.

'He has gone! At daybreak, when I went forward to have a look, there
was no sign.'

We surprised ourselves at the sadness we felt. Life at sea was so simple,
so uncluttered by the trappings that are integral with shoreside living in the
hurry, hurry world of today, that the simplest of events like this was not just
a basic, matter-of-fact experience. It meant more. Part of the life we were
living had gone.

If our companion had indeed been a native of the Galápagos, it would have explained why it would sit with us showing no concern. The birds, like all of the wildlife of the archipelago, with so little exposure to predators, including the human kind, had no fear. There had been a link between us. We were both essentially land animals, albeit from an originally aquatic ancestry, and as such out of our depth, literally, in surroundings totally alien to us. We were the minutest of specks sitting on top of an enormous volume of water at the bottom of which was an unknown world, completely devoid of light and occupied by creatures beyond anything we could imagine. Beneath us were depths of 35,000 feet or more, 5,000 feet greater than the height of Everest. The means of support for the continued existence of one bird and two men were so vulnerable and so insignificant in such a panorama that the thought of sinking down through this vast abyss to total black oblivion was frightening to contemplate.

Progress from Academy Bay had been painstakingly slow, with the lightest of winds from east of south bringing with them slight seas which had provided a stable platform for our companion. Las Encantadas had kept their hold on us. They evidently did not want us to leave their shores, as they were to demonstrate. *Tern* came close, far too close for comfort, to leaving her remains on them. It was a replay of the not infrequent scenario of no wind and no engine. Now into January, the Galápagos climate was entering the wet, warm season, with a lightening of the trade wind wafting through the islands and with the currents swirling amongst them, being subject to change in their general drift. At this time of year the usually dominant Humboldt Current, or if one prefers it the Peru Current, is upset by a strong flow coming down from the Gulf of Panama. The net effect of these influences is to create uncertain conditions for sailing. Such was our experience as we attempted to clear the southern, broken, rock-bound shoreline of Albemarle Island, known today as Isabela. After a night of uncertain winds, conspicuous for their absence much of the time, we had ended up largely at the mercy of the current. We tried falling back on the engine. It started, stopped, started again, then went into a sulk, evidently not happy with the state of health of its fuel system, once again contaminated with paraffin. We let it rest in peace to enjoy its sulks.

Come the morning, Brattle Island, otherwise known as Tortuga, off the south-eastern coast of Albemarle, was close aboard, with the width of clear water between us closing at an alarming rate. The wind had chosen to leave us completely. Back to the engine once more, and now with a sense of considerable urgency pressing down upon us. Repeated flushings through of the fuel system brought no response. The sea, reaching up to the foreshore, which was now looming perilously close, was too deep to anchor. Our only resource left was to get the dinghy, lashed upside down over the skylight, over the side to try to pull *Tern* clear. About this we were not too optimistic, in view of the strength of the current, and a sense of desperation was now starting to envelop us. It was at this moment that the witch, in whose dominion these bewitched islands lay, relented and let us go. A gentle breeze rippled across the completely smooth surface of the sea and we gathered way. We were free from Las Encantadas.

The road to the Marquesas now safely opened up clear ahead, we hove to for a swim to reinvigorate and de-stress ourselves. Around us were whales blowing, paying no attention at all to us – two completely different planetary species at peace with each other, with no sense of concern in either party and each species totally to itself.

In the early hours of the following morning we were treated to a heavenly extravaganza – a total lunar eclipse. It was an unexpected delight as *The Nautical Almanac* does not list the phenomenon, it being of no particular navigational interest. The ephemeris devotes a couple of pages to solar eclipses but not those for the moon, so it came as an enjoyable surprise to watch the event unfold. The setting was perfect. Clear skies, uncontaminated by artificially induced light pollution, which we would have had if we had been onshore, with a smooth surface to the sea reflecting the brilliant shining path of the moon beaming towards us. From our grandstand view we watched the slow progression in sharp relief of the Earth's shadow across the amazingly brilliant surface of the full moon. As it did so, the shining white surface gave way to a warm, copper glow covering the lunar face. Then slowly the process was reversed, as the shadow moved on and the brilliance of the moon started to emerge again as the startlingly bright arc of the rim reappeared.

Although we understood the scientific reason for what we were witnessing, we still had a feeling of awe. To have observed it without the benefit of this knowledge the spectacle would have been even more awesome, almost to the extent of fear. It is on record that Christopher Columbus 'in 1504, landing in Jamaica and, wanting help from the natives, announced he would darken the moon. And, lo, it darkened.' Western knowledge of astronomy was such that he knew a lunar eclipse was due, and the trick worked with dramatic effect.

Thursday 21 January Noon OP 02° 00′S 93° 40′W. Course 235°C. Weather: Bright and sunny. Very hot. Sea: Calm. Wind: Light S. Day's run: 35 M.

Ship under all plain sail plus balloon foresail, Yankee jib and main topsail.

Wind has been tricky all day, mainly S or SSE and very light. The rising and setting of the sun kills it and it takes several hours before there is any sign of it returning.

Big haircutting operation in the forenoon. Peter seems better at it than I but fortunately we can't see our rear views.

Attacked, or so it seemed, by orca whales in the afternoon, one under the counter and two under the bows. No impact but quite alarming. Considered possibility of starting the engine to frighten them off but decided this might have made matters worse, the sudden noise making them cross.

Trade wind clouds about. With luck we may be entering a new phase in the passage. They are what we want.

Obtained a time signal at supper time from the BBC with very clear reception. Never know with our radio. Tends to the temperamental and like the engine has spells of the sulks.

Apart from the lack of wind the evening was perfect. The sun on setting left a copper sheen on the surface of the sea with the whole western sky a gentle, light shade of pink. Then the moon came up with a brilliant path across the rippled water stretching up to and over us, lighting up everything in and around the boat like day.

The following day, despite the wind encouragingly picking up to a moderate S by E, which lifted our day's run to 110 miles, our way of life took a turn for the worse. Peter had a particularly bad attack of asthma. This affliction tended to come on without warning and completely laid him low, leaving him with no option but to attempt to find refuge in his bunk. This meant I had to engage full-time in the sailing of the boat. During the periods I could get her to sail herself I would grab catnaps, and when this gave inadequate sleeping time it would be necessary to heave to with the helm lashed. I could then benefit from longer spells of essential, uninterrupted sleep. Fortunately, we were still under fore-and-aft rig, with weather and sea conditions helpfully reasonably benign.

Although Peter had come provided with medication, he found the only really effective treatment was fasting and resting with plenty of fresh air. This meant he could not get any real relief in his bunk and he had to get out on deck to take up a position on the foredeck with his back against the mast. Here, with brief spells back in his bunk when exhaustion overtook him, he coped with his misery for five long days. He was in great distress but never complained, and I admired enormously how well he handled it all. However, the strain was taking its toll on both of us.

Sunday 24 January 2000 Peter still bad with his asthma and myself quite worn out, with a headache from lack of sleep.

Hove-to on the port tack. Crew of *Tern II* turned in with an attempt to get some sleep.

We were over the worst as next day saw an improvement all round. Peter was coming out of the attack, so much so he picked up his watch again. This in itself speeded up the recovery process, as throughout his ordeal he had hated not pulling his weight. Although the wind did not correspondingly improve its performance, remaining stubbornly light in the SSE, our day's run managed to struggle up to 95 miles. However, we were still not back to the good life.

Tuesday Wind dropped during the night and we had the usual accompaniment of the sound of jerking sails and slatting gear. These calm periods are such a curse, making us feel so helpless. Peter takes it all so well, which is so much to his credit as his asthma is still hanging on, but I am afraid I lose control and just about get beside myself with irrational rage and frustration. Perhaps tiredness has something to do with it.

Three days later it all looked so different.

Friday 1700 All's well, wind freshening from SSE. Days' runs have risen now to around 130 miles. Our spirits have risen accordingly.

Passed the first 1,000 mile position and somewhat of no particular relevance crossed the magnetic equator at the same time.

Monday 01 February A landmark day. Crossed the halfway line, going off the American chart Sheet 1 of the Pacific Ocean, which had been showing on it our departure point of the Galápagos. Changed over to the Admiralty Pacific South East sheet which brought up the Marquesas Islands and lost the Galápagos. Big boost to morale to see our objective now on the chart ahead of us and getting closer as the daily position plottings march towards it.

Dropped the fore-and-aft working rig of main and headsails. Hoisted the squaresail and raffee. Drawing well with the wind continuing to back further to east of south. The trades are now upon us and very welcome they are too.

Served a tot of rum (perhaps a little heavy-handed) to all hands.

At the end of the week there occurred another memorable day but for an altogether different reason. I fell overboard.

Friday 05 February Noon OP 06° 57′S 121° 40′W. Weather: Bright and sunny. Very hot. Short breaking sea from SE. Wind: Moderate ESE.
Course 260° C. Day's run 130 M. Ship under squaresail and raffee.

The day had started well enough with 'hands to bathe' dunking from the end of the bowsprit, always an enjoyable refreshing treat. In the afternoon it was pleasant sailing. Peter was soundly asleep below and I was having an easy time on the tiller with the boat holding a steady course, marred only by the occasional lurch down to leeward. The wind being broad on the quarter, the boat's motion running before these south-east trades was not so subject to the incessant rolling we had endured in the north-east trades. Life was, as a result, more congenial on deck and below. *Tern* was no longer throwing water over the helmsman, and the watch below was getting more restful sleep.

Responding to the call of nature, and lashing the tiller, I went forward to attend to that call. Leaning my shoulder against the after lee shroud left both hands free for the operation. This was the moment for one of those occasional lurches to happen. My shoulder slipping off the shroud, I found myself in slow motion pitching head first into the water sluicing along the topsides. Landing flat on the water, I twisted and tried to swim back to catch hold of the gunwale, but it was just out of reach and moving fast past my outstretched hands. Now left swimming off *Tern*'s rapidly receding stern, the gap widening fast between me and my sole life support system, the realisation undramatically flooded over me, pragmatically and quite matter of fact, that I was going to drown. It was as if I were just a witness to a scene of which I was not part. I was calling out to Peter but I knew that, snugged down, deeply asleep in his sleeping bag, he would not hear me over the sound of wind and rushing water. It was at that moment I remembered the 'fish'. Trailing for some way astern of the boat was the thin plaited line that held at its end a metal, finned rotator, the fish, which in turn rotated the line to give a reading on a dial mechanism mounted on the boat's stern, the whole device being known as Walker's Patent Log. Its function was the determination of distance run through the water. It was to save my life. My only hope now was to get across to where the log line was trailing and hang on to it. I thought the line might possibly take my weight but I was not sure if the mounting on the deck would be able to accommodate the sudden shock of my deadweight abruptly coming on to it. I also had to be quick to catch the line running out to the fish before the whole lot went past and disappeared ahead, taking my only hope of survival with it. I made it. Letting it slip through my hands, I slowly tightened my grip on the twisting line to avoid any sudden load as my weight came on it. Everything held, and I was now safe and once more connected with my sanctuary. *Tern* had been doing the best part of 6 knots when I went over the side, and although her speed had slowed with me in tow, the line was cutting into my hands and my head frequently dragged under water. The question wa: how long could I hold on until the boat wandered off course and stopped by eventually coming head-to-wind, thereby bringing the squaresail and raffee flat aback, or until such time as Peter woke up? By great good fortune I did not have long to wait. I told myself I could see, although most probably it was just wishful thinking, *Tern* starting to veer up to windward, and almost at the same time Peter appeared in the cockpit. I was saved. He said afterwards he did not know why he had woken from such a deep sleep. Perhaps it was a change in the boat's motion as she had slowed with my load on her, or was it something else? He knew not what, he said, but I suspect he had a private conviction. He was, I knew, a believer, possessing a strong faith. Unlashing the tiller, he brought the boat to the wind and laid the sails to the mast.

Slowly hauling me in, hand over hand, he got me under the counter and lowered a bight of rope over the side such that, with his help, I was able to drag myself over the toe rail on to the afterdeck. Neither of us said anything. Peter got *Tern* sailing again and whilst I climbed out of my dripping gear he broke out the rum bottle.

It was only some time later that Peter spoke of his shock when he emerged into the cockpit and, looking round, saw no one. He felt so desperately alone until he saw me way astern being towed, half submerged but still part of his existence.

Next day we passed the 'last thousand to go' mark. The wind had inconveniently hauled round to ENE and become lighter, creating the conditions for an unwelcome return to rolling and an unstable platform which reinforced the need to heed the lesson of the day before. Belatedly we now rigged waist-high lifelines along the sidedecks and, moreover, agreed that in future, when alone on deck, we would not leave the cockpit without tying a line around our waists with the tail secured to a nearby fitting on deck. We were two chastened men. We were more or less to obey this agreed discipline from then onwards, but to this day I remain unconvinced about the merits of the present-day practice of religiously 'hooking on' whenever one sets foot on deck in the open air. Safety first in the modern world is all pervading, with life jackets, lifelines and deck jackstays integral with going to sea in small boats. There is, however, a downside to this philosophy. In *Tern*, as we were not in possession of any of this gear, we would usually make sure we were following the old sea rule of 'one hand for the ship and one for oneself'. We watched our step, literally, when moving about the deck whilst engaged in 'the ordinary practice of seamen', in the words of the ColRegs. The danger is one can become careless if there is a feeling of false security fostered by the wearing of safety gear. An element of over-confidence can be engendered.

However, in our real-life man-overboard situation I had certainly been too relaxed and paid the price accordingly. It is food for thought, though, that if I had been wearing a harness and lifeline, the chances are I would have still ended up in the sea before the lifeline had taken up its slack as I pitched over the low guardrail. I probably would then have drowned by being dragged under because of the high speed of the boat. An interesting scenario, this. In this hypothetical situation, assuming I had been able to release the lifeline or myself from it, or alternatively unbuckle the harness, I would still have drowned, the boat sailing on without me. The moral, of course, is not to become overconfident by putting too much reliance on safety aids. This includes lifejackets. We did not carry these in *Tern*, so there was no debate about whether or not to wear one. The latest designs of these suitable for the leisure market are light and unobstructive to the wearer's free movement, so much so that in recent times there have been campaigns by the RNLI and others, pushing for lifejackets to be worn at all times when afloat and, heaven forbid, this could even become law. It could be argued that this is a somewhat dubious practice to foster. It is reactive rather than proactive, in that it is a safety measure applicable to the wearer who has fallen over the side rather than focussing on the need not to fall over in the first place. The dangerous inference is that all one has to do is to wear a lifejacket and all will be well. On the contrary, the emphasis should be 'prevention is better than cure' as the guiding principle. Even if we had had lifejackets on board, I doubt if we would ever have worn them. That was not the way we saw things in those days. Safety was not the god it has now become.

If I had, in fact, been lost overboard, Peter would have been presented with a major dilemma over what action to take. Initially there was the psychological hurdle to overcome of coming to grips with the situation and adjustment to the realization he was completely alone. He would then have to think calmly through the recovery steps he should take. Crucial decisions, obviously, but ones that had to be devoid of panic. First he had to get the boat in a state able to be sailed back up to windward again. This would have involved dropping the raffee and brailing up the squaresail. Then he had to get the engine started to begin heading back whilst he set the fore and aft sails so he could beat back against the trade wind, progress under engine alone being severely limited. To get the mainsail hoisted it would first be necessary to get the sail cover off, this having been put on to protect the sail from the weather over the weeks at sea whilst out of use. Next would be the task of resetting the working jib, which had been taken off and stowed down below. With the boat now back under control he had to try to determine her position, as she would have been blown some way from the original position during all this time. He needed to know this to determine the mean track to sail back along the reciprocal of the course we had been steering at the time of the misadventure. Not knowing the time when this had occurred, he had, however, no real idea where I was in all that empty space of water.

The decision now to be addressed was whether to persist with the reciprocal course tactic or to undertake what can be described as a 'square search'. Again a crucial decision, bearing in mind that Peter was having, entirely on his own, to do everything: sail the boat, navigate and concentrate on the visual search. Because it was not possible to proceed directly back into the wind along what he estimated the reciprocal course to be, Peter would have to follow a zigzag path, beating to and fro across the target mean track. To have done this whilst keeping a check with any accuracy on his changing position would have been almost impossible. The alternative, and more precise, approach was to embark on the square search. In the end, this would have been more likely to be successful, but correspondingly more difficult to execute, even for a fully crewed craft, let alone a single-hander. What would be entailed was first to make a best guess where the victim might be, then, having assessed one's maximum range of vision, establish a search area in the shape of a square box around this possible position. Along the sides of this box the boat is sailed in ever increasing parallel legs, covering a wider and wider area, until hopefully the person in the water is sighted. The underlying objective is to avoid wasting crucial time by repeatedly sailing over the same ground. The difficulties for Peter in achieving any degree of precision with this method would have been formidable. Apart from anything else, a head in the water, even with only the slightest of seas running and relatively smooth water, is a very tiny object indeed to see, especially when being sought from the deck level of a small boat.

Whatever practice Peter had followed, in the end, with fading hope of success, the ultimate decision would be how long to keep searching.

Eventually he would have had to decide when to give up and turn back onto our original course. For the rest of his life he would have been beset by nagging, dreadful doubt. Had he failed me by abandoning the search too soon? Should he have continued just that little longer? All hypothetical, perhaps, but it could well have happened.

A similar misfortune had overtaken that redoubtable character, Bill Tilman, 'mountaineer, sailor and one of the great explorers of this century', whilst on passage to Montevideo in 1966 in *Mischief*, his Bristol Channel pilot cutter. In *Mischief Goes South* he tells of the awfulness of losing a man over the side.

'Coming on deck at 7.40am I found the ship on course, the helm lashed, and no sign of the helmsman. It was hard to believe but it did not take long to satisfy myself that David, who had the watch from 6am to 8am, was not on board. After a hasty look in the peak, the galley, and the cabin I gave the alarm, turned out all the hands, and gave the order to gybe. In a few minutes we were sailing back ENE on a reciprocal course with all the hands up the shrouds scanning.

We soon noticed that the patent log had stopped rotating, and on hauling in the line we found this had broken about two-thirds of its length from the counter. It is by no means unusual to lose a rotator; on the present voyage we lost two. Either it is bitten off by a shark or a porpoise, or the line frays at the point where it is attached to the rotator. But the line is less likely to break or be bitten through at any other point, accordingly we assumed that it had broken when David grabbed at it, or even later when his weight on it had combined with a sudden lift and snatch of the counter to put too much strain on the line. We concluded that if the line broke when David grabbed at it, as seemed most probable, this must have happened about 6.15am (derived from the log reading), so that he had already been overboard for an hour and three-quarters. My heart sank. In so far as we were not shipping any water on deck the sea could not be called rough, but for man swimming it was far too rough. I did not see how a man unsupported by a lifebelt could long survive.' It was a sobering thought that the patent log line was the same as the one we used in *Tern*.

They did not find him, having searched for 12 hours until it got dark. This was in a fully crewed boat, with enough persons available to scan the water continuously, handle the boat and navigate. What chance was there in our situation for Peter on his own? There was also, of course, the small matter of sharks in both situations.

On arrival at Montevideo, Tilman reported the fatality to the British Consul and had no problems with the local authorities or the press. There was no official enquiry, presumably because he had witnesses to confirm his account. Peter, however, with no corroborative evidence to hand, would have come under close scrutiny and, in the face of inevitable suspicion, be unable to prove his innocence of wrongdoing. All of this would have added immeasurably to his distress.

Life moved on. We were, as it was soon to turn out, about to have another crisis on our hands, almost literally. We ran out of toilet paper. I took this somewhat personally, as it could have been construed as a reflection on my stores planning, but in fact it was easy to flush out the reason for the shortage and to get to the bottom of it. So why had it happened? We had restocked in Cristóbal at the commissary, and of course, the toilet tissue on the shelves there was of American manufacture. Tissue was the right description, being appreciably less robust than the British dreadnought variety. Americans, it would appear, preferred the softer touch. Knowing how many rolls we had consumed during the Atlantic passages, I had restocked accordingly for the next legs. After changing over to American stocks the usage rate rose dramatically, so much so that whilst we were still some way out at sea our stock was wiped out, so to speak.

What to do? We were to find there was more to a book than just reading it. *Tern* being an easy boat to steer, full concentration on the tiller was not needed much of the time, which enabled us to develop the practice of reading and steering at the same time, with only the occasional look up to check on what the boat was up to. When the toilet tissue issue came upon us we were reading Compton MacKenzie's *The East Wind of Love*. Peter and I tended to have similar tastes in literature and would read the same book. Part of the watch changeover routine was the handover of the common book, albeit a little soggy at times, to the ongoing helmsman. MacKenzie's work was ideal, with the pages of the right size, soft but strong and easily removed, the book getting progressively thinner as we sailed on. The covers being hardback they were not used, it being mutually agreed they were 'not fit for the purpose'. I am sure the author would have been gratified that his creation was being so widely distributed across the Pacific.

Most of the way across on this leg, life had been more comfortable than the rather trying periods we had experienced on occasions when in the NE trades. On the Pacific run, much of the time the wind had been further round on the quarter, the boat steadier as a consequence with appreciably less of that aggravating rolling. The direct result of this was that the squaresail yard had not been sawing to and fro across the mast as it took up the give in its wire jackstay. The much reduced chafe was kept under control with leather strip binding and liberal applications of tallow. The main beneficiaries were, however, *Tern*'s crew, there being a greater measure of placidity in their lives as a result. There was an unexpected side effect of the permanent heel to starboard in the form of quite remarkable growth of weed along the lee topsides and extending well up onto the waterways. It was a mystery how this had managed to attach itself and stubbornly adhere to the smooth surface of the painted wood with the water flowing fast past it. The accumulation was quite dense and took some effort to remove when we were at anchor in the Marquesas.

Now well into the passage, we were enjoying pleasant conditions, and a typical log entry reads:

> All around us is bright, winking phosphorescence. Much warmer now, the South Equatorial Current heating up as it sweeps west away from its origins in the Humboldt Current, which had been bearing all that cold water up from the Southern Ocean.

We were living in conditions akin to those for Thor Heyerdahl and his companions on *Kon-Tiki* as they drifted along on the same friendly current towards the Tuamotu Archipelago, the endgame for them. They had been only just to the south of us. He caught the moment in his inimical style in his *The Kon-Tiki Expedition*.

'When night had fallen, and the stars were twinkling in the dark tropical sky, the phosphorescence flashed around us in rivalry with the stars and single glowing plankton resembled live coals. When we caught them we saw that they were little brightly shining species of shrimp.'

Also like them we had our retinue of those marvellous little creatures: pilotfish. They are about six inches long with zebra stripes, swimming in shoals just ahead of a shark's snout, darting off when they see food. We had two of these little fellows in their football jerseys permanently swimming a few inches ahead of our stem, one above the other, maintaining perfect station on us regardless of any variations in our speed. They appeared to have an unshakeable belief that we were a shark, albeit of rather unusual form. They were always there, and what they did for food was a mystery. Perhaps from time to time they did go off to find a real shark, their natural support system, providing morsels for them after it had made a kill. On the passage across we had not seen much in the way of sharks, but the presence of the pilotfish indicated they were not far away. This left me wondering again about my fate if I had been left for any length of time in the sea after my earlier involuntary immersion. The thought was something I did not want to dwell upon.

Although sharks had not made their presence felt, other forms of more friendly marine life were keeping us company. Frigate birds had been appearing for some time, signifying land was not too far away. With their long, split tails and equally long, high-aspect-ratio wings, they were easy to identify as a breed, our best guess being that our particular companions were of the species known as 'lesser frigate birds'.

Then, of course, there were the ubiquitous flying fish. They were also welcome visitors, as they had been in the Atlantic, in the NE trades, featuring regularly on the breakfast menu. Most mornings would see one or two at least lying on the sidedecks.

They were in a no-win situation, these nocturnal visitors. They had escaped the jaws of predators below the surface of the sea, only to end up between the waiting jaws of others on top of it.

As we closed the Marquesas the 'even tenor of our ways' gave way to more unfriendly conditions.

Sunday 14 February Sea rough. Wind fresh ESE to SE. Weather bright and sunny with heavy patches of cumulus. Day's run 134 M. Under squaresail only.

Another rather boisterous night with the almost continuous roar of water in the scuppers and across the afterdeck. Sounds are much more pronounced when heard from below but it is certainly pretty wet on deck. If this wind stays steady expect to pick up Ua Huka early tomorrow morning. Nearly there!

Sure enough, next morning at 0330, shortly after I had turned in, Peter called me to exclaim with some excitement in his voice that he could see land. It was Ua Huka Island, clearly visible in the bright moonlight. A wonderful sight. I had been only too happy, for once, to climb out of my bunk to share with Peter the excitement of the landfall. It was our first glimpse of a South Sea Island, which added to the excitement. There is a romanticism about these islands which has endured over the years despite all the changes that have occurred, unfortunately mostly for the worst. In spite of it all, their exotic attraction remains, as does their beauty.

I felt satisfaction over our landfall. It had been navigationally accurate, confirming that the chronometer watch was not out from its estimated rate. Comparing an observed position with a fix on a piece of land of known position on the chart provides a very accurate check on the chronometer's performance, and particularly so in our case, as it had been some time since I had been able to get a radio time check. It was a method I was to use more than once in the absence of any help from our temperamental radio. I had, however, been helped over the past few days by being favoured with good conditions for sight taking. The horizon was generally free of haze and the heavenly bodies readily visible, despite intermittent patches of immense cumulus cloud banks. Moreover, the platform for using the sextant was steadier than it had been in the Atlantic trades, the rolling being much more restrained. Conditions for astronomical observations were thus happily more user-friendly. With constant practice, my sextant skills had developed to the point where its use had become second nature, such that I knew instinctively when a sight was a good one or should be rejected. I had long before abandoned the textbook dictum when shooting the sun of taking several sights and averaging them out on a straight line drawn on graph paper. I was at sea, not in a classroom. Another classroom pearl of wisdom on using a sextant concerns making a correction to the observer's height of eye above the sea to accommodate wave and swell heights. In theory, such an adjustment should be made to ensure the correct altitude is obtained, as its reading otherwise would be too high. The rise and fall of the sea could vary between 8 feet in trade wind conditions and twice or more in a gale, thereby affecting the accuracy of the sextant shot. The prescribed procedure is to estimate the wave height from trough to crest and divide by two to give the mean height. This figure is then added to the observer's height of eye, measured from the level of the sea around the boat when she is at rest. I found this all too complicated and not meaningful in practice.

Assessing wave heights at sea is notoriously difficult and a hit-or-miss guessing game at best. One reads yachtsmen's desperate accounts of waves they have encountered, cheerfully claiming heights as much as 40 feet. Pure flights of fancy. This is hurricane stuff. I did not engage in best-guessing wave heights, preferring to be heavy-handed when applying the height-of-eye correction in the calculation for true altitude. I relied on 'gut feel' as to whether a sight was likely to be accurate or not. After all, if there is any run to the sea sextant accuracy, in a small boat, to give a position within the nearest mile or two is all that can be expected.

In partnership with the sextant the chronometer is central to the determination of longitude. As Henry Raper, in his monumental 1840 work *The Practice of Navigation and Nautical Astronomy*, expressed it: 'The most convenient method of finding longitude is by comparison of the time at place with the time at Greenwich, as shown by the chronometer.' The 'time at place' is the mean time of the observer deduced by computation from the altitude of the most appropriate heavenly body, be it sun, star or planet, or even the moon. Raper's very detailed work, with its significant mathematical content, was the basis of the navigational method I had adopted, known as 'longitude by chronometer', using spherical trigonometry in its methodology.

The fact that Raper's principles were still in practice in my time was indicative of the slow rate there had been in technological development in nautical astronomy, but in a few short years all that was to change dramatically with the invention of the satellite.

Several times on passage I had expressed concern to Peter that he really should know something about celestial navigation. This concern had resurfaced after my overboard misadventure and the possibility that I might not have got back on board again. He would have been faced with a problem in the event that I was unable to continue to function as the navigator, as his knowledge of the practice was virtually non-existent. He would have had to rely on dead reckoning – the flat Earth system, in effect – to know where he was going. He did not worry about this, however. There were two reasons, as far as I could see, for this lack of interest. In the first place he would inevitably, in due course, make a landfall somewhere. It was only a matter of time. When crossing the Atlantic there was ahead of us the vast length of the Americas, but, more precisely, short of them were the West Indies, a long chain of islands stretching north and south across a wide latitude spread. In the Pacific there was a similar spread of places to 'hit'. The French Polynesian group of islands extend over a large area, with no great distances between each of them. Peter would have had as starting point my last plotted position, and the simple laying off of course and distance run from then onwards would have sufficed, more or less. I think, however, the more important reason was his inner conviction, his faith and his firm belief in the presence of a higher authority. He never paraded any of this but I sensed it existed. It was certainly manifested whenever we were in a place where he could attend a church service; this he invariably did. Whatever one's feelings are about such matters, it is certainly true that those with faith have something going for them, a greater surety in life which is denied the 'materialist'. Peter had this quiet confidence, whereas I had to rely on a piece of man-made clockwork.

By breakfast time we had the black bulk of Ua Huka abeam, starkly dominated by a high mountain range, down which deep valleys ran to the sea. Like its neighbours, the volcanic origins were very evident, witness to its violent birth. The island was the lead-in to Nuku Hiva, now dead ahead. Forty miles south of us lay Hiva Oa, where almost up to the last day or two of the passage I had considered stopping off, but from what I had read Nuku Hiva seemed the more appealing. Hiva Oa was the most fertile and populous island in the Marquesan group, but this in itself was not of particular interest. The principal village of Atuona had, however, attracted international attention to itself by being the last resting place of the French post-Impressionist painter, Paul Gauguin. He had lived in Tahiti for some years and ended his days in Atuona, dying in 1903 at the relatively young age of 55 from venereal disease, the scourge of the Pacific Islands. One had to wonder how much he personally had contributed to spreading this white man's gift, given so generously to the Polynesians.

It was time to change from the trade wind square rig to the more manoeuvrable fore-and-aft rig. Brailing in the squaresail, and after setting jib, mainsail and mizzen, we entered the sweep of Hakapehi Bay on the south shore of Nuku Hiva, wherein lay the 'fairest haven' in the Iles Marquises.

> *Monday 15 February* 1330 Anchored off the jetty in Taiohae Bay in 4 fathoms after a drifting match up the bay, the engine refusing to co-operate.

The log goes on to record the occasion of our arrival in this French outpost. It was to be our only contact on an official basis with what was to prove the most relaxed of bureaucracies, with the ensuing proceedings, short-lived, reduced to the point of non-existence.

> Visited soon after our arrival by the doctor, Pierre Truc, and his wife Karin, plus the gendarme. It was evident our crawl up the bay had been viewed with much interest. Yachts were a rarity it seemed. Pierre and the gendarme were fulfilling their official roles of health and immigration respectively. It was the most glamorous inspection we have had by port authorities or likely to have. They are not normally that way inclined. Karin, Swedish, is lovely. Our perception was not coloured, of course, by having been at sea for a month with only each other to look at.

There was a surge coming in and we were lying beam-on, rolling heavily, which no doubt helped to bring official business somewhat abruptly to an end. Quite possibly there might also have been present a strong boat smell, of which we were unaware, and this would not have helped. Politely declining our offer of tea, the team took to their boat and our guests were soon ashore – thankfully, no doubt.

We got our heads down soon after this and slept for 15 hours with hardly a stir.

Chapter Nine

Polynesian Pleasures

*So we come to the disputed
question whether conditions in
Polynesia really were, and still
are, paradisal.*

BENGT DANIELSSON, *LOVE IN THE
SOUTH SEAS* (1956)

'Don't like the way you have left that jib sloppily stowed at the end of the bowsprit. Slovenly. Unseamanlike!'

So said Bob McKittrick sitting on his veranda studying *Tern* through his telescope. She was lying at anchor in full view of this ex-trading schooner seaman with the critical eye and very much one of the old school. He knew a 'harbour stow' when he saw one, and in this case he did not see one. *Tern* had the bay to herself and was thus receiving the full force of his undivided attention. Watching her rising and dipping in slow motion in response to the swell rolling languidly up the bay from the ocean outside, I had to agree with him. Our excuse was that we had been only too anxious to get ashore. All we had done in the morning, on surfacing from our long overnight sleep in, was to launch the dinghy and lay out, on a long warp from the stern, the kedge anchor to keep her riding at right angles to the swell, which had effectively reduced the rolling. Apart from making our own life more comfortable, we had the hope that next time Karin and Pierre came on board they might be induced to stay longer. We had enjoyed their welcoming 'official' visit, albeit short. They were good company and Karin had made a most favourable environmental impact. I found myself apologizing to Bob, assuring him we would be squaring the boat off when we returned on board. He seemed satisfied and suitably placated. Point made and taken.

'Have a beer. Plenty of cold stuff in my fridge!'

Faced with an offer like that he could criticize as much as he liked. The last cold beer we had enjoyed had been in Wreck Bay and that seemed a long time ago. It transpired he had the only fridge in the bay and, as far as I was aware, on the island. We were to see a lot of Bob.

The sum total of Westerners living on Nuku Hiva came to six, all of whom resided in the tiny, rather scattered village of Taiohae at the head of the beautiful, lushly wooded bay. The line-up consisted of Bob, Karin and Pierre Truc, the administrator for the island in the form of *Commisseur* Reboul and his wife, plus the gendarme. Bob was the only Englishman, the remainder being French, apart, of course, for Karin. With the exception of the police force, a pleasant, quite jolly man who kept very much to himself, we saw a great deal of the island's permanent residents. So much so that we spent very little time on board, for sleep and not much else. The extent of the hospitality we received was quite remarkable, almost embarrassing, in fact, particularly as we could do little to return it. No one really wanted to spend much time rolling around out in the bay as our guests.

The practice developed of us going ashore each day to Bob's house, to which was attached a small general store, the only one, to buy fresh bread, have the daily philosophical discourse and drink cold beer. Bob was a remarkable man, a character who could well have been plucked straight out of a Somerset Maugham story. Born in Liverpool, he had globetrotted over the oceans, ending up in the South Seas as a seaman in inter-island sailing trading schooners, to become, in due course, a trader in his own right. He was one of those many men of widely different backgrounds who had come to the islands intending to stay for a short time, only to end up seeing out their days in those havens for lotus eating. In Tahiti he had married a Chinese girl, the Chinese being strongly represented on the island, coming to the Marquesas to retire but still maintaining an interest in trading on a small scale. Taiohae suited him very well. I would sit for hours on his veranda, sometimes accompanied by Peter, listening to his tales about Polynesia and partaking in quite intense discussion with him about what we thought life was all about. When the glasses began to run low he would shout out a command for his wife to bring more refreshment. She seemed devoted to him, always around in the background but never joining us. She looked very old.

Had he ever thought about returning home, if only for a visit? Yes he had, even to the extent of contemplating taking one or two Marquesan youngsters with him to advance their education in a modern, civilized society. But, as he said, who really were the more civilized? The islander, with his live-and-let-live philosophy, carefree and virtually crime-free way of life, or the denizen of a backstreet of a large city at home, as in one in which he had been raised, where deprivation governed conduct and where the red claws in the fight for survival predominated? He had decided not to put it to the test. Trader Bob, as he liked to be called, may at times have been homesick but he had been seduced by the charms of the Enchanted Isles and was happy.

> *Few men who come to the islands leave them; they go grey where they alighted; the palm shades and the trade wind fan them till they die, perhaps cherishing to the last the fancy of a visit home, which is rarely made, more rarely enjoyed, and yet more rarely repeated.*
>
> ROBERT LOUIS STEVENSON

I have written a lot about Bob, but he was one of the most memorable personalities we met on the passage out. Polynesia, like the rest of the post-war world, was changing, with an ever quickening pace. His likes would not be seen again.

Alongside the warm, entertaining company of Bob was the equally warm welcome and friendship coming from the Trucs, 'who have gone out of their way to look after us and give us a great time. They have been marvellous hosts.'

Very early on in our stay, Pierre and Karin asked if we were interested in being shown something of the upper reaches of the island and they suggested there was no better way than on horseback. Both of them were keen on outdoor activities and riding was a particular favourite, indulged in at every opportunity. This had been a good policy on their part, as the climate and general mode of living were more conducive to somewhat unhealthy relaxation than any urge for action. Peter and I were keen to explore the beautiful, exotic backdrop to our anchorage and accepted the invitation with alacrity but were rather apprehensive about doing it on the back of a horse.

Neither of us had much experience of these, to us, rather frightening beasts but we were prepared to have a go, albeit with some trepidation. We fancied ourselves as sailors not equestrians. We also had some concern that riding in company with two tyros would make for a boring ride for our experienced guides. They brushed aside these reservations, and in the event it was to work out very well for all. The plan was to make an early-morning start and for the four of us to ride up the valley and over to Taipivai, returning the same day. The Taipi Valley, at the head of the Baie du Contrôleur, adjacent to Taiohae Bay, was of particular interest to me, having read Herman Melville's *Typee*, a world classic and a particularly fascinating read; a snapshot of Polynesian life, pertaining especially to Taipivai. The essence of the story is that Herman, with his shipmate Toby, in pursuit of a more pleasant existence, desert their American whaling ship, which he refers to as 'the detested old vessel', with the unlikely name of *Dolly*, in Taiohae Bay and climb up the valley to shake off pursuers whom they expected would be organised by the captain to recover them. He was already short of good seamen and could be expected to bribe the natives, possibly with a musket, to chase after them. The islanders often did not know how to use firearms but they were a highly valued commodity. Herman and Toby's plan was to clamber up to the top, where there was a convergence of deep valleys, and escape down one of them. The question was: which one? They knew that cannibalism was practised in one of the valleys but not the neighbouring one.

Inhabiting one vale were the Happar tribe, known to be friendly, with a reputation for gentleness and humanity. In the other were the ferocious Typees, renowned cannibals. Fear of recapture being the spur, there was nothing for it but to make the best guess they could and hope for the best. It was the wrong choice. With hunger and growing exhaustion driving them on, they were soon to learn to their horror that they were in the valley of Taipivai, the home of the dreaded Typees. Their reception by the tribesmen, however, was not what they expected. They were treated as honoured guests, pampered and indulged, under the benign patronage of the supreme chief, but there was one slight drawback. It was made clear they would not be allowed to leave. Although there were drawbacks to being a captive guest there were also compensations. The scene was set on the first day of their new life. The house which had been allocated to them was 'nearly filled with young females, fancifully decorated with flowers. The proceedings of these unsophisticated young creatures were altogether informal, and void of artificial restraint. Long and minute was the investigation with which they honoured us, and so uproarious their mirth, that I felt infinitely sheepish; and Toby was immeasurably outraged at their familiarity.'

Something over 100 years later, Peter and I were about to travel over more or less the same route, but for us it was to be the easier way, on horseback, devoid of cannibals and maidens. As it was to be an early start we slept the night at the doctor's house, which was in itself something of an occasion, being the first time away from *Tern* for six months. I rather regretted it, though, as the mosquitoes were bad and I seemed to be awake much of the night. Peter appeared to be unaffected and snored his way through my torment. It is a strange thing about mosquitoes, sandflies and other insects of that ilk. They will savage one human and have nothing to do with another. To this day I have the same problem with my wife. I resent her immunity. I suppose someone knows why this natural selectivity occurs. The near invisible beach-inhabiting sandfly, the 'no-seeums', did not trouble either of us out in the boat lying some way offshore, either because it was too far to fly or they were unaware of the existence of the tempting flesh on offer. It was a different story on the foreshore when we were using the dinghy. They made a meal of me but once again, irritatingly, ignored Peter.

In line with the plan for the impending expedition we found ourselves saddling up early next day and mounted our horses. Close up they looked twice the size they had appeared out in the paddock, but we were now committed. On climbing up into the saddle the animal's back seemed the width of a football pitch. I had forgotten what it was like to be up there in space with the accompanying somewhat helpless feeling and wondered how I was going to control such a large powerhouse. The last time I had been riding was with a girlfriend, a keen horsewoman, and I had not been shown up at my macho best. However, I was getting plenty of help from Karin, who walked my steed around whilst I got a feel for what I was trying to do. Pierre did the same for Peter. Putting on an air of bravado, we set off. The horses were splendid, and as we progressed, with our confidence building up, a degree of empathy developed with them. It was hard going up the broken beds of the ravines, through the heavy woodlands and over the rough surface of the clearings, but with my feeling of being in charge growing, I found my nervousness retreating to the point of allowing enjoyment to creep in.

Below us was laid out the full splendour of the bay of Taiohae, supremely beautiful, epitomising the grandeur of the Nuku Hiva sea and landscapes. As Melville wrote: 'No description of the bay can do justice to its beauty.' From our vantage point we could see its full extent, the intense blue water stretching out to the ocean, which was streaked with white caps. The deep indentation, a mile and a half long and half as wide, its steep sides thick with lush growth, dropped down to stretches of tree-fringed, golden foreshore. Lying to her anchor at the head of the bay, clearly in sight, was the small shape of our home.

Our efforts were finally rewarded by reaching a ridge above our destination, Taipivai, to give us an overarching, uninterrupted view of the inlet. It was somewhat larger than Taiohae but of no less beauty. It was stunning. The overused travel guide phrase 'breathtaking' was a totally appropriate description. The slog up to our viewpoint had been so worthwhile, completely transcending the discomfort occasioned by our hard-worked backsides. 'We were very tired when we got back to the Trucs' house, but it has been one of the most enjoyable days I have spent for a long time. It is difficult to know how to thank Karin and Pierre enough. We have been riding again since and have quite got the bug, thirsting for more.'

During the ride we had frequently come across some rather curious piles of rough-hewn stones, but there was an order to them. They had a special significance, as Pierre explained. They were symbolic, sad remains of the way the island had once been, teeming with people before tragic depopulation had overtaken it. Resorting again to Melville helps to explain their meaning.

'The dwellings of the islanders were almost invariably built upon massive stone foundations, which they call pi-pis. The dimensions of these, however, as well as of the stones composing them, are comparatively small, but there are larger erections of a similar description comprising the 'morais', or burying grounds and festival places, in nearly all the valleys of the island. Some of these piles are so extensive, and so great a degree of labour and skill must have been requisite in constructing them, that I can scarcely believe they were built by the ancestors of the present inhabitants. If indeed they were, the race has sadly deteriorated in their knowledge of the mechanic arts. To say nothing of their habitual : by what contrivance within the reach of so simple a people could such enormous masses have been moved or fixed in their places? And how could they with their rude implements have chiselled and hammered them into shape? All of these larger pi-pis bore incontestable marks of great age.'

These stone piles were still being used in our time there. Whenever a local wished to build himself a house, all he had to do was to use a convenient pi-pi for the foundations. It seemed to be a free-for-all as regards taking over these stones and the land around them. Acquisitiveness of possessions and property did not register with us as a Polynesian trait, and as far as we could see, thieving was not a social problem. It was therefore disappointing that the one piece of gear that we lost on our trip went missing in Nuku Hiva. It was our practice to leave the dinghy hauled up on the foreshore when we came ashore: the oars, bailer and various items of gear left in it. Nothing was ever disturbed until the occasion when we returned to find the bailer missing. As bailers go, this was rather a good one, with its aluminium bowl and nicely turned wooden handle, albeit its monetary value not being particularly great. We were surprised this had happened as it seemed out of context. The honesty displayed by the Typees had impressed Melville and he refers to 'the integrity of the Marquesans in their intercourse with each other. In the darkest of nights they slept securely, with all their worldly wealth around them, in houses the doors of which were never fastened.' However, he then goes on to say: 'The strict honesty which the inhabitants of nearly all the Polynesian Islands manifest towards each other is in striking contrast with the thieving propensities some of these evince in their intercourse with foreigners. It would almost seem that, according to their peculiar code of morals, the pilfering of a hatchet or a wrought nail from a European is looked upon as a praiseworthy action. Or rather, it may be presumed that bearing in mind the wholesale forays made upon them by their nautical visitors, they consider the property of the latter as a fair object of reprisal.'

The loss of our bailer was an inconvenience. Our handsome dinghy was of wooden, clinker construction and quite possibly the boat's original tender. At sea it was carried upside down over the cabin skylight, which was a drawback in that it was fully exposed to the sun, quite apart from darkening the interior. The result was that on a long passage, such as that from the Galápagos, it dried out and the planking opened up. For the first few days in harbour whilst the strakes 'took up', the bailer was in some demand. We never saw it again and had to live with an empty can of beans. Claud Worth would have turned in his grave. Not at all Royal Yacht Squadron.

The history of depopulation in Polynesian islands would seem to have been a long one and not confined only to the last century or two following the arrival of the white man. Undoubtedly, though, the advent of the whites dramatically and tragically accelerated the process. Venereal disease, smallpox and tuberculosis epidemics, opium, alcohol, firearms, 'blackbirding', which was the ruthless deportation of labour, and the misguided zeal of the missionary (the litany of disasters just goes on and on) precipitated the demise of large swathes of the populations of Hawaii, Tahiti and the Marquesas. However, one has to ask what fate befell the races who built the pi-pis and morais. Did they just die out or were they exterminated by other waves of invaders?

Although theories abound, virtually nothing is known about the Marquesas prior to their discovery in 1595 by the Spaniard Alvaro Mendaña de Neyra on his way to the Solomons, six weeks out from Peru. He claimed them for Spain and named them after the Marqués de Mendoza, Viceroy of Peru, his benefactor and patron, who in fact, like his fellow *Conquistadores*, was more interested in plunder than exploration. Next visitor of note was Cook, who fixed the islands on the chart, discovering in the process a hitherto unknown small island which he named Hood after 'the young gentleman (midshipman)' who first saw it. Hood was aged all of 14 and came from one of the most distinguished names in Royal Navy history. Cook was most impressed by the Marquesans: 'They are, without exception, the finest race of people in this sea. For fine shape and regular features, they perhaps surpass the other nations.'

In 1842 the French, their colonizing ambitions rampant, having set themselves up in Tahiti and Moorea, claimed the Marquesas and installed a garrison with a coterie of priests. Faced with the guns of a protective naval squadron, the local inhabitants had little option but to acquiesce. For the next few decades it was all downhill for the Marquesan race. No islands in the South Pacific suffered the impact of the white man more disastrously.

A keen observer of the Marquesas was Robert Louis Stevenson, who spent some time in Nuku Hiva and was captivated by it, duly recording his observations. A discerning student of life in the South Seas, he was only too well aware of the depopulation that had overtaken some of the islands, both in earlier and more recent times.

'Over the whole extent of the South Seas, from one tropic to another, we find traces of a bygone state of overpopulation, when the resources of even a tropical soil were taxed and even the improvident Polynesian trembled for the future. The Polynesians met this emergent danger with various expedients of activity and prevention. These were insufficient for the teeming people, and the annals of the past are gloomy with famine and cannibalism. Meanwhile, over all the island world, abortion and infanticide prevailed.'

Stevenson expanded on the theme to attribute 19th century depopulation in large measure to the missionaries, who prohibited indulgence in pleasure, superstitious practices and belief in ancient gods, thereby stifling the will to live in their converts.

Nothing can, of course, excuse the excesses of the white man in all his different guises, but perhaps what happened over time from prehistoric days was just part of the Darwinian evolutionary process.

We had from the outset planned to have an extended stay in Nuku Hiva, partly to get some refitting work done but principally because of the tropical storm risk. About this, our 1946 edition of the Admiralty *Pacific Islands Pilot Vol III* had this to say:

'Cyclonic disturbances – tropical hurricanes – affect the region south of latitude 10°S and west of longitude 135°W where they occur mainly from December to April.' The Iles de la Société, which take in Tahiti, lie squarely in this danger zone, but the Iles Marquises, embracing Nuku Hiva, are free of risk, lying to the north of the hurricane belt.

What we had not anticipated were the benefits we were to gain from that extended stay in the form of the hospitality we had been so privileged to enjoy and the friendships we had made. We had no evenings on board alone, and apart from breakfast, no meals in the boat. The evening after our Taipivai ride the Trucs gave a dinner party which included the Rebouls. This was the first time we had tried raw fish. About this I had been somewhat dubious when Karin announced it was to be on the menu. It took a little adjustment of the palate but, well marinated, it went down quite well, to my surprise.

It had been a good dinner, and of course, with the company being French, the wine flowed. The mood was relaxed. Karin left the room for some reason and on reappearing said with a smile:

'Come outside, you salty sailors, there is a sight that will do you no harm.'

In fact, it did us no good at all. Under a shower that had been installed at the back of the house, their maid, a most attractive young girl, was bathing, her long black hair streaming down her back to the waist and the water flowing over her body. She waved gaily, quite at ease. She was, after all, just being Polynesian and no doubt would have known of no reason why the beauty of nature should not be seen and enjoyed.

Confident the risk of a 'cyclonic disturbance' had sufficiently retreated, the time had come once more for us to get on our way. But how reluctant we were to take that step! Sunday, the last day of February, was to be sailing day, but it was not to work out quite that way. By the time we had enjoyed a last beer with Bob, stopped at the Trucs (with inevitably the appropriate hospitality) and stayed for lunch at the Rebouls (this was the usual session, rendering us incapable of doing much for some time after), we decided it would make more sense to leave first thing on Monday.

But perhaps we were just prevaricating and wanting to put off the evil hour. We knew how much we were going to miss all those people, particularly Pierre and Karin. Both of them had done so much during our stay, but there was just something special about Karin. What was there about that name? We had known two appealing women with it and it was just a little intriguing that both were living unusual lives in out-of-the-way exotic places, sharing both a common name and same region of origin, Scandinavia, but had no knowledge of the other's existence. William Albert Robinson had, for sure, been just a little in love with the one in Galápagos, and I found it easy to entertain similar feelings about the one in the Marquesas.

Monday 1 March Recovered the kedge. Lifted the dinghy on board and lashed it down. Secured for sea.

0900 Got under way under jib and main.

0930 Set all plain sail.

Desperately sorry to leave this place and it is with a real feeling of homesickness I think of those delightful people we are leaving.

As we cleared the two islets, the East and West Sentinelles, which guard the entrance to the bay, I heard:

Someone's in the kitchen with Dinah,
Someone's in the kitchen I kno-o-ow.

When I expressed mild surprise at the sudden eruption into song, Peter explained he had the same feelings about leaving and there was the need for some cheering up. I cannot hear that song, even to the present day, without vivid memories of Taiohae flooding back. Peter had a tuneful voice and I liked to hear him giving forth on a range of currently popular, if somewhat incongruous, tunes. One of these,

How much is that doggie in the window?
The one with the waggly tail.

was also long to remain with me.

I suppose in the world of ocean cruising today music of infinite choice comes out of an electronic box at the turn of the switch. For us it was a DIY operation and I was lucky with Peter as he had talent. He was not quite so fortunate with me.

We took a last lingering look at what had been for us our Enchanted Isle. The mountains, rising to two thousand feet, were by happy good fortune clear of cloud, and the dark, broken tops with their abrupt jagged peaks were outlined in sharp clarity against the vividly blue sky. I can never forget Nuku Hiva.

It is the fate of most voyagers, no sooner to discover what is of most interest in a locality, than they are hurried from it.

CHARLES DARWIN

It was back to reality as we left the relative tranquillity and security of Taiohae to emerge once more into ocean conditions, to feel again the friendly trade wind on our cheeks and the white-capped, flowing sea rolling under us. The meteorological data contained in the *Pilot* suggested we could expect a generally benign passage through the Tuamotus to Tahiti. For March, the wind direction was shown as predominantly from NE to ESE with a mean wind speed of 5 knots, this figure kept low by the high percentage of the calms recorded, particularly in the vicinity of Tahiti. Interestingly enough, a zero incidence of gales is shown, a not unwelcome observation. The indications were that the spinnaker was going to earn its keep and so it did, the square yard having been lowered to the deck. The run to the Tuamotus was to prove an enjoyable interlude, a typical log reading being:

Weather: Beautiful day, bright and sunny with small cumulus.
A very quiet night with cloudless sky and amazingly bright stars with a warm breeze.

The conditions favoured the taking of astronomical observations to the extent that on the fifth day out a good midday fix, run up to an afternoon sight for longitude, placed us with a high degree of certainty in close proximity to an atoll on the fringes of the Tuamotu Archipelago, although nothing was to be seen. We hove to for the night with the intention of making the transit of this conglomerate of coral reefs and atolls in daylight the next day. I felt it was not a good idea to attempt a night passage. They were unlit, with no navigational marks of any sort, and being beset with uncertain currents, coupled with a wind tending to fickleness during the dark hours, all added up to suggesting we stayed put until dawn at least. It is not called the Dangerous Archipelago for nothing. The *Pilot* reinforced this view. 'The currents in the vicinity of Archipel des Tuamotu are particularly irregular, and great caution is necessary when navigating among this mass of low-lying atolls.' The group, straddling our path to Tahiti, consisting of 78 islands, almost all of them small atolls, is spread over a large area, 950 miles long and over 300 miles wide. And as another reference in the *Pilot* stated: 'They barely break the surface of the ocean and are so difficult to see from ships and boats that the French naval officer, Comte Louis de Bougainville, gave them their name of the Dangerous Archipelago.' That name, and the alternative title of the Low Archipelago, have remained through to the present day. The chart added its note of caution with the warning that the surveys on which it was based were old and longitudes taken off it could be markedly in error. Bougainville stumbled almost literally onto the island group in 1768 and was one of the earliest of explorers to make their acquaintance.

The first European settlers arrived on Rangiroa Atoll in 1851 and, with their Protestant attitudes, would change for ever the indigenes' way of life. Over the preceding years, however, the atoll's inhabitants had not been idle, periodically attacking their neighbours, killing each other and on occasion eating the vanquished. The islands, unhappily, were in due course to experience the ultimate in barbarism when the French commandeered Mururoa Atoll and exploded a nuclear bomb in 1966, detonating over the next 30 years, regardless of international sentiment, a further 170 of these ecological disasters.

The largest atoll, Rangiroa, was in recent times to see the wreck of Francis Chichester's restored *Gipsy Moth IV* whilst she was in the course of a round-the-world commemorative cruise. This misfortune brought home the difficulties of sailing in these waters, even with all the help that modern, sophisticated electronic equipment can provide. Over the centuries the Polynesians developed systems for finding their way across the seas, and nowhere were the demands of accurate pilotage more exacting than in the Tuamotus. In the words of Thor Heyerdahl: 'The whole formation has been entirely built up by coral polyps and consists of treacherous submerged reefs and palm-clad atolls which rise only 6 or 7 feet above the surface of the sea. Dangerous ring-shaped reefs fling themselves protectively round every single atoll and are a menace to shipping traffic throughout the area.'

So how did the islanders get about in safety? Study of the stars told them much, but many and varied were other techniques employed to help tell them where they were. Movements of birds were a certain clue. Particular species were known to fly quite precise distances offshore in search of fish, the return flight home giving an indication of direction and sailing distance to the unseen land. Something akin to 'tidal atlases' were known, having been derived by watching the flow of water round and between the islands. Individual atolls had their almost unique flow pattern as the currents divided on impact with the surrounding coral reefs to re-form into identifiable configurations. Detailed knowledge of this had been handed down over the generations. Then again, there was a bank of knowledge about cloud formations over different islands, giving quite precise indications to the informed observer of their identity and location. A remarkably innovative navigational system we had been told about was calling on the services of a pig. When a boat was expected to be nearing land, as yet below the horizon, the boat's pet pig would be launched. Being a land animal, it would strike out boldly in the direction in which its senses told it lay its natural habitat. It would only do so, however, if it knew it could make it. Without this surety it would not leave the boat. The boat's navigator, knowing from experience his pig's swimming range, would be able to assess how far off the land lay and its bearing when the pig finally set off. It is for speculation that if *Gipsy Moth IV* had carried a pig, rather than relying on an array of fiendishly clever electronic aids to navigation, she might well have avoided landing up on the Rangiroa reef.

Whilst the Polynesians were honing their navigational skills by interpreting what the natural world had to tell them, the Europeans were developing methods of finding their way around at sea, not only by observing natural phenomenon, but also by devising instruments and methods to achieve infinitely greater precision. It is for speculation why the intellectual development of one species of the human race was on arrest and the other on growth. Perhaps again it simply was the Darwinian theory of survival, whereby the Polynesian, enjoying a more benign climate and food in profusion, readily available just for the picking, had no imperative to develop, whereas the Eurasian had a harsher environment in which to exist. The different rates of development would also seemingly not be directly related to skin colour, but evidence exists that some very early inhabitants of Polynesia had white skins with light-coloured hair and near blue eyes.

In our situation, having reassured myself that enough allowance had been made for drift due to the current, and also for our own leeway,

I succumbed to temptation. Following an early supper and leaving *Tern* hove-to on the near flat sea, we retired to our bunks. The intention was that after a good night's sleep we would rise early, have a leisurely breakfast together at the table in the cabin and set off to thread our way through the atolls. Confident we would wake in plenty of time, we did not bother to set the alarm clock. In fact, we slept on. When I did finally surface and became conscious of my surroundings I was aware something had changed. The boat's motion was more lively, and from outside there came a strange continuous roaring sound. Peter was still deep down as I spurred myself into action, to emerge out in the cockpit and promptly go into shock. Alarmingly close under our lee were seas breaking onto a coral reef, spray flying high above it as the reef resisted the impact of the ocean swell bursting over it. The sound I had heard was that of this crashing surf, and the change in the boat's motion the effect of the roll of the swell as its crest curled over on to itself, and under it the surge of the backwash rushed out to sea again. Shouting out to Peter, I let the staysail draw, and with him now on deck, he having shot out of the cabin as though from the proverbial gun, we wore the boat round in the lightest of airs and stood clear. There had not been much room to spare. We only just made it, as in the process we had closed further the turbulence. We looked at each other and this was another occasion when nothing was said.

The drama now behind us and our heartbeats slowing, we enjoyed the passage through the atolls, a gentle breeze wafting us along. Making an unscathed exit from the archipelago we took our departure from Toau Atoll, identified by sun sights. Lying not far to the east of us was Raroia, which had claimed *Kon-Tiki*, the raft broken on its reef. A similar fate had so very nearly overtaken us, but for us it would have been a different ending. Heyerdahl's vivid account of *Kon-Tiki*'s stranding makes for sombre reading, as although the conditions at the time were, it would appear, more robust than ours, all reefs in the group are of the same configuration with similar hazards. We would have had something of the same experience had not the gods intervened on our behalf.

'The swell grew heavier and heavier with deep troughs between the waves. A sea rose straight up under us and we felt the *Kon-Tiki* being lifted in the air. The great moment had come; we were riding on the wave-back at breathless speed. A new sea rose high up astern of us like a glittering green glass wall; as we sank down it came rolling over us ... the whole mountain of water rushed on with an ear-splitting roaring and crashing ... then I saw the next sea come towering up, higher than all the rest ... we must have hit the reef that time.'

At best, *Tern* would have been dumped, still hopefully more or less in one piece, on top of our reef, but what then?

Reflecting subsequently on the incident, it might have been prudent for me to have taken some evening star sights to compare with the afternoon fix. The distance between the two positions, albeit not large, might perhaps have helped to have given a better idea of the current's drift and rate. Uncertainty about these and inadequate allowance for the current had been central to the cause of our near mishap. I had not got into the habit of taking regular star sights, as much of the time they were not needed. They could be something of an added chore, and their timing, before sunrise and after sunset, intruded into the boat's routine. Most of the time at sea, and bearing in mind extreme accuracy of position in ocean sailing is not too meaningful, daily sun sights usually suffice quite adequately. However, I was forced to admit that the real culprit in the reef scare was my laziness. It was inexcusable, purely in the interests of having all night in our bunks, to have left the boat drifting unattended in such uncertain waters. The warning in the *Pilot* had been clear enough. I could hear Bob McKittrick's voice:

'Slovenly. Unseamanlike!'

Robert Louis Stevenson had also gone on to visit the Tuamotus in his chartered schooner, *Casco*, after leaving Nuku Hiva. In the account of his travels he goes on to make interesting comparisons between the Marquesans and the Tuamotuans. He, like all other visitors, was impressed by the Marquesans, referring to them as 'the most beautiful of human races and one of the tallest', as well as being childishly self-indulgent. The Tuamotuans, on the other hand, were appreciably shorter and certainly not good-looking, with a tendency to the ascetic. It is strange that such near neighbours should be so different.

We could not comment on the racial comparison issue as we were not to see any Tuamotuans, all the atolls we passed being deserted. These were just what one imagined South Sea islands to look like. Coral reefs under foaming breakers, ringing a clear blue lagoon with sparkling, calm water, and gleaming, white-sanded beaches overhung by leaning, wind-rustled, densely packed palm trees. There was not a human being to be seen to spoil the picture of nature in all its perfection. We were sorely tempted to land on one of them, but that curse of modern living, shortage of time, dictated otherwise. Moreover, the *Pilot*, seldom guilty of being light-hearted, was rather off-putting.

'When entering [the reef], a vessel should always proceed through the pass at high speed, especially if there is a strong outgoing tidal stream; with an outgoing stream, eddies and whirlpools may cause the vessel to yaw unless quickly countered by the helm. High speed should also be maintained even with a strong ingoing stream, otherwise the vessel may yaw dangerously.' High speed was not associated with our little engine, even assuming it was not in a sulk. The wind being light, sailing in with ideas of emulating Robinson Crusoe was not an option.

We sailed on, laying a course for Venus Point on the north-western tip of Tahiti. Two days later, still in quiet sailing conditions, under spinnaker, we sighted fine on our port bow the small island of Mehetia, the most easterly of the Iles de La Société, abrupt and steep; a dramatic contrast to the Tuamotus. This was the signpost leading us on to Tahiti. The *Pilot* informed us that Mehetia was visible on a clear day from a distance of over 60 miles. We were not so lucky, its upper reaches being enshrouded in low cloud. From the very earliest days of South Pacific exploration, Mehetia has fulfilled its signpost role. Apart from this function it was of no particular interest to us: the main beach, said the *Pilot*, was of uninviting black sand and, moreover, the island was only occasionally inhabited, it appeared. However, it does have a place in multinational exploration. The Spaniard, Pedro Fernández de Quirós, who went on to discover Tahiti, was the first European to sight it and actually landed there in 1606. He was followed in 1767 by the Englishman Captain Samuel Wallis RN, and a year later by the French naval officer Comte Louis Antoine de Bougainville who, for a reason best known to himself, called it Boudoir. Then along came Captain James Cook RN, who referred to it under its native name, Maitea, which subsequently, inconsequentially, became Mehetia. In his use of the name Maitea, Cook was being Cook. One of his great strengths was his sensitivity to local sentiment. It was a characteristic which contributed so much to the warmth of the reception afforded him and his men in the Society Islands. It was so unfortunate that this same sensitivity was not emulated by the missionaries who were to follow after him.

Five hours later we had the famed, exotic Tahiti itself ahead, and what a dramatic sight it presented! All too often, of course, reality does not match expectation, but this was not such an occasion.

Chapter Ten

Enchanted Isles

Happy it would have been for these people had
they never been visited by Europeans; for, to
our shame be it spoken, disease and gunpowder
is all the benefit they have ever received from us
in return for their hospitality and kindness.

SURGEON HAMILTON OF HMS *PANDORA*,
SOCIETY ISLANDS, 1791

'Pester, get up here! Your drink's waiting.'
I groaned. The best part of another morning would now be lost and
the planned work programme for *Tern* put on hold yet again. The call
had come down from the balcony of a bar overlooking the main street of
Papeete, along which I had been walking, hoping not to be observed. A vain
hope. I should have known better.

In the early days of our arrival in the port we had met, in a bar, a bunch of
tough-looking characters who had welcomed us into their group. It transpired
they were captains, and in some cases owners as well, of a mixed bag of inter-
island trading schooners and small steamers. The voice I was hearing could
well have been that of a Cape Horn master hailing the fore upper topgallant
yard. I could not ignore it, and nor could the rest of the street.

The vessels they commanded were moored in a row a little further up
the roadside quay from us and, like us, stern to the main thoroughfare with
anchors out ahead. This bunch of old reprobates, at least they seemed old to
me, came here each year in their ships to sit out the tropical storm season. It
now being near mid March, they would be gone in two or three weeks time,
but they did not give the impression they were in any great hurry to get
back to business. Their tempo was the tempo of the islands. They were Bob
McKittricks, and it might well have been that he had known some of them
in the past. I must confess I enjoyed being with them and was somewhat
flattered they wanted to include me in their company as a fellow skipper,
even if only of a small yacht. A new face, it would seem, was perhaps a
refreshing change, or perhaps more prosaically, a new recipient of their
yarns was what they needed. Be that as it may, I learned a lot about life in

the islands. Most of the inter-island schooners had local native captains, but there was this small enclave of white skippers, their annual get-together being important to them. The rest of the year their lives were involved with Polynesian crews, so this time off with others of their own kind had therapeutic value, a necessary break.

A recurring problem they all had was the enactment of the farewelling ritual each time they left Papeete. It did not matter whether the forthcoming voyage would be protracted or only for just a few days, as many of them were, the farewell afforded by the families to their departing menfolk was always a big event, enjoyed to the hilt by all except the captain. The families of each crewmember assembled en masse at the time of departure, dressed in their most colourful attire. In varying states of inebriation, they filled the decks with laughter and uninhibited displays of affection. The captains knew the form and exactly what to expect. There would be an untidy unberthing from the quay, and the first night at sea would be one of some stress for the captain whilst his crew sobered up.

We had, as it happened, an awareness of the ramifications pursuant to these farewells. We were berthed alongside a large American-owned steel yacht, *Vega*, a schooner rigged of some 90 feet overall. Her masts were not standing, lying instead along the length of her deck. She was deserted. We had been on board to have a look and were appalled at what we saw. Gear was lying everywhere and she had the appearance of being completely neglected. Of particular interest was her big steering wheel on the afterdeck, only half of it being there. The missing half had been neatly sliced off. It was evident she had been dismasted and the mainmast coming down had sheared the wheel in two. What, we wondered, had happened to the helmsman? *Vega* was a well-known sight on the waterfront and it was not long before we heard her story.

Hailing from the west coast of the United States, she had been sailed down to Papeete the year before and for some reason had then been sold. The new owner, also American, had employed another skipper and sent him down to bring *Vega* back to her home port. He engaged a crew, all Tahitian including the mate, and prepared to sail from Papeete. It would appear he was not conversant with Tahitian farewells. The night before sailing the whole crew slept ashore, to arrive on board in the morning complete with families and all drunk. Later that day the skipper, with some difficulty, managed to get the well-wishers ashore and then got under way. It was apparently a beautiful afternoon and the mate insisted on setting every sail *Vega* could carry. What had not been noticed was a small cloud up to windward, rapidly building and getting blacker. The captain saw, with growing alarm, the approaching danger. They had to get sail off, and quickly at that, but he was unable to get any sense out of the mate or the crew. The heavy squall hit them and something had to go. What went was the lower shackle on the forestay at the point of attachment to the stem fitting. The pin on the shackle sheared and the whole rig arrived on deck. One could only begin to imagine the ensuing utter chaos: all the spars, the full outfit of sails and a tangled mass of running and standing rigging about the ears of the panic-stricken and now, no doubt, stone-cold sober crew. We understood that in the States a battle over insurance liability was raging. In the meantime, poor *Vega* sat and sat. She was still doing just that when we left. It was sad that what had been a gracious ship was in such a state, but at least we had now a feel for what a Tahitian farewell meant.

We were uncertain about our feelings about Papeete, our reaction being a mixed pot of impressions of this multi-racial seaport, but what was clear was how much we had enjoyed making a landfall on this fabled superstar amongst South Sea islands. Over the centuries it has had more praise of its charms and beauty heaped upon it than has any other in the Pacific. Charles Darwin, homeward bound in *Beagle*, was one of the many to add his share of the outpourings, referring to it as 'the island to which every voyager has offered up his tribute of admiration'. We, in *Tern*, would add our voice to the songs of praise. Tahiti is reported as being visible in fine weather 100 miles away, but we were not so lucky in our approach to it by having to sail on some distance past Mehetia before the clouds enshrouding it lifted. Then we suddenly saw our objective. Rising to sharp, lofty peaks, the highest of which is Orohena at 7,300 feet, the volcanic island displays to dramatic effect the torture to which it had been subjected during its creation. Ravines and valleys with precipitous flanks form, as a hugely impressed Darwin informs us, 'mountain gorges far more magnificent than anything which I have ever before beheld.' All of this was laid out before us as we sailed close up to the barrier reef of coral that almost completely surrounds Tahiti, a mile or so offshore. Within the reef were the calm waters of the intensely blue lagoon and turquoise shallows washing up to the narrow sandy shore, with its encroaching dense covering of palm trees on the mountain's lower slopes. The impact on the senses was one of admiration for absolute beauty.

At 0600 next morning we had Venus Point on the port bow, and on gybing ship we set the spinnaker to head down the coast, keeping clear of the breakers smashing over the reef. Nine miles away to the west lay Moorea, with its jagged, broken silhouette so similar to Tahiti and of comparable beauty; so much so that we resolved we would visit it when we sailed for home. If we had known how much the perfect island of the South Seas it was, we would have gone there much earlier. By early afternoon we were off the small town of Papeete – 'the best sheltered harbour in Tahiti,' said the *Pilot*, but for us to be received in its embrace we had to negotiate Passe de Papeete, the narrow opening in the barrier reef. This, according to the *Pilot*, was a 'navigable channel reduced in width to about 65 yards by a shallow spit which extends from the reef on each side. In the summer months, November to April, there is sometimes a considerable sea on the bar in the pass. At times a heavy swell sets in from north-westward without any apparent cause, rendering the pass a mass of breakers. A speed of at least 7 or 8 knots should be maintained in the pass. Pilotage is compulsory.' The speed stipulated was for us hopelessly out of reach. We would just have to hope for the best. We hoisted our International Code signal flags to identify ourselves, and with them up went flag G, 'I require a pilot'.

We hove to and awaited developments. Sure enough, in surprisingly quick time, out through the pass came the pilot boat, to range alongside and deposit the pilot on board. His English was passable and, reminiscent of the last pilot we had had when in the Canal Zone all those months ago, he indicated a marked degree of unease about the task ahead of him. Expressing concern about a problem with currents, he confirmed what the *Pilot* had been on about, there being 'very strong currents found in the pass'. Like our previous man he also was unimpressed by the shortage of horses in the power of our engine. Under full main and jib, with the engine working its little heart out, we shot through the pass with no drama, with the joys of Papeete then laid out before us to take unto ourselves. The pilot directed us over to a clear spot on the waterfront quay, his boat helping us into our berth by pushing us round to put our stern against the shore. Handling the boat with precision, the pilot boat coxswain most obligingly laid our bow anchor and kedge out ahead. A couple of onlookers amongst the little crowd that was assembling on the foreshore took our stern lines, and dropping them over old cannon buried upright in the ground, we were safely secured in place without any fuss. I was reminded of the last time we had engaged in this manoeuvre in Cristóbal: it had taken seemingly the best part of a football team to get us into position. We expressed our appreciation to our friendly pilot for his help and that of his team. We were tempted to think the French were not so bad after all.

We liked to think we had made a little bit of a splash on entering harbour, with a brave array of bunting and flags on display. At the mainmast head was the RNSA's (Royal Naval Sailing Association) burgee, at the mizzen head on a staff which Peter had made, was our 'house flag', which in its other life had been a flag from Peter's sailing club and was now serving as our wind direction indicator. At the starboard mainmast spreader were our four signal flags, plus flag H: 'I have a pilot on board'. On the other spreader was the yellow flag Q: 'My vessel is healthy and I request free pratique'. To add to it all, at the mizzen mast was the plain blue ensign. The long-established maritime flag for Great Britain is, of course, the red ensign, and probably this is the one we should have worn, rather than the blue version. Because of my membership of the RNSA I was entitled to hoist the undefaced blue ensign, but in fact, this was to cause the occasional difficulty in places remote from home waters. Its meaning was often not understood. Perhaps most importantly of all in the full display was our 'courtesy flag', conveying a mark of respect to our hosts. Above the signal flag hoist we had this flying in the form of the French national flag, the Tricolore, which remained hoisted the whole time we were in French Polynesian waters. The courtesy flag had a somewhat deeper meaning, however, because it indicated that we accepted the islands were part of the Republic of France, albeit there was in reality no legitimate right of ownership, they having been stolen from the previous owners at gunpoint. In actual fact, the group of islands could well have been British, but Cook, and before him the discoverer of Tahiti, Captain Wallis of the Royal Navy, well before the arrival of the French gunboats, had deliberately chosen not to claim it for the British crown. It was not theirs to claim.

Whilst we were settling down in our berth, the multi-ethnic crowd of onlookers had grown. They gave us a happy welcome with a cheer and the hope we would enjoy their island. We could not help but notice in their midst quite a few young girls, all smiles and prettiness, who had arrived riding side-saddle on motor scooters behind their boyfriends. They were to become a familiar sight, night and day, as they rode along the boulevard close to our stern, long hair blowing in the wind and laughing.

Accompanied by some of the bystanders, acting as guides, I walked into the town centre to call on the port authority, police and customs. These were all quite relaxed. I paid the modest harbour dues, demanded in advance, which included the services of the pilot for both entry and exit and repaired back on board. It was time to sample the delights of Papeete. Evening was coming on and the bright lights beckoned. The passage from the Marquesas had been the easiest of all our passages to date, with benign weather, gentle breezes and an absence of those blinding squalls, peculiar in the tropics, which can make life so uncomfortable. We had consequently not arrived in Papeete tired out the way we had been on previous landfalls. We were ready for those bright lights.

Having attended to ship's business I felt it was due time I let someone in the navy in New Zealand know where I was, having last sent a situation report way back in Colón. That had been over three months ago. During this span of time of no news, I could only surmise on what conclusion had been reached in far off Wellington: a) it was presumed I had sunk without trace; or b) there was some confidence I would report in from somewhere, sometime; or c) naval command had its mind on other things.

Next morning, after a lie-in to compensate for the delay there had been in getting to bed the night before, we turned up at the British Consulate wondering, a little doubtfully, what sort of reception we would receive. Our previous experience with the consulate in Las Palmas had not been too encouraging. The Papeete branch of Her Majesty's Consular Service was a different animal altogether. The consul himself was home on leave and we were in the hands of the vice-consul. He was to prove kindness itself, throwing the consulate open to us with an immediate invitation to enjoy a shower and at all times use the place as our own, including a suggestion we should sleep there every night. The vice-consul, David, already knew about us, it transpiring that the Navy Office in Wellington had reached conclusion b) by informing the consulate of our movements with the hopeful prediction we would turn up sometime.

Over coffee it became apparent that David felt it his duty to inform us about a certain aspect of life in the islands, and one particularly relevant to Papeete.

'Clap is rampant in the town. You are two young chaps and there are plenty of very attractive young girls around. Take care!'

During our time in Polynesia we had become aware of the ills bestowed on the natives over the last 200 years, two of the principal ones being venereal disease and missionary domination. The origins of sexual disease in the islands are obscure, except that it had been introduced by westerners. Before Cook's time it was unknown amongst the islanders. Although the Society group was visited by Quirós in the early 17th century, the discovery of Tahiti is usually attributed to Wallis in 1767, who fully documented his stay on the island. There appears to have been no perception that his men may have infected the local women, although given every opportunity to do so. In 1768 the next known visitor was Bougainville. Sometime later, when Cook was in Otaheite, the native name for what was to become Tahiti, his men contracted the scourge. In the intervening period after Bougainville, the Spanish had tried to establish a Roman Catholic mission, but this had been short-lived. It is generally accepted that neither Wallis nor Cook were the guilty parties, so it has to be assumed that either Bougainville's French seamen or the Spanish sailors from the mission ships brought the disease to Polynesia. It spread rapidly, vastly assisted by the sexual freedom naturally enjoyed by the Polynesians. It was a major cause of the massive depopulation that ensued throughout the islands.

On his return home, Bougainville wrote a book, *A Voyage Round the World in 1766, 1767, 1768 and 1769*, which reveals some special difficulties of his own whilst in Tahiti.

'As we came nearer the shore, the number of islanders surrounding our ships increased. The canoes were full of females and most of these fair females were naked. It was very difficult, amidst such a sight, to keep at their work four hundred young French sailors, who had seen no women for six months. In spite of our precautions, a young girl came on board, and placed herself upon the quarterdeck, near one of the hatchways, which was open, in order to give air to those who were heaving at the capstan below it. The girl carelessly dropped a cloth, which had covered her, and appeared to the eyes of all beholders, such as Venus showed herself to the Phrygian shepherds, having, indeed, the celestial form of that goddess. Both sailors and soldiers endeavoured to come to the hatchway; and the capstan was never hove with more alacrity than on this occasion. At last our cares succeeded in keeping these bewitched fellows in order, though it was no less difficult to keep the command of ourselves.' We don't know how successful he was with this latter endeavour.

The problems presented to those early captains by Tahitian maidens, not demonstrating any great sense of shyness, were first to be experienced by Wallis in HMS *Dolphin* on anchoring in Matavai Bay. A large fleet of canoes, containing an estimated 4,000 Tahitians, came out to greet the new arrivals. In the canoes were many bare-breasted young women, which did not escape the attention of Wallis's 150 seamen. Suddenly, for some unknown reason, the natives started throwing stones, to be repulsed by broadsides from the ship. However, fences were mended and trade began. Top of the list were iron nails, metal being unknown in Polynesia, and so was launched prostitution. This practice did not exist in the islands, being totally irrelevant to the Polynesian culture of free love. It did not take long for the islands' women to catch on to the fact that they had an asset, invaluable to the visiting sailors, which could occasion the acquisition of the equally invaluable iron nail.

Cook was also not unaware of what was around him, confiding to his journal:

'The young girls whenever they can collect eight or ten together dance a very indecent dance, which they call Tumorodee, singing most indecent songs and using most indecent actions in the practice of which they are brought up from their earliest childhood.'

Cook's journal was published on his return home and, coupled with Bougainville's book, ensured that Europeans, pruriently inclined or otherwise, now knew for the first time about this paradise on Earth in the South Seas. The Tahitians' fate was sealed.

Very little is known about how Cook, as a man, coped with Tahiti's indulgence of total sexual freedom and 'its women warm in welcome'. Innumerable biographies and his own writings do not reveal much. It is difficult to accept he remained throughout just a dispassionate observer, restricting himself merely to making objective comments on the Polynesian attitude to life such as: 'There is a scale in dissolute sensuality, which these people have ascended, wholly unknown to every other nation.' His own special position in the scheme of things put him in a particularly difficult situation. As captain of the ship, the maintenance of discipline and preservation of his authority demanded a high degree of exemplary behaviour in the way he appeared to his men. Added to this he was, it is evident, of strong moral code and faithful as a husband. What he had to contend with, however, were the pressures on him when dealing with the locals. His was a world of high society, mixing with the chiefs and tribal elders. They would consider it the most natural act in the world, not to mention their duty, to offer a favourite daughter to their honoured guest, the girl herself assuredly a most willing participant. To have declined such a gift, no matter how politely done, would have been taken as a major insult, so major that Cook would have found it next to impossible to contemplate such an action.

Having done his best to frighten us to death, David then invited us to lunch for the next day. This, cooked in the traditional native way, was to be a delight. We collected our mail and returned on board to catch up on family affairs and rediscover there was still a life out there in the world apart from ours of boat and sea.

The other major contributor to the islands' depopulation and the demise of the Polynesian traditional way of life was the 'missionary effect'. Following national publicity about Cook's voyages, it did not take long for well-intentioned would-be purveyors of the Word to perceive that in Tahiti lay fertile ground, ready to receive the Gospel. In 1797, under the command of Captain Wilson, the ship *Duff*, which had been chartered by the London Missionary Society, arrived with the first load of lay preachers. It was to take them and their successors over 20 years before the first conversion was made, but thereafter, with the full co-operation of the local chiefs, responding to bribery and threats, progress was rapid until the domination of the Tahitians' lives became total. A way of life which had existed for thousands of years died, and with it large swathes of the population. The missionaries, it would seem, were unabashed at what they had done.

A discerning and sad reflection on the 'missionary effect' is contained in Somerset Maugham's short story, *Rain*. Maugham had been through the South Seas in 1917 and had spent some time in Tahiti. One of the central characters in the story is an English, totally dedicated missionary, and here we have him expounding on his attitude to the Polynesians, as conveyed in a 'sermon' to a visitor from Britain.

'We'll save them in spite of themselves. Yes, with God's help I'll save them. I must save them. You see, they were so naturally depraved that they couldn't be brought to see their wickedness. We had to make sins out of what they thought were natural actions. We had to make it a sin, not only to commit adultery and to lie and thieve, but to expose their bodies and to dance and not come to church. I made it a sin for a girl to show her bosom and a sin for a man not to wear trousers.'

'How?'

'I instituted fines. Obviously the only way to make people realise that an action is sinful is to punish them if they commit it. I fined them if they didn't come to church, and I fined them if they danced. I fined them if they were improperly dressed. I had a tariff, and every sin had to be paid for either in money or work. And at last I made them understand.'

'But did they never refuse to pay?'

'How could they? You must remember that in the last resort I could expel them from their church membership.'

'Did they mind that?'

The missionary smiled a little and gently rubbed his hands.

'They couldn't sell their copra. When the men fished they got no share of the catch. It meant something very like starvation. Yes, they minded quite a lot.'

A fictional scenario perhaps, but uncomfortably portraying reality.

Whether the influence of the missionary was good or bad or something of both is, of course, open to wide debate, and views on the issue, like the perception of beauty, lie 'in the eye of the beholder'. Opinions on the matter have been aired in the writings of innumerable visitors to Tahiti, but all too often the views expressed are those of 'overnight experts' who have spent only the briefest of periods on the spot. An observer not of this breed is Herman Melville, much admired by Robert Louis Stevenson as 'a writer who has touched the South Seas with genius', and one whose opinions carry real weight.

'Let the savages be civilized, but civilize them with benefits, and not with evils; and let heathenism be destroyed, but not by destroying the heathen.

Among the islands of Polynesia, no sooner are the images overturned, the temples demolished, and the idolaters converted into nominal Christians, than disease, vice, and premature death make their appearance. Enlightened individuals…clamorously announce the progress of the Truth.'

So what were our impressions as yet more visitors in a long line? Tahiti, for us, lived up to its reputation of unsurpassed beauty, but unfortunately that was more than could be said for Papeete. It was witness to the ravages that western cultures had imposed on what had once been a South Sea *paradis*. Most of the indigenous population had been driven out or died off as a result of the white invasion. In its place was now a motley collection of French, Americans, British and other Europeans, Australians, New Zealanders, Chinese and half-castes, but happily there were also some full-blooded Tahitians, or nearly so. Also happily included in this mix were very pretty girls. Overall, the impression was one of vibrant life. Constant movement of people, motor vehicles racing up and down in the shape of trucks, runabouts and obscenely large American automobiles; vehicles of all kinds in varying states of repair, bicycles and scooters all adding to the noise and pollution.

Music was everywhere, day and night, but most of the time of a type that one would not term easy, enjoyable listening: American-style, mixed up with westernized Tahitian renderings, dominated. When we stepped off our stern onto the quay beside the road into town, we could turn left or right from one contrast to the other. To the right were berthed the inter-island vessels, and further along the pleasant, cool residential area of the more well-to-do, overlooking the lagoon. The leafy lawns and shady verandas suggested relaxed, comfortable living. A left turn took us into the business sector, civil administration centre and shopping area. White-owned shops jostled for a place in the sun with those of the Chinese, and amongst them one could get most things. Back of the main street was the central vegetable and fruit market, an unattractive building in itself, with close to it more interesting satellite small stalls. Between them all we had a wonderful choice of exotic tropical fruits and island-grown vegetables. Shopping was all action and noise.

Dominating the commercial scene were the Chinese. Originally imported into the island in the 1860s as cheap labour, the Tahitians not being work inclined, to tend the newly established white-owned plantations, they had stayed, multiplied and become prosperous until it was estimated at the time of our visit they accounted for a fifth of the population. With them was associated opium which, combined with the white man's alcohol and firearms, exacerbated the afflictions bestowed on the Tahitians.

The Tahitians of today would be of a very different race to that which Darwin and, even more so, Cook knew. A 'one-liner' had it that the missionary and the French took control of their lives, the Chinese took control of their economy, with the Polynesians left with just their land. In Tahiti, this perhaps rather simplistic observation was unhappily evidently only too true. However, we were told that in more recent days there had been in the islands amongst the young a reversion to the beliefs, customs and culture of their ancestors, but one has to doubt how long this trend would withstand the seductive, escalating power of technology, with its so-called benefits to all peoples.

Throughout the town ran a theme of liquor and sex. So-called nightclubs catered for those seeking an evening's entertainment and satisfaction. Two of the principal ones, Quinns and Col Bleu, had been recommended to us on our arrival, but we found them not quite as exciting as we had been led to believe. They were tawdry. However, they were alive with people and the food was cheap and good, the former feature being of particular interest to us and our pockets.

Where Cook, Wallis and Bougainville had anchored their ships, in the northern reaches of the harbour, flying boats came down, bringing in hopeful travellers looking for the paradise they thought would be there for them to enjoy. In the main they were middle-aged males with pot bellies and they were too late. Quinns and Col Bleu did quite well, though. The flying boats of Tasman Empire Air Line (TEAL), the predecessor of Air New Zealand, stopped bringing in their pot bellies when, in 1960, the international airport was opened, to welcome in today a quarter of a million camera-wielding tourists a year.

In fairness to the French, their attitude to the Tahitians was one of tolerant understanding of their free morals. This was remarked on by the Swedish ethnologist, Bengt Danielsson, who had been one of the crew of *Kon-Tiki*. He had stayed to live with the Tahitians, study their habits and write about them. His book, *Love in the South Seas*, was being written whilst we were in Papeete. It is not an erotic account but brings out vividly the Polynesians' love of sex which played such a major role in their lives. They indulged themselves in it and they enjoyed it so much because it was such fun. That is until the Anglican missionaries came along.

One of the 'must-see' landmarks on the island was where Cook carried out his famous observations of the transit of the planet Venus across the face of the sun. Pointe Vénus, the northern extremity of the island, was in its way something of a shrine to which we duly made our pilgrimage. A lighthouse and a church with a couple of radio masts were located in near proximity to a stone in the ground on which was marked a meridian line where Captain Cook made his observations. Cook had been in Tahiti largely because he had been sent there by the Admiralty, specifically to make these observations. As a biographer records:

'Calculations having been made that the planet Venus would pass over the sun's disc in 1769, the Royal Society, under the patronage of King George the Third, presented a memorial to Government, requesting that a vessel might be fitted out to convey proper persons to observe the transit.' The government, in the form of the Lords Commissioners of the Admiralty, appointed Mr Cook 'to the distinguished post of the commander of the expedition and promoted [him] to the rank of lieutenant in the Royal Navy.' In the ex-collier *Endeavour*, Cook, now entitled to be addressed as Captain, duly arrived in Otaheiti (Tahiti) and executed his orders to watch Venus, like a model on the catwalk, strut across the sun. This was 3 June 1769. The purpose of observing this beauty parade was an attempt to determine more accurately than had been achieved hitherto the distance of the sun from the Earth. Having an idea of what was the diameter of the sun, and also of the distance of Venus, our closest neighbour from Earth, the time taken for the planet's transit would hopefully enable the sun's distance to be worked out by geometry. Cook, to be on the safe side, set up two observation posts, separated by some distance, and in good conditions took his readings. They were not a resounding success but the right spin was put on them.

'Both the parties that were sent out to make observations on the transit met with good success, though they differed more than might have been expected in their records of the contact.' Cook laid the blame for this squarely on the shoulders of the girl herself in that she was behaving like a woman – difficult.

Cook went on to open up the Pacific, up till then largely a blank space, apart from various cartographers' flights of imagination colourfully shown on the world's maps. He was, of course, an extraordinary man, respected for his exemplary conduct, for which history has rightfully treated him kindly. On arrival in Tahiti in *Endeavour*, amongst his first actions was to draw up a code of practice for the guidance of all hands 'for the better establishment of a regular trade with the natives'. This exhorted his men to be humane to the inhabitants and to cultivate friendly relations with them. The cynically minded would say his edict was commercially driven rather than out of respect for those inhabitants' human rights. However, he has always, and justifiably so, been considered humane. The maximum punishment handed out by Cook was two dozen lashes, which compares favourably with many hundreds – which frequently was the case. It is all a matter of degree, as not long before this 'flogging round the fleet' was still in vogue, the offender being rowed around the fleet to be handed out a dozen lashes by the boatswain's mate of each ship in the anchorage. Cook undoubtedly merits his reputation, but consider this cameo: *Endeavour* is at anchor off an island in the Society group when a canoe paddles alongside. A ship's officer hands down a piece of Otaheitean cloth for barter to an occupant. It was of particularly high quality and the recipient decided to keep it.

Furthermore, he refused to pay for it or give anything in exchange. He 'paid dearly, however, for his temerity', being shot dead on the spot. His companions, rather understandably, 'fled with great precipitancy'. Interestingly enough, the tribal elders felt he had deserved his fate. It would seem Cook held the same opinion, as seemingly no further account was taken of the incident, and certainly no punishment, it would appear, was administered. If this murder had been committed back home in England, it might be surmised that Cook could well have been subjected at least to a court martial as being party to an act of unlawful killing. What does this tell us about the man? Although his moral standards were certainly higher than many of his contemporaries, he was still 'a man of his times' and as such imbued with the conviction, shared wholeheartedly by the missionaries, that natives and heathens were lower down the human scale and certainly did not have the right to possession of their lands, let alone their souls. That right rested solely in the hands of the whites. It was their God-given preserve. The arrogance of the early voyagers, and especially the missionaries, was staggering. Although Cook's attitude was commendable over not annexing Tahiti, with the hope it would never be colonized, he did take possession of other islands 'in the name of his sovereign'.

Back at the ranch, or rather our berth at the quay, we were in contact with the other yachts around us, all American and from the US west coast. We had given up on the likelihood of ever seeing a British yacht. Our immediate neighbour was a plush schooner of 70 foot out of San Francisco, *Nordlys*. Next in the trot was another ketch of about our size, *Mandalay*, also American, which was of some interest. She was owned by Pebble, a young member of one of America's most illustrious families, the Rockefellers. Apparently he had been, he told us, something of a thorn in the family's side, to the extent that they had bought him the boat and told him to push off and not to be in too much of a hurry to return. This he gave no indication of doing. Judging by the frequency of visits by young maidens with long flowing tresses, and the sound of laughter and guitars, day and night, he was not feeling too much pain over his banishment. Pebble and his graceful companions were good company, and Peter in particular spent many a happy hour on board, joining in the music and enjoying the entertainment. So did I, but for me a few days of rest were called for as

I wrestled with a complaining stomach. Was it Quinns or Col Bleu? The hygiene police would have had a field day there whilst they took time off to investigate first-hand the other attractions those places had on offer. Our departure date was coming up and it was agreed that when we left for our projected stop off in Moorea, *Mandalay* would sail over with us in company.

Stored and watered with the ship ready for sea, it was time for farewells. A final drink, or two, with fellow skippers up in the bar brought home how much I would miss that hard-drinking, warm and convivial gang. Then a thank you visit to David and the staff in the consulate, with whom I left a cable to be sent off to the Navy Office breaking the news I was off and they should start to hold their breaths towards the end of April. The final call was at the Harbour Office to obtain clearance and to arrange for the pilot. I really need not have bothered. The same relaxed mood prevailed, but even more so than when I had first presented myself. They inferred that actually nothing needed to be done. With our harbour dues already paid I could go whenever I felt like it. But what about the pilot? The response was one of those lifts of the shoulders which convey so much expression; a physical feat excelled in by the French and one with which no other race on Earth can compete. In other words, it was entirely up to me. The message evidently was that it was only important to have a pilot on arrival to ensure we got into the harbour safely so we would be able to spend our money in the town. Now we were leaving we would be making no further contribution to the economy. If we landed up on the reef, so be it. I said not to worry about the pilot, and about this the officials were quite happy. Less trouble for them and they already had my money in the till, his services covered both ways. Pragmatic people, the French.

Tuesday 23 March 1100 Slipped from the quay. Recovered our anchors.

It was quite extraordinary how the word of our departure had spread. The same small crowd assembled off our stern. Someone let our lines go, accompanied by much laughter and expressions of goodwill, with wholehearted exhortations for us to return. The voices sounded as though they really meant it. My memory of our departure, as the gap between our stern and the quay widened, was of smiling faces and white teeth.

We passed through the reef without incident, leaving astern of us Tahiti, the Pearl of the Pacific, its beauty on full display. The sharply broken skyline was outlined in clear, sharp contours against a cloudless sky, and down the side of the mountain to the sea plunged the heavily wooded clefts, their depths emphasised by the dark shadows which lay in them. It has long been the touching little custom for voyagers leaving a Pacific island to cast upon the waters a lei, the sweet-smelling garland of intertwined flowers, to make sure that one returns. We did not leave a lei in our wake. We did not want to return. The island, which has suffered so much from change, would be undergoing yet more, and I for one did not want to see it.

As we cleared the pass in the reef, laid out before us was Moorea, rising abruptly out of the sea, dramatic and imposing like its neighbour but with an even more jagged silhouette of starkly defined peaks. Ahead, on full display as we closed it, was the Gem of the Pacific, transcending the Pearl, its sister beauty. At 1600 we passed through the reef into Pao Pao Bay. It was just lovely, quite the most beautiful setting I had ever seen; a South Sea island to perfection. It was deserted, the silence broken only by the crashing of the surf on the enclosing reef. The sense of isolation totally enveloped us before it was intruded into by the arrival of *Mandalay*. She anchored a little way off. We had had our moment of sublimity and did not resent her intrusion and, at one with the world around us, we respected her privacy. On board was Pebble and he was not alone. It was evident he was not proposing to exchange the way of life in Tahiti for a monastic one in Moorea.

We woke to a glorious morning and wished so much we had come over here earlier, at the expense of our time in Papeete. The town had been of considerable interest and well worth the visit, but it was unnatural and it had been spoilt. Pao Pao was natural and completely unspoilt. We would have enjoyed a few lotus-eating days, immersed in its loveliness and tranquillity, but we were compelled to get started on the last leg, the long haul to Auckland. After all, there in New Zealand we would still be in Polynesia, but how different!

With the thought of a long ocean passage ahead of us, it seemed to me to be a wise seamanlike precaution to recheck the chronometer's time and rate before we launched into space. We were anchored in the lagoon, protected by the reef, in calm water, with a clear view of the horizon. This was an ideal spot for taking an astronomical fix from a steady platform to compare with our known exact position on the chart, determined terrestrially by taking compass bearings of features on the shores around the bay. Any discrepancy between these positions would throw up the time error on the chronometer watch, which could be calculated by working back the sight for longitude to give the correct time. I had not been able to pick up any time signals whilst we had been in the islands, that being beyond the powers of our radio. However, the conditions for taking celestial observations were good, such that having taken them I worked out our position with some degree of confidence. I was somewhat surprised at the result.

'Take your hat off, Peter!'

'Why?'

'You are standing in the nave of Coventry Cathedral.'

As it did not appear from our surroundings we were in a holy setting, there was obviously a navigational glitch somewhere. I rechecked our position obtained by the terrestrial bearings and could find no error. I then reworked my astronomical calculations and again could detect no error. What had put us where we obviously weren't? We might well, however, have been in holy surroundings, because suddenly a blinding light of revelation shone forth from on high. I remembered the time of year! In the southern hemisphere, winter was upon us. Sure enough, the *Nautical Almanac* confirmed that a couple of days before we had left Papeete, the sun had deserted our hemisphere and gone north. It had crossed the equinoctial, but we had been a little too occupied with life in the town to have noted the occasion of the autumnal equinox. It was not something they worried too much about in Papeete: the seasons did not change to any significance. For so long I had been accustomed to reading the letter 'S' for 'South' before the figures for degrees and minutes in the *Almanac* for the sun's declination, and I had failed to register that this was now an N for North. Feeding this into the calculations changed everything.

'Peter, you can put your hat back on again!'

The difference between the two positions in Pao Pao Bay was now gratifyingly small. The error in the time shown by the chronometer now known, and its rate re-established, we were ready to depart. With our hearts heavy at leaving, we got our anchor and passed close by *Mandalay* to exchange greetings and farewells. Peter and I were as one in wishing we were staying on in that superb scene, but it was now too late for second thoughts. We were on our way. We told ourselves without conviction it was always better to leave when not wanting to do so rather than staying too long.

At 1100 we passed through the reef under jib and mainsail, turning west to cross the entrance to Opunohu Bay, from which we took our departure. It looked so inviting that the thought welled up we should weaken and sample what was so invitingly on display before our eyes. It was a picture postcard view of gently waving palm trees, golden sands and smooth, unruffled vividly blue lagoon against the backdrop of deeply fissured, wooded mountain slopes. We diverted our eyes and sailed on. The Enchanted Isles had the power to have held us irresistibly in their embrace. How fortunate we were to have known them.

The exercise to check the accuracy of our chronometer could not help but bring home the problems facing those early navigators as they blundered about the enormous sweep of the South Pacific, with only the vaguest idea where they actually were most of the time. There was no mercy in a coral reef if they got it wrong. We were still in Cook territory, and how, for example, had he found his way so confidently to these islands, having criss-crossed large swathes of the ocean on the way? It is difficult for a modern navigator to fathom this out. On his first voyage he had no chronometer, the longitude problem still in the process of being solved, or rather the Admiralty was having difficulty in accepting its solution. John Harrison, a carpenter employed on a country estate, amateur mathematician and clockmaker, had finally succeeded in constructing the first timepiece accurate enough to determine longitude at sea. This was some years before Cook had set off on his voyage, but through official prevarication he was denied its use. Rather he had to fall back on 'lunars', a longitude-finding method based on measuring the angle between the moon and selected stars, considered fixed in the firmament, and their position in it shown in the almanacs of the time. The procedure was prone to error in taking the observations, exacerbated by a heaving deck, and required lengthy calculations, providing in themselves further sources of error. It was ironic that this method had been dreamed up by Dr Maskelyne, the astronomer royal, who had done his best to rubbish Harrison's efforts, because it was Maskelyne's unshakeable conviction that the right way to determine time, to the required accuracy, was not by some man-made contraption but rather by using what God had provided, the heavenly bodies.

Maskelyne was a brilliant mind and compiled the first *Nautical Almanac*, in which he included the positions of various stars to enable the lunar system to be used. However, in the end, Harrison won the day, and four copies of his final masterpiece, a watch known as the H4, went with Cook on his second voyage. Remarkable accuracy was achieved. Only the Admiralty could afford the cost of a chronometer, and although the cost came down progressively, it was many years before its use became widespread in the world's merchant fleets, lunars holding a place until the 20th century. It is a snippet of history that on the eve of Cook embarking on his second voyage in his replacement ship, *Resolution*, a time check was carried out in Plymouth on the same lines that I had done in Pao Pao Bay, nearly 200 years later. Observations were made on Drake's Island which established the latitude and longitude with the time ascertained to 'put in motion the timepieces and watches'.

As we progressed along the northern shores of Moorea, the wind came and went such that we had to fall back on the engine on brief occasions to keep us clear of the breakers as we cleared the north-west tip of the island. Our relations with the engine had improved somewhat, mainly because we had come to realise that it was inclined to behave more favourably if we fed it the nourishment it needed and, when it needed it, in the form of petrol, rather than trying to force paraffin down its throat. Daybreak saw us on course for Auckland before a light east-north-easterly wind, under all plain sail, plus the spinnaker doing more than its share of the work. The log records:

'A very quiet night with Tahiti just visible in the bright moonlight. Little wind but the boat keeps ghosting along. Saw a shark very close, gently swimming around us.'

Ahead of us lay a period of frustratingly slow progress in light, uncertain winds. The prevailing wind through the Society group is predominantly easterly but the region is beset by a high incidence of calms. According to that never failing source of knowledge, the *Pacific Islands Pilot*, over the last 60 years of record taking the frequency of calms in March ranged from 21 per cent in late afternoon to a staggering 55 per cent in early morning. We could not say we had not been warned. However, the not unreasonable expectancy was that once we got clear of the islands we would feel the effects of the south-east trade wind, now free-ranging and free of land interference, and start to make progress. We were wrong. The wind continued fading away to nothing, with lengthy periods of total calm becoming ever more frequent. We felt aggrieved and started to take it personally. Writing up the log became a helpful way of relieving feelings.

Flat calm with no steerage way. Have been becalmed all day and now into the second one; this is becoming a record. However, the sea in close proximity to the boat is marvellous, the deepest blue I have seen yet and the surface completely smooth. These are without doubt the calmest spells we have had in the entire passage, beating even the Gulf of Panama. These days which keep repeating themselves are so tedious and it is particularly irritating to see our fresh provisions vanishing with nothing to show for it.

Desperation coming over us, we tried running the engine for an eight hour stint to help our morale by giving the illusion we were going somewhere. In the scheme of things it achieved little. Twenty miles was nothing in just over 2,200 on a Great Circle track to cover, and we could ill afford the fuel for such an extravagance.

There was another point of concern over our slow passage. With the approach of winter in New Zealand, *Ocean Passages for the World* told us westerly winds would be likely. They would also be fresh and I did not relish having the wind well forward of the beam again, with water continuously over the decks and everything, including us, getting wet. I wanted to get to Auckland before those westerlies set in. On the plus side, we were getting significant help from the ocean current. The South Equatorial Current, having threaded its way through the Societies, turns south-west and was giving us a good push along. The other plus was, as compensation for the lack of progress, the calm spells meant relaxed living. We were having meals on deck or at the table together in the saloon, enjoying swims over the side and, moreover, with the boat going nowhere, we could harden in sheets and sleep our heads off. These consolation prizes did little, however, to relieve the overall sense of frustration and tedium.

Despite the paucity of wind, we had nevertheless been making southing, albeit pathetically slowly, and quite suddenly everything was about to change.

'Nobody has found a substitute for the sweet chuckling of water, like the laughter of young girls, that you hear outside the hull whilst lying in a small yacht's bunk.' So said Samuel Eliot Morison and he was right. In the midst of yet another flattest of calms I had stretched out below on my bunk. There was no movement to the sea, no movement to the boat, no sound of wind and no rustling of gear. Peter was dozing at the idle tiller. I must have drifted off because I suddenly became aware of a strange sound that had not been there before. And then I realized what it was. It was the laughter of young girls trilling sweetly along the boat's side just beside my head. A feeling of joy swept through me. I got up and there was Peter, his hand firmly holding the tiller and he was grinning.

'Yes, we have wind!'

The wind had suddenly come true and steady out of the south-east and slowly building. We were under Yankee jib, balloon foresail with main, topsail and mizzen full of wind. The lot was up. Everything drawing on a reach and we were making six knots; the sea around us still quite flat and sparkling under the sun. 'It was a day to remember.'

We were to stay like that for the next few days, the despondency and state of near despair we had been in during the preceding days, forgotten. The only cloud on our horizon was Peter suddenly once again developing toothache. This could have been serious and we debated the best course of action. Auckland was maybe three weeks away, and that was a long time to have to endure toothache. Rarotonga was within reach and we could have fetched it with the wind we now had, but Peter said the pain was intermittent and thought we should carry on, if necessary with doses of painkillers. What might have been at the back of his mind were the options. Chief of these was extraction. The scenario for this was not good. Our medical kit did not embrace the dental tools and gum injection equipment to ensure a non-agonizing operation. Pliers out of the boat's tool kit would be less than ideal. I also lacked a dental assistant to hold him down. We decided to press on to Auckland, the decision being swayed by us now having wind and the wind charts suggesting we would keep it. I just had to hope it was the right decision. The problem was Peter belonged to the 'stiff upper lip' brigade, and in such circumstances I never knew if I was getting the truth. It was, as it turned out, the right decision, as by great good fortune the tooth seemed to cure itself.

Sterner days were now our lot, the days of warmth and idleness just a memory. The wind had settled down, fresh and cutting, south of east and slowly veering into the south bringing the cold with it. For the first time for what seemed ages we were sailing under reefed mainsail, and out came oilskin coats over thick woollen jerseys. The helmsman's bare feet readjusted to the change in temperature as once again they got used to the cosy feel of cold sea water swilling about the cockpit sole. We were back to reality. I was later mindful of a somewhat relevant remark by Kevin O'Riordan, who had accompanied Humphrey Barton on their demanding, and often wet, epic crossing of the Atlantic in *Vertue XXXV*. When subsequently I had occasion to be sailing with Kevin, an exponent of bare feet, he related that when once asked if he ever wore socks he replied, 'No, they give me colds.'

In the log entries, such as 'Sea state: rough' started to appear. For most of the journey out from Plymouth we had largely escaped seriously bad weather, and although experiencing some unpleasant conditions down the west coast of France and off Portugal, most of the way across the North Atlantic and the South Pacific gales had not featured. Our time was about to come. The classic build up heralding the advent of a gale appeared in the heavens high above our heads as the day progressed. Streaking thin cirrus cloud, with its distinctive, curved 'mares' tails', progressively covered the sky, and the barometer inexorably started its downward fall. That night there was a multicoloured vivid halo ringing the moon and shining through the cloud veil. With the wind steadily increasing in strength and veering round to WNW, the message was becoming all too clear. We were soon to have a full gale on our hands.

In an attempt at precision in the imprecise art of weather prediction, which it tries to convey in the shipping forecast, the Meteorological Office would today define 'soon' as '6 to 12 hours from time of issue', and that was to be right. By mid-morning next day we had its full force upon us. Although we were without any way of measuring wind speed, the state of the sea told it all. Gale 8 on the Beaufort Scale has the wind at 34 to 40 knots, resulting in 'moderately high waves; edges of crests begin to break into spindrift. The foam is blown in well-marked streaks along the direction of the wind.' But for those unfortunates onshore and deserving of every sympathy it 'breaks twigs off trees; wind impedes progress'. Around us the scene measured up well to the former description. We gave the situation best. Leaving the boat quietly hove-to on the starboard tack under reefed staysail, we retired below, pulling the hatch over our heads to turn in for the duration. In closing off the hatch opening we had shut out the sound of wind and sea, it feeling so much more secure in the sudden quiet of the cabin. The noise on deck associated with a full gale is dominating and threatening. The sea tumbling over itself with the crests breaking has the roar of crashing surf. The wind tearing through the rigging and swirling round the masts sets up a pronounced moaning sound which rises dramatically in tone to a near howl as the boat, following the action of the sea, rolls and lurches up to windward, the relative wind speed rising sharply. A gaff-rigged boat has a mass of lengths of rope hanging down the mast, and these hauled taut resonate like the strings of a large musical instrument. The change from the clamour on deck to the peace down below is most marked. The noise is possibly the most frightening feature of a gale.

The front moved through, the wind shifting back into south of west and slowly moderating such that we started sailing again just about on course under No 2 jib and trysail. During the blow, the use of the galley had been denied us. Trying to work at the stove up in the forepeak was unacceptably difficult, the motion being just too much. In anticipation of this situation, the frame I had made – in which swung a Primus stove in its gimbals, the whole assembly being mounted when needed on a shelf at the after end of the cabin – made life much more tolerable. This was another occasion when the Heinz self-heating cans came into their own, due recognition of which featured prominently in my final report to the company. They did much for the helmsman coming on watch when emerging into a cold, wet cockpit.

The big day came up. We went off the South Eastern sheet of the South Pacific chart onto the South Western sheet, and in doing so passed the 1,000 miles to go. Now showing on the chart was New Zealand. It could be seen to be within reach. The waters in which we were now sailing are particularly noteworthy to the ornithologist and that special breed of person, the 'birder', being the northern limit of the world of the black-browed albatross. On cue, the first one appeared, and henceforth one or more kept us permanent company up till our arrival in New Zealand. The sighting of this great bird had its own significance for me, bringing into focus awareness we were nearing my homeland. The first time I had seen one was when sailing from Wellington for England nearly 12 years before, in 1942, in these selfsame waters.

It is a feature of the black-browed albatross, the most widespread of the species, to follow ships, and many had been the hours spent standing on the afterdeck of our passenger ship, *Rauhine*, absorbed in watching and admiring the fluidity of movement and grace of these creatures.

Although not identified as such by Samuel Taylor Coleridge through the haze of laudanum, it was most likely a black-browed albatross that played the pivotal role in *The Rime of the Ancient Mariner*. Albeit we were not sharing, self-inflicted or otherwise, the Mariner's misfortunes, we nevertheless knew something of what he had endured when we were locked in the depths of windless periods in the Doldrums.

The last leg, we knew, was not going to be easy, the pilot charts making that only too clear. *Ocean Passages* emphasised the point, talking about 'unsteady trade winds' and 'variables' for the region we were now entering. The Good Book also gave warning of the threat of tropical storms, known as 'cyclones', in the south-western part of the Pacific, as still in season until the end of April. These usually generated to the east of Australia and the north of New Zealand, then to track westward. The risk to us was not great, but nevertheless it was there and sufficient to cause me enough concern to do my homework and read up about the warning signs of a cyclone coming our way. The *Pilot* also took the subject seriously with helpful hints to the mariner. 'The indications of the approach of a tropical storm include: a swell not caused by the wind then blowing.' I made it a point when I took over the watch to study the run of the sea, explaining what it was I was looking for to Peter. His response was to laugh.

'You are always worrying about something or other. Is this the latest one? If one hits us, so be it. Not much we can do about it!' What a gift, I thought, to have such fatalism. But I had not given up completely.

'Yes, but the swell's direction would give us a clue on which quadrant of the storm is ahead of us. Could be the dangerous one.'

'Ben! Come on!'

The fickleness of the weather was noted in the log.

Strong gale force wind from WNW. Hove-to on starboard tack under staysail and trysail. Frequent violent squalls with drenching rain and bitingly cold spray lashing over the helmsman. A b***** awful day.

But to reinforce the point about also being in the variables there was next a completely different story:

Have been praying for an easterly wind and now have one but only just. Under all plain sail and spinnaker with little real progress. It is unfortunately only too plain to see we now have the anticipated countercurrent flowing NE at 25 miles per day or even more against us. Along with the south-east trades the favourable South Subtropical Current has gone.

Back, of course, came the wind and this time out of the south, very fresh and bringing with it a particularly uncomfortable sea, rolling relentlessly and unceasingly towards us from the far-off horizon. I suddenly felt I had had enough of it. I found myself standing up in the cockpit facing the wind and that cold, remorseless sea, cursing its spitefulness, directed personally at me, perverse and hostile. It was a living being, full of malice.

Fortunately, Peter, sound asleep below, or so I hoped, was not witness to his skipper out of control. The mood wore off and on we sailed, passing one milestone after another. Five hundred miles to Auckland and then came up 30 days at sea, the longest time yet, with our routine working well, one day flowing into the next. The only change in our lives was the change in wind and weather with the infinitely varying moods of the sea. A strong southerly brought rough, cold and boisterous sailing under storm jib and trysail with the decks running water continuously and heavy driving spray, but then soon afterwards it was all change again and it was a wonderful night's sail over a calm sea in bright moonlight with 'the old lady doing a steady 7 knots and no fuss'.

With the nort-east coast of New Zealand just a few days away, the realization came over us that the adventure was nearing its end, and with it went the feeling we didn't really want this to happen. It had all been so fulfilling. Peter and I had been through so much together in complete harmony, and sadness gripped me at the thought that it was all but over. I had come to grips with the dispassionate aggression of the sea, accepting this as just a fact of what life at sea is all about, and had recovered to a large degree my equanimity. Although, of course, looking forward to seeing again my country and family, I had become so at one with our way of life that I would have been relaxed about sailing on. *Tern* also indicated she was happy about continuing. All she needed was fresh water plus some fresh provisions and a new supply of torch batteries. Peter seemed to be of the same mind but would have been torn. He was keen to see New Zealand and looking forward to that experience. The country's reputation was good, being a part of the world looked upon with favour by many of his countrymen and women, quite a few of whom having strong family links with it.

Navigationally the final days were to be difficult. The weather was overcast, dull and cold, thin altostratus cloud covering the sky and obscuring completely the sun and stars, effectively preventing the taking of sights. We were closing the land on dead reckoning, about which I was not relaxed. In other words, I did not know exactly where we were. Then there was a breakthrough, albeit temporary. The outline of a watery sun suddenly appeared during the forenoon through the cloud coverage and the lower rim was sharp enough for an observation. I grabbed it. Then just after midday the sun, for a second time, put in a very brief, shy appearance and once again I grabbed it. It was now 20 minutes after the time for a standard meridian altitude at noon, when the sun and the observer share the same meridian, but it was still within the time span for an ex-meridian altitude to give a latitude position line. I had almost given up hope. Running up to it, the result of the earlier forenoon shot of the sun gave us our position. We had been fortunate as the heavens closed shut again and remained that way for the rest of the day and into the evening with no chance of star sights, but I was now happy. I knew where we were.

Monday 26 April 1900 Sighted Mokohinau light right on the nose ahead.

2200 Picked up loom of Cuvier Island light on the port bow; where it should be.

We were home! Ahead lay the entrance to the Hauraki Gulf, the large, semi-enclosed stretch of water at the bottom of which lay Auckland Harbour. At 0300 next morning we were bang in the middle of that entrance channel, making fast time in smooth water under full sail, and the memory of that moment has remained with me ever since. High above my head the mainsail, black against the night sky, was full of wind. Astern stretched a long glittering wake, alive with phosphorescence, our final link with the South Pacific, our home for the last 35 days and long before that, way back to the Galápagos.

Near the top of the gulf lay the beautiful little island of Kawau, in which was contained a sheltered anchorage where we anchored mid afternoon that day. *Tern II* had done her job. To bring us back from our ocean existence and into the world around us, the appropriate transition was as noted in the log: 'Advanced the clocks one day.' We had crossed the International

Date Line on the passage down from Moorea but had not bothered to change the day and date on board. We had been at sea long enough for these not to be of any importance in our daily lives, apart from having been noted to meet navigational dictates.

There had been no debate between us about anchoring in Kawau's Mansion House Bay rather than carrying on down to Auckland. We needed to adjust from a sea routine which had been a world of our own, shared only with boat, the elements and each other, to a world of people and structured society. We needed to catch our breath. To help with the adjustment process we launched the dinghy and went ashore to the island's only hotel for dinner. First off, I made the duty call to report in to the naval officer in charge, Auckland, checking in with the duty officer, it being out of working hours. That telephone call was, for me, hugely symbolic. I had handed back my 'ticket of leave'. Henceforth, others would dictate my life. No longer would my actions be under my sole direction, governed only by wind and sea, *Tern* and my obligations to Peter. Suddenly I had ceased to be my own man, whereas Peter would continue to be his. Perhaps I envied him. Then, after also reporting in to my parents in Christchurch, it was high time for a celebratory drink. The hotel manager assumed the role of host, insisting drinks and dinner were on the house. Things were going well.

Interrupting our first 'happy hour' on dry land, there came a telephone call from the Auckland daily newspaper requesting an interview. We were suddenly famous. I was not sure, however, how I felt about being the local lad made good. It would seem the duty officer in the naval base had embarked on a PR exercise with the press. The only guests in the hotel were a young, newly married couple on their honeymoon, no doubt expecting to have a full measure of exclusivity to enjoy it. We could only hope that the advent of two sailors straight out of their boat with tales of the high seas was not stealing the young man's thunder and spoiling the sweetness of the lovers' moment. We also had to hope that after five weeks at sea, sweetness still prevailed in our near proximity.

Next morning we were nearly to become even more famous. After a leisurely breakfast, aware of there being only a short final sail ahead of us, we hoisted our full set of canvas, perhaps to show off a little by making something of a display, and then got our anchor. Rather, that is what should have happened. Heaving in the anchor cable it came up short, fouled on something on the seabed. With the breeze picking up, we finally succeeded in sailing the anchor out, but as it came free we found ourselves heading for the rocky beach. *Tern*, with her long keel, takes some time and distance to turn. We came uncomfortably close to those rocks before we sailed clear.

Dear old Claud Worth would not have approved, being a great exponent of buoying one's anchor on an unknown seabed. We had not been far off a highly embarrassing ending to our cruise, but the press would have loved it.

In a failing wind we arrived in the approaches to Auckland's harbour to be met by a naval launch from the dockyard sent out to tow us in, casting us off when we were in the yard's confines. We were somewhat surprised, and pleasantly so, at the appearance of the launch. Apparently, the signal tower overlooking the approaches to the harbour had been co-opted to monitor our progress and alert the naval base when we closed the entrance. It was a thoughtful gesture, we having no means of ship-to-shore communication to report our arrival, apart from International Code flags or Morse code by flashing light. In this regard we would have been, 30 years on, more or less literally in the same boat as Claud, with maritime communications unchanged, but I suspect again not meeting with his approval, as our expertise in flag signalling was not likely to have been up to his standards. In his other work, *Yacht Navigation and Voyaging*, he relates how in the course of a circumnavigation of the British Isles in *Tern III* he had occasion to report in to his own authority, the redoubtable Mrs Worth.

'A little before noon we stood in towards Flamborough Head to get a telegram sent to Mrs Worth to tell her that we intended going into the Nene (or Wisbech river) instead of the Ouse. Fourteen hoists were required, but it took only a few minutes, because each hoist was read and acknowledged almost as soon as it was clear of the deck. The telegram was delivered within a couple of hours. They are smart signallers at the Flamborough station.' In our case, if the need had arisen, hopefully the signallers at the Auckland station would have been equally accommodating, having to exercise a full measure of patience.

Peter and I then carried out the last manoeuvre we were to execute together in *Tern*. The engine obligingly started and I went forward with the bow line whilst Peter put the boat alongside. I heaved my line up onto the quayside to welcoming waiting hands who secured it. As I walked aft to join Peter in the cockpit I saw him send his line ashore. It was all too apparent he was not pleased.

'Ben! I thought we had agreed a long time ago that because *Tern* is so hopeless in going astern we would always get the stern line ashore first to stop her and then get the bow line ashore.'

'Peter, I am sorry. You are right. What would I have ever done without you?'

Epilogue

What Happened to Tern II?

Shortly after our arrival in Auckland I was back at sea in a ship of war. Knowing I would not have time to sail *Tern*, and more importantly not be able to give her the attention she deserved, I reluctantly sold her.

The years passed and it was not until 1999 that I heard of her again, reading in an article in *Classic Boat*, headed '*Tern II* in NZ' that she was still sailing on the Hauraki Gulf and up for sale on her 100th birthday. Later I heard from her owner, Linn Avattar, an American from Hawaii and now in Auckland. She had rescued *Tern* from a period of neglect in a mud berth. The poor old boat's fortunes had varied over the years at the hands of a succession of owners. At some time she had been vandalized, having her lovely, classic, long counter amputated and converted to cutter rig. She had suffered additional abuse, with her interior gutted and the gracious saloon joinery torn out. Her dignity was further affronted by a ghastly deckhouse and coach roof built onto what had been a clean sweep of flush deck with handsome skylights.

Linn ran a charity, 'NameSail', aimed at fostering awareness of domestic violence. The idea was to display on the boat's mainsail the names of donors to the charity, the cause being promoted by sailing *Tern* round the world and ending back in England. In the course of sailing to Hawaii they ran into bad weather, the boat taking such a beating that they had to seek shelter in Tonga. The cost of repairs was beyond Linn's resources, all her money having been spent in returning *Tern* to health in Auckland. The boat was left in the sympathetic care of a local, Jon Beacham.

Then events took a turn for the better. Whilst cruising in the Pacific, an Australian shipwright, Mike Lyon, with his English wife Rachel, came into Vava'u and saw *Tern II*, which they identified from Worth's *Yacht Cruising*. They were able to take possession of her and have her shipped back to Auckland, where she is now, stripped down to the bare hull. The plan is restoration to the way she was in Worth's day and largely as I knew her. On completion, Mike and Rachel will sail *Tern* back to Falmouth, inviting me for part of the passage. Perhaps Dick Durham and I will indeed 'get that sail together yet'.

Appendix One

Tern II

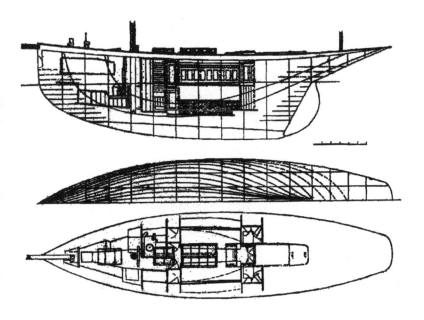

Built by Messrs Stow and Son,
Shoreham in 1899

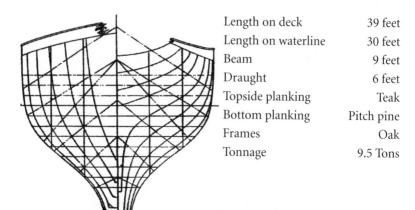

Length on deck	39 feet
Length on waterline	30 feet
Beam	9 feet
Draught	6 feet
Topside planking	Teak
Bottom planking	Pitch pine
Frames	Oak
Tonnage	9.5 Tons

Appendix Two

Tern II *Sail Plan*

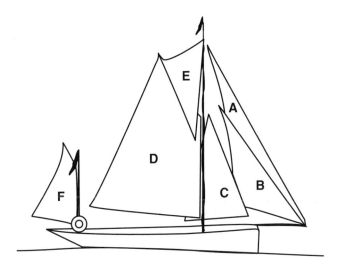

A	Yankee jib
B	No. 1 jib
C	Staysail or Balloon foresail
D	Mainsail
E	Topsail
F	Mizzen

Appendix Three

Glossary of Navigational Terms

Astronomical or celestial triangle. See also Observed position, OP. Known as the PZX triangle, it is used for working out a sight with spherical trigonometry wherein P is the celestial pole which projects down to the pole on Earth. Z is the zenith of the observer, ie the point immediately above his head, and X is the position on the celestial sphere of the heavenly body.

Beaufort Scale. Compiled in 1808 by Admiral Beaufort to provide a measure of wind strengths with an accompanying description of the associated sea state. Expressed in 'forces'. Scale runs from force 0; a calm, to force 12; a hurricane.

Cable. Measure of distance, one tenth of a sea mile, equalling 183 metres or 100 fathoms, ie 200 yards.

Course. Direction in which the boat is set to steer. True course is relative to true north. Magnetic course is relative to magnetic north. Compass course is when the magnetic course is corrected to compensate for compass error.

Dead reckoning, DR. Gives the boat's approximate position on the chart by drawing from the last known position the true course steered and distance sailed through the water.

Departure. Position on the chart, after the vessel has cleared harbour, to mark the start of the passage and from which the measuring log records the distance sailed.

Estimated position, EP. Gives a more accurate position than that by DR. The courses and distances sailed through the water are adjusted to allow for the effects of leeway and tidal streams or currents.

Ex-meridian altitude. A sextant observation to determine latitude by taking the altitude of a heavenly body within a short time before or after its meridian passage.

Fathom. The measurement for the depth of water; used over the centuries until metrication. Equals 6 feet or 1.83 metres. Believed to come from the medieval English word 'faedm' meaning 'to embrace', and was the span across the outstretched arms of an average man of the day, having a spread of 6 feet.

Leeway.   The drift laterally through the water due to the force of the wind. The angle between the course steered and the actual course made good through the water.

Log.   A device to record the distance sailed through the water. In *Tern*, in common with many older boats, this was Walker's 'Excelsior' IV patent log: a rotator towing astern on a plaited line, the log line, with the distance-recording instrument mounted on a bracket on the stern. To give the actual speed, the instrument's flywheel had a white mark on it; the frequency of rotation as seen through an aperture in the casing enabled the boat's speed to be derived.

Log or logbook.   The ship's journal. An hourly or daily record of everything happening in or to the boat and her crew.

Meridian altitude.   The altitude of a heavenly body, taken by sextant, when the body is on the observer's meridian, that is due north or south, to give the latitude.

M.   Symbol for sea mile and equates to one minute of latitude at the boat's position. Also indicates a magnetic course or bearing, the angle relating to the meridian through magnetic north, which differs from true or geographical north.

Observed position, OP.   The boat's position at sea as found by observation of heavenly bodies. The method used in *Tern II* was 'longitude by chronometer'. The requirement is to find the Local Hour Angle, LHA, which is the angle at the pole between the meridians of the body and the observer. This is done by calculation, incorporating the sextant observation and the estimated latitude. The difference between the LHA and the Greenwich Hour Angle, GHA, which is the angle at the pole between the meridians of Greenwich and the body, gives the longitude. The GHA is extracted from the *Nautical Almanac*. The position line through the longitude, so calculated, when crossed with the actual observed latitude, gives the observed position, the OP. The astronomical triangle, the centrepiece of celestial navigation, is depicted *right*:

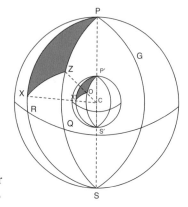

   In the diagram, O is the observer and C the centre of the Earth, PZQS

is the observer's meridian, PXRS is the meridian of the body, and PGS is the Greenwich meridian. The haversine cosine formula is used to calculate the LHA, the equation being solved with logarithms.

$$\text{Hav LHA} = \frac{\text{havZX} - \text{hav (latitude declination)}}{\cos \text{latitude} . \cos \text{declination}}$$

The zenith distance, ZX, is the angular distance between the observer's zenith and the body, being equal to 90° minus the altitude. The declination is the angular distance of the body from the celestial equator, XR, and the latitude is that estimated at the time of the observation.

SAT, Ship's Apparent Time.   The time kept on a daily basis relative to the true sun, ie the one apparent or visible in the heavens, as would be indicated by a sundial.

Sextant.   An optical instrument for measuring the angular distance of a body above the visible horizon. Called a sextant because the measuring arc on the frame is one sixth of a circle.